Banking in North America:

NAFTA and Beyond

Series in International Business and Economics
Series Editor: Khosrow Fatemi

Related Elsevier Science Journals—Sample copy available on request

Banking in North America:

NAFTA and Beyond

Edited by

Jerry Haar

Dante B. Fascell North-South Center
University of Miami

and

Krishnan Dandapani

Florida International University

1999
PERGAMON
An imprint of Elsevier

Amsterdam - Lausanne - New York - Oxford - Shannon - Singapore - Tokyo

ELSEVIER SCIENCE Ltd
The Boulevard, Langford Lane
Kidlington, Oxford OX5 1GB, UK

First edition 1999

Library of Congress Cataloguing in Publication Data
Banking in North America : NAFTA and beyond / edited by Jerry Haar and
    Krishnan Dandapani.
        p.   cm. – (Series in international business and economics)
        Includes index.
        ISBN 0-08-043457-6 (hc)
        1. Banks and banking–North America.   2. Financial services
    industry–North America.   3. Canada.   Treaties, etc.   1992 Oct. 7.
    I. Haar, Jerry.   II. Dandapani, Krishnan.   III. Series.
    HG2398.B36   1999   99-22911
    332.1'097–dc21   CIP

British Library Cataloguing in Publication Data
A catalogue record from the British Library has been applied for.

ISBN: 0 08 043457 6

♾ The paper used in this publication meets the requirements of ANSI/NISO Z39.48-1992 (Permanence of Paper).

Typeset by The Midlands Book Typesetting Company, Loughborough, Leicestershire, UK.
Printed in The Netherlands.

In memory of
George B. Simmons
Banking professor, humanitarian, colleague and friend

Contents

The Editors

Jerry Haar is Senior Research Associate and Director of the Inter-American Business and Labor Program at the North-South Center, University of Miami, as well as Research Affiliate at Harvard University's Rockefeller Center for Latin American Studies. Dr. Haar was a Visiting Scholar at the Harvard Center for International Affairs in 1994. He has also been an Adjunct Scholar of the American Enterprise Institute in Washington, D.C., and a business professor at Florida International University.

From 1981 to 1984, Dr. Haar was Director of Washington Programs for the Council of the Americas, a New York-based business association of over 200 corporations comprising a majority of U.S. private investment in Latin America. He was a Research Fellow in the Institute of Latin American Studies at Columbia University from 1974 to 1976, and from 1972 to 1973 a Fulbright Scholar at the Fundação Getúlio Vargas School of Public Administration in Rio de Janeiro, Brazil.

Dr. Haar received his B.A. cum laude from the School of International Service, American University, master's degree from the Johns Hopkins University, and Ph.D. from Columbia University. Dr. Haar is also a graduate of Harvard University's Executive Program in Management. He has written seven books, including *Making NAFTA Work: U.S. Firms and the New North American Business Environment*, co-authored with Stephen Blank, and more than twenty articles. Consultancies include: Exxon, IBM, Mobil, Microsoft, ING Barings, Arthur D. Little, FMC, Young & Rubicam, Disney, and YPF oil company of Argentina. He has appeared in media such as *The Wall Street Journal, The New York Times, The Washington Post, The Financial Times* (London), *The Journal of Commerce, Business Week, Newsweek*, Fox Cable News, CNN, and NBC.

Krishnan Dandapani is currently the Professor and Chairman of the Finance Department at Florida International University, Miami, Florida.

He received his Ph.D. in Finance from The Pennsylvania State University (1985) and an M.B.A. from the University of Madras, India, in 1977. He has won several honors and awards including Excellence in Research Award, State of Florida (1991), Excellence in Teaching Award, State of Florida (1992), Excellence in Service Award, State of Florida (1997).

Dr. Dandapani is an internationally known scholar in the area of financial markets and institutions and has done pioneering work in financial derivative securities. He has published extensively in the areas of business finance, financial markets and banking. He is the author of several research and professional articles, numerous book chapters and one co-authored book entitled *The Return Generating Models in Global Finance.* He is an active member of the Financial Management Association and the International Trade and Finance Association. He also serves on the Editorial Board of the *International Journal of Finance.* He has taught a variety of courses at the under-graduate, master's and doctoral level. He has taught in the executive education programs also and has received numerous teaching awards. He is currently the Director of the M.S. in Finance Program. He has extensive experience in performing research and financial analyses for a wide variety of corporations, governments and institutions, both in the United States and overseas.

His current research work is with the State of Florida's Department of Community Affairs and is focusing on developing financial incentives and tools for mitigating hurricane risk.

The Contributors

I. Jerry Haar, Senior Research Associate & Director, Inter-American Business & Labor Program, Dante B. Fascell North-South Center, University of Miami

Krishnan Dandapani, Chair and Professor of Finance, College of Business Administration, Florida International University

II.Harry Makler, Stanford University and Professor Emeritus, University of Toronto

III.Stephen Lande, President, Manchester Trade Ltd

Manuel Mindreau, Professor of International Relations, Universidad del Pacífico (Peru)

Michael Lande, Vice President for Research, Manchester Trade Ltd

IV. James R. Barth, Lowder Eminent Scholar in Finance, Department of Finance, College of Business, Auburn University

Ray Y. Chou, Associate Research Fellow, Institute of Economics, Academia Sinica, Nankang, Taipei, Republic of China

John S. Jahera, Jr., Colonial Bank Distinguished Professor & Department Head, Department of Finance, College of Business, Auburn University

V. James L. Darroch, Associate Professor of Policy, Schulich School of Business, York University

VI. Ignacio Perrotini and Luis Miguel Galindo, Professors of Economics, Universidad Nacional Autonomá de México (UNAM)

VII. Carlos Palomares, Chairman, Citibank International, Latin American Consumer Bank

VIII. Emmanuel N. Roussakis, Professor of Finance, Department of Finance, College of Business Administration, Florida International University

IX. John A. Adams, Jr., Senior Investment Consultant, Banc One Securities Corporation

X. Saturnino E. Lucio, II, Partner, Lucio, Mandler, Bronstein, Garbett, Stiphany & Martinez

Acknowledgements

We gratefully acknowledge the cooperation and support of Ambassador Ambler Moss, Director of the Dante B. Fascell North-South Center; Deputy Director Robin Rosenberg; Jeffrey Stark, Director of Research and Studies; and Arun Prakash of the Department of Finance, College of Business Administration, Florida International University. Invaluable research assistance was provided by former North-South Center Fellows Manuel Mindreau (who also co-authored a chapter in the volume) and María Eugenia Mújica.

Additionally, we extend a special note of gratitude to both the Center for International Affairs and David Rockefeller Center for Latin American Studies of Harvard University and ING Baring Securities for their research and financial support, respectively. Finally, the editors and authors wish to express enormous thanks to Kathleen A. Hamman, editorial director of the North-South Center; Jayne M. Weisblatt, editor; and Mary M. Mapes, publications director for their excellent production assistance.

1

Introduction

JERRY HAAR AND KRISHNAN DANDAPANI

The decade of the 1990s has been a turning point for the world economy. Trade, commerce, and finance have expanded dramatically exceeding $6 trillion in 1996. Concurrently, developing as well as industrialized nations have forged agreements to liberalize, rationalize and harmonize economic relations. A largely integrated world economy could well be a reality by the first decade of the 21st century. Recognizably, there continues to be friction and floundering over issues such as telecommunications, maritime services, intellectual property rights, and environmental and labor standards. Nevertheless, bilateral and multilateral accords aimed at tearing down barriers and opening up markets are proliferating. The Summit of the Americas, held in Miami in December 1994, produced an agreement signed by 34 democratic nations of the western hemisphere to create a Free Trade Area of the Americas (FTAA) by the year 2005. An Asian-Pacific free-trade area, involving 18 nations including the U.S., is envisioned by 2020. A translantic dialogue launched in November 1995 could well result in a U.S.-European free-trade area; and an enlarged European Union, to include Eastern and Central Europe and more Mediterranean nations may also materialize. Most impressively, nearly three dozen regional and subregional trade pacts in the Americas, Southeast Asia, Europe and Africa are emerging, widening and deepening commerce throughout the world. Undoubtedly, it is the North American Free Trade Agreement (NAFTA), creating the largest free-trade agreement in the world (encompassing a gross domestic product (GDP) of $6.8 trillion and a population of 379 million), which produced an enhanced, if not catalytic, effect on trade integration in the western hemisphere.

The evolution of the General Agreement of Tariffs and Trade (GATT) into the World Trade Organization (WTO) with a large mandate and expanded powers will ensure continued progress in global trade and commerce.

Simultaneous with multilateral, regional and subregional trade expansion has been the dramatic growth of financial services worldwide. To illustrate, world stock market capitalization exceeds $16 trillion, more than 2.5 times the GDP of the U.S.; pension fund assets in the U.S. exceed $3 trillion; and the world bond market holds more than $18.5 trillion in publicly traded debt. Banking, in particular, has undergone structural changes and an expansion of activities in both the bank and non-bank areas. The financial environment of the1990s has been shaped—and will continue to be shaped—by the globalization of financial markets, technological and financial innovations, emerging capital markets, deregulation, the emergence of supraregional banks, and the liberalization and harmonization of cross-national banking rules and regimens.

The dynamism and synergy of regional trade integration and financial services expansion are vividly illustrated in the case of North America. The Canada-U.S. Free Trade Agreement came into existence on January 2, 1989; five years later, Mexico joined what was renamed the North American Free Trade Agreement (NAFTA). Accounting for 80 percent of western hemisphere trade, NAFTA provides duty-free treatment for most products over a 10 to 15 year transition period. Integrating the three disparate economies is a daunting task (Saborio, 1992; Randall, 1992; Winham, 1988; Heilleiner, 1991; Lustig, 1993), and will be determined as much (or more so) by domestic macro-economic and adjustment policies (Bouzas and Ros, 1993; Shaiken, 1990; National Planning Association, 1993). In the meantime, the NAFTA partners are attempting to deepen their economic relationship (Waverman, 1994) and widen the agreement (Weintraub, 1994) as their hemisphere neighbors proceed to expand and integrate their economies bilaterally and multilaterally (Hufbauer and Schott, 1994; Starr, 1995).

Far more portentous and significant than the NAFTA agreement itself is a deeper and more structural integration, one of 'complex interdependence' (Keohane and Nye, 1977), that has produced a North American 'economic space'. In fact a new 'architecture' of North America has been taking form during the past two decades:

> The economic logic of an emerging North American economic space is eroding the political logic of national economies. The Canada-U.S. FTA, an emerging 'new jurisprudence' in North America, and new corporate structures and strategies are all responses to the same phenomenon—a new economic 'architecture' of North America (Blank, 1993, 2).

The gradual emergence of a new jurisprudence (Gotlieb, 1991), indeed, 'challenges' national sovereignty, as new legal and regulatory structures provide an overarching North American framework. Environmental codes, labor and safety rules, sanitary and phytosanitary standards are but a few of the areas in which domestic laws and regulations are modified to accede to harmonization and/or mutual recognition by all signatories to the NAFTA.

Arguably, the NAFTA—as well as other trade agreements—validates more than it creates international commerce. The economies of Canada, Mexico and the United States have become increasingly integrated through the investment, trading, licensing and financing activities of business enterprises—national as well as multinational—in all three nations (Blank and Haar, 1998). To illustrate, Northern Telecom, Kodak, and Cemex do business in each NAFTA country; and products, services and personnel flow relatively freely among these nations.

Additionally, 'clusters of excellence' have emerged whereby the competitive advantage of entire sectors and industries are highly localed in regions or cities (Porter, 1990a; Porter, 1990b). Just as the high technology corridors of the Silicon Valley and Route 128, (also in northern California) have enhanced the competitiveness of industries, and in turn regions, NAFTA corridors are spurring increased business as well, especially: Montreal-Boston-New York; Rocky Mountain region (Colorado, Idaho, Montana, Utah, Wyoming, Alberta, British Columbia); Cascadia (British Columbia, Alberta, Washington, Oregon); U.S.-Mexican border states; and the U.S. and Mexican Gulf states. The trucking deregulation provisions of NAFTA will expand commerce from northern Mexico through the western states to Canada's western provinces; and telecommunications, maritime and air transportation will be linked more closely as well.

In essence, NAFTA is the trilateral, governmental recognition of the increasing and expanding commercial cooperation, linkages and transactions which had been set in motion long before the North American Free Trade Agreement was conceived.

The explosion in global financial services has produced changes in the banking sectors of Canada, the United States, and Mexico concurrent with NAFTA provisions which have impacted banks as well. The 1989 U.S.-Canada Free Trade Agreement fostered cross-border integration, equalizing access and treatment for Canadian banks in the U.S. and U.S. banks in Canada—*de jure* national treatment. Under NAFTA, the principle of national treatment was widened, subnational governments (U.S. and Mexican states and Canadian provinces) were required to oblige by the accord's provisions. 'Most favored nation' principles were applied to North American trade, and transparency was established throughout. NAFTA provisions also bolstered the Mexico's privatized banking system as well as its modernization and internationalization; and they did so in a way which protected Mexico's financial services sector, in its delicate process of transition, while providing the flexibility for Mexico to go beyond the NAFTA provisions, which it did.

The aim of this book is to present, analyze, and discuss the evolution, current state, and outlook for financial services in North America, with special attention to the banking sector. Towards this end, authors from all three nations and representing differing policy perspectives, were called upon to address the theme within the context of the globalization of trade and financial services; changes in domestic banking and regulatory policies in Canada, Mexico, and the United States; and the impact of NAFTA and its financial services provisions on the banking sector of each nation. It is hoped that both the descriptive and prescriptive features of the volume will be of use to professionals in business and banking, government, and academe and, in general, broaden and enrich the knowledge base in the field of trade and financial services.

One caveat is in order. As this book evolved over time, it was not possible to capture and report all the significant developments within the rapidly changing environment of global banking and finance. Major upheavals in capital markets, dramatic changes in merger and acquisition activity (e.g., Chase and Chemical Bank, Bank of America and NationsBank, Deutsche Bank and Bankers Trust), along with the reengineering and refocusing of a number of leading financial institutions, combine to make it very difficult, indeed, to be as timely and up to date as one would like. Be that as it may, there is clear value, we believe, in capturing the historical context of banking reform in North America in that this provides a clear understanding and appreciation of the current panorama in all three NAFTA countries.

The book begins with 'Regional Integration and Trends in Financial Services,' in which Harry Makler introduces the main features which characterize the banking systems in all three North American countries in the 1990s. Despite the recent reprivatization of its banking sector, Mexico is described as an underbanked and highly concentrated system—with two banks controlling 60 percent of the market—whose total assets represent only 4 and 25 percent of those held by U.S. and Canadian banks in respectively their own countries. In addition, banks in Mexico are usually at the core of *grupos financieros* (multi-company enterprises). Canadian legislation, on the contrary, shows a preference for widely-held ownership, while at the same time preventing linkages between financial and non-financial enterprises. Nevertheless, this has not prevented concentration. Even today in 1999, the six largest Canadian banks hold over 90 percent of the banking assets.

In the U.S., because of the branching prohibition within and across state-lines imposed by the McFadden Act of 1927, the picture of the banking industry is one of fragmentation and diversity as the largest 100 banks accounting for only 51 percent of the market. Furthermore, the Glass-Steagall Act of 1933 prohibits U.S. commercial banks from providing investment and other financial services. Within this framework, Makler argues that both the 1989 U.S.-Canadian Free-Trade Agreement (FTA) and the NAFTA marked the first steps toward the integration of financial services across borders: the FTA by permitting U.S. financial subsidiaries to operate like Canadian chartered banks, and the NAFTA by setting the ground for a metered entry of foreign banks over a ten-year horizon in Mexico. Makler argues that from now on the challenge and opportunities rely on the ability to form mergers or joint ventures with prominent local capital in other countries.

The effects of the FTA and the NAFTA on the integration of financial services in North America are more deeply examined in Chapter 3. Stephen Lande, Manuel Mindreau and Michael Lande start by comparing the provisions of the FTA dealing with commercial banking to provisions of NAFTA in this same area. The FTA basically confirmed the status quo for Canadian banks in the U.S. and guaranteed their future equal treatment *vis-à-vis* U.S. banks, while exempting U.S. subsidiaries from ownership restrictions in Canada. However, it is made evident by the authors that the FTA was not directed toward the integration of financial markets through harmonization in regulation. The Landes and Mindreau argue later that although the NAFTA built on the FTA provisions, there was not a significant movement to eliminate the barriers left untouched by the FTA. However, improvements were made in terms of structuring the NAFTA around specific trade principles—like the concept of 'equal competitive opportunities,' which ensures that foreign banks will enjoy the same rights and privileges as domestic laws change. Furthermore, NAFTA was negotiated as a tool for gradually opening the Mexican market for North American banking over a ten-year transition period. However, as the financial stability of many Mexican banks was threatened—not by competition from North America, but from the number of non-performing loans held by the privatized banks and the shrinking profit margins of a number of banks in the aftermath of the December 1994 peso devaluation—the Mexican Government actually impelled the liberalization process by accelerating the pace of removal of its transitional restrictions beyond what was required under NAFTA. Mexico also liberalized its laws allowing foreign banks to take control of any of the banks which found themselves in financial trouble. The authors conclude by stating that, once the current economic crisis is over, opportunities for strategic alliances will again be fully explored resulting in both a stronger Mexican banking system and a more integrated North American financial market.

In Chapter 4, about the transition the U.S. banking industry has undergone in the last two decades, James Barth, Ray Chou and John Jahera argue that due to restrictions imposed by the existing legislation, between 1980 and 1992 a significant number of credit unions, commercial banks, and savings and loans institutions have failed. Moreover, given that most large businesses are now able to bypass banks and borrow directly on more favorable terms through the issuance of commercial papers, the deregulation process started in recent years has come too late to solve the problem, while the lack of uniformity in regulation still persists. However, Barth *et al.* point out that advances in computing and telecommunication are helping reduce banking costs. Furthermore, banks have not been totally passive and are moving more assets into all types of real estate loans to replace their lost commercial and industrial loans, while at the same time getting involved in off-balance activities—such as foreign exchange, interest-rate swaps, and other derivatives—and broadening their menu of products and services. In this way, U.S. banks are relying more heavily on fee income as compared to traditional interest income. However, Barth *et al.* conclude that, since inadequately capitalized banking institutions have a proclivity to engage in excessively risky activities, there is an underlying risk with this new pattern of behavior in U.S. banking. Therefore, it should be incumbent upon regulators that both capital and risk be properly monitored. They argue that risk be prudently reduced through greater geographical diversification, and thus propose the dismantling of the regional compacts under which U.S. banking has traditionally operated.

As observed by James Darroch in Chapter 5, Canadian banks have traditionally focused on the domestic market where weak competitors provided easy prey. Concentration in the Canadian banking sector is the result of more demanding customers and tougher competition among roughly equal rivals. However, in the last decade, with clients going abroad as well as foreign clients coming into Canada, the strategic objectives of Canadian banks were realigned. This movement required efforts to harmonize the differing federal and provincial jurisdictions. Today, the Federal Government has power over the banking sector, while the provincial government has power over securities exchanges, investment banking, and other key financial services. In this respect, Quebec has been the leading voice for change. Furthermore, since 1980 foreign banks are fully allowed to operate in Canada, and in 1987 Canadian banks were allowed to offer trust and insurance services through subsidiaries, investment counseling, portfolio management, financial planning, and to establish networking arrangements. Darroch argues that neither the FTA nor NAFTA significantly affected the powers of Canadian banks in the U.S.; however, these agreements brought about strategic implications for Canadian banks, which in addition to shifting to a North American strategy, are generating more fee-based revenues and have increased price competition. Darroch concludes by arguing that with Canadian banks now profiting from cross-border trade and investment, future opportunities will emerge from different market segments such as export financing, multinational companies reorganization in global terms—Canadian banks will follow their clients entering new markets—and retail banking on a North American scale.

On the other hand, as asserted by Ignacio Perrotini and Luis Miguel Galindo in Chapter 6, the major outcome of the privatization of the banking sector in Mexico and the subsequent financial liberalization process started in 1988 was the strengthening of oligopolistic financial groups. Within this context, the authors argue that the Mexican financial opening departed from the 'optimal path' of balanced public finance and prompted the Mexican economy and banks to eagerly seek foreign loans. Furthermore, the exchange rate was used as an anchor for inflation—a quasi-fixed exchange rate triggered a real appreciation of the peso, reducing the relative cost of U.S.$ loans and easing the negative impact of import liberalization on domestic output and employment. Furthermore, expectations after the external debt renegotiation and the approval of NAFTA helped increase the level of financial intermediation. However, the financial fragility of the banking system to external shocks was made evident by the amount of short-term capital instruments issued during that period: speculative investment accounted for 75 percent of inflows attracted via high nominal interest rates.

The peso depreciation of December 1994 which created liquidity constraints, and in turn had the immediate effect of increasing provisions for capital and loan defaults, has turned mergers and acquisitions into appealing solutions to fight widespread bankruptcies and capital inadequacy. So far, the Mexican Government has been using a combined strategy: let the banks with the highest risk rates fail and rescue the big ones; bail out the banking system; and accelerate the opening of the financial system to foreign investors. The first choice is costly in political terms, the second one is costly economically, and the third one requires the active role of foreign banks. Nevertheless, Perrotini and Galindo conclude that the major outcome resulting from the current financial crisis is that the Mexican financial system is liberalizing at a much faster pace than the NAFTA ten-year gradualism.

In Chapter 7, Carlos Palomares makes an analysis of the implications for competition resulting from the globalization of financial services in the North American market. As can be imagined, the most of the opportunities for foreign entrants are expected to emerge in the newly liberalized and rather underbanked Mexican banking system, as a result of the attractive current pricing and fee structure—determined in an oligopolistic environment in Mexico—and its prospects of future growth. However, Palomares argues that in the early stage foreign banks will postpone their penetration into Mexican retail banking in favor of exploiting other areas, such as cross-border mergers and acquisitions, trade and equities, where they have comparative advantages in terms of bypassing large expenditure and sunk costs associated with initial construction and equipment purchase. Furthermore, strategic alliances seem to be a good option to test the market, and to establish links with the local institutions. Mexico is also seen as a first step toward the penetration of Latin America by U.S. and Canadian banks.

However, Palomares points out to the dynamic effects of technology in the shaping of the global financial service industry in North America. Palomares argues that, as technology advances and product lines expand, the distinction between bank and nonbank institutions is being blurred. In addition, large technology and computer firms are allocating significant amounts of resources to bank technology in targeted areas such as 24-hour access to accounts through automatic teller machines (ATMs) and remote delivery options; improving efficiency in lending practices by using optical imaging to store and immediately access loan documentation; development of pre-authorized debits/credits. As transaction times are reduced, applied technology will have an impact on the four areas of a bank's profitability: cost control/reduction, pricing, service quality, and revenue opportunities. Today, more than half of all current bank transactions are conducted outside of traditional physical bank branches. Similarly, it is expected that the number of banks within the industry will continue to shrink dramatically, while a continued affinity for strategic alliances—engineered by the larger global banks—will become the norm. Smaller boutique-type community banks will be essentially niche players, catering to the needs of particular individuals and extremely well-defined target markets. Personal relationships with their clients represent their major competitive advantage. Palomares concludes that the increased presence of global banks in local markets, the co-existence of both banks and nonbanks, and NAFTA provisions will all contribute to the formation of an almost uniform North American banking sector in the next century.

In Chapter 8, Emmanuel Roussakis looks beyond NAFTA at relevant banking trends in the Latin American region. After tracing the development of commercial banking in Latin America, Roussakis analyzes the consolidation of the banking industry in Argentina, Chilie and Mexico and the growth of regional banking, along with the strategies pursued by banks to boost competitiveness. He notes that open markets have increased the size and scope of banking services, catapulting banks as catalysts in the consolidation of the financial system as a whole. Roussakis concludes that market reform and prudent regulation are creating a Latin American banking environment in which the chief beneficiaries will be Latin American firms, small businesses and consumers.

In Chapter 9, John Adams examines Mexico and the IMF, in terms of the global consequences of a regional banking crisis. He chronicles the evolution and aftermath of the 1994–95 Mexican banking crisis and the IMF's role as global watchdog. Adams subsequently identifies seven key factors in evaluating the financial stability of a nation's economy. He asserts that, while the globalization of banking and financial services has spread the exposure, it has increased the concern with portfolio management and credit policies. As for the recent Asian financial crisis's relationship to North American banking, Adams contends that banking reforms in all three NAFTA countries have cushioned the impact of turmoil in financial markets.

The effect of Nafta on the entry of foreign banks in Mexico and in the U.S. is the focus of Chapter 10. Saturnino Lucio details the reasons that NAFTA's intent to create a 'borderless' regional financial market has not materialized. His historical analysis and assessment of recent developments illuminate the interplay between regulatory policies, privatization, the peso crisis and NAFTA implementation. Lucio argues that Mexican measures to liberalize banking following the peso crisis have done more to open the market to foreign banks than the NAFTA agreement itself, although NAFTA has indeed brought the three North American economies closer together and stimulated cross-border banking activities and transactions.

European Banking

While the focus of this book is on NAFTA and its impact on banking in North America, we recognize the possible implications for banking in other major markets such as in the European Union. The banking landscape of Europe is vastly different due to the fact that there are no limitations on banking structure and no regulations such as the Glass-Steagall on U.S. banks. Additionally, the functional and geographical separation that had dominated U.S. banking until the 1990s are also conspicuous by their absence. In Europe, the concept of universal banking is taking a strong hold due to global competitive pressures. In most European banks, along with the traditional commercial functions, investment and trust services are available and the major sources of revenues are the interest earnings from commercial banking, fee earnings from investment trust and the transaction earnings from equity and money market security trading. Unlike the U.S., but like Mexico, European banks can simultaneously make loans, and sell securities, insurance and mutual funds. This wide range of activities provides a competitive advantage over U.S. banks and does not constrain their operations.

Walter identifies four factors which will affect the future of universal banking in Europe.[1] These are de-regulation, re-regulation, globalization and technology/information-induced strategic forces which direct the banks to become information companies. The drive towards efficiency induced by cost-conscious clientele, who demand customized solutions using innovative technology to access a wide range of services, shall accelerate. In such instances, technology will be more of a tool than the driving force.

The banking organizations in individual countries are also variedly affected. German banks historically have been the most stable, with no instance of any crisis such as speculative bubbles in real estate or share markets impacting a serious repercussion for the entire economy. The dynamic growth of financial markets and the global integration has posed new challenges for these banks. The tremendous growth of the derivative markets has led to a refinement of market transparency reporting in French banks. The lack of demarcation between banking, security and insurance industries has given rise to a technological monster of valuing risk exposure. The most pressing need for these banks is the necessity of extending the Basle Accord for evaluating the market risk of derivative securities. In Swiss banks. mergers and acquisitions are converting holding company structure banks to fully integrated structure banks carrying out a collection of activities.

The accelerated implementation of Europe 1992 has been responsible for the globalization of European banks. Competition induced by foreign banks' entry, expansion of electronic stock exchanges, the erosion of fixed commission structures and the shrinking of spreads has provided an added impetus to the universal banking structure of Europe. The two additional factors of technological change and uncertainty induced by financial market cycles have necessitated all institutions to focus on value-added services, be flexible to change and focus on size to achieve economies of scale both in their domestic and international operations.

Two important evolutionary trends taking shape in Europe are first the concept of 'one customer, one bank' and second the possible merger of the banking and security industries due to the complementary nature of their business.

Note

1. Based on the guest address of Professor Ingo Walter at the Financial Management Association International meetings at Zurich, Switzerland, May 29–30, 1997.

References

BLANK, STEPHEN and JERRY HAAR (1998). *Making NAFTA Work: U.S. Firms and the New North American Business Environment.* Coral Gables: North-South Center Press.

BOUZAS, ROBERTO and JAIME ROS (1993). *The North-South Variety of Economic Integration: Issues and Prospects for Latin America.* Buenos Aires, Argentina: Facultad Latino-americana de Ciencias Sociales.

GOTLIEB, ALLAN (1991). "International Law in a North American Economic Space." Lecture delivered at the Americas Society/Canadian Affairs, November 21.

HELLEINER, GERALD K., ED. (1991). *Trade Policy, Industrialization, and Development: New Perspectives.* New York: Oxford University Press.

HUFBAUER, GARY CLYDE and JEFFREY J. SCHOTT (1994). *Western Hemisphere Economic Integration.* Washington: Institute for International Economics.

KEOHANE, ROBERT O. and JOSEPH S. NYE (1977). *Power and Interdependence: World Politics in Transition.* Boston: Little, Brown and Company.

LUSTIG, NORA (1993). "NAFTA: Potential Impact on Mexico's Economy and Beyond," Paper presented at the Conference on Economic Integration in the Western Hemisphere, University of Notre Dame, April.

NATIONAL PLANNING ASSOCIATION (1993). "Adjusting to NAFTA: Strategies for Business and Labor," *North American Outlook*, vol. 4, no.1-2.

PORTER, MICHAEL (1990a). *The Competitive Advantage of Nations.* New York: The Free Press.

PORTER, MICHAEL (1990b). "Japan Isn't Playing by Different Rules," *The New York Times*, July 22.

RANDALL, STEPHEN J. ED. (1992). *North America Without Borders?* Calgary: University of Calgary Press.

SABORIO, SILVIA, ED. (1992). *The Premise and the Promise: Free Trade in the Americas.* Washington: Overseas Development Council.

SHAIKEN, HARLEY. *Mexico in the Global Economy*, Monograph Series, 33. San Diego: Center for U.S.-Mexican Studies, University of California, San Diego.

STARR, RICHARD, ED. (1994). *Hemispheric Trade and Economic Integration After NAFTA.* Indiannapolis: Hudson Institute.

WAVERMAN, LEONARD (1994). "Post-NAFTA: Can the United States, Canada, and Mexico Deepend Their Economic Relationships?, " in Sidney Weintraub, ed., *Integrating the Americas: Shaping Future Trade Policy.* Coral Gables: North-South Center Press.WEINTRAUB, SIDNEY (1994). *NAFTA: What Comes Next?* Westport, CT: Praeger.

WINHAM, GILBERT (1988). *Trading with Canada: The Canada-U.S. Free Trade Agreement.* New York: Priority Press Publications/Twentieth Century Fund.

2

Regional Integration and Trends in Financial Services

HARRY M. MAKLER

Introduction

As the internationalization of economic activity becomes ever more important, a growing number of countries within specific geographical regions are entering into economic compacts or agreements.[1] Such regional compacts are designed to reduce barriers to the free flow of goods and services across borders. They are also designed to enable financial service firms to more freely conduct their activities without regard to national boundaries. The eventual outcome under these agreements will be greater interdependence and integration of both the goods and financial markets of the countries participating in these compacts.

Evidence of these growing trends manifested itself in early 1994. First, the North American Free Trade Agreement went into effect. Second, the United States Congress removed a 'cross-border' obstacle to the passage of a nationwide banking bill. Taken together, these measures represent a real breakthrough for the emergent process of regional integration. They serve as a sign that the competitive barriers which prevented out-of-state and foreign banks from free movement within the United States are now down. As a result, Canadian, Mexican, and northeastern American banks will soon be opening branches in the southeastern United States, currently the fastest growing region in the Americas, but one which has historically closed its doors to 'foreign' activity.

And yet, while such regulatory liberalization in the financial sector reinforces the larger process of hemispheric integration, the financial industry also represents one of its greatest challenges. This tension becomes vivid when the size, structure, and regulatory environment of the banking sector within the three countries of North America are compared. Such a comparison reveals that despite the freer flow of financial goods and services at the national level, a number of questions remain unresolved, including its impact on the concentration of ownership within the financial sector, rules governing cross-border and out-of-state entry, and above all, the 'threat' which sub-national compacts within these countries pose to larger efforts at liberalization.

In light of these observations, this chapter examines the challenges and opportunities to the financial industry raised by the new NAFTA compact. After a brief comparison of financial industry structure in Mexico, Canada, and the United States, I discuss their implications for regional integration, with particular emphasis on the pending issues outlined above. While the focus is primarily on the Mexican and American commercial banking sectors, all three countries raise issues which will require increased policy attention as the process of hemispheric integration unfolds.

The Structure of the Commercial Banking Sector

This section lays out some basic information regarding the banking systems of the three North American countries. For each country involved, I describe the size and structure of the commercial banks, provide relevant background information on the development of the banking system, and discuss its regulatory environment.

A. Mexico

Mexico's 18 banks are free to open branches in all areas of the country, but unlike Canada and the United States, there are no sub-national regulatory authorities. In 1992, the total assets of these banks was $158,846 million, roughly equivalent to 4 percent of the assets held by American banks, and 25 percent of those held by their Canadian counterparts. But despite this relatively low level of overall activity, the Mexican banking system is highly concentrated with respect to its ownership, particularly when compared to the U.S. banking system. While Mexico's three largest banks—Banamex, Bancomer, and Banco Serfín—hold 58 percent of the financial assets listed above (roughly comparable to the 61 percent held by Canada's three largest banks— Royal Bank of Canada, Canadian Imperial and Toronto Dominion banks), the three biggest American banks at the time—Citicorp, Bank of America and Chemical Banking—hold only one-seventh or 12 percent of the total assets (*American Banker*, October 5, 1993; Gruben,

1993: 15). This difference is also reflected in the concentration ratios, the number of branches, and the number of automatic teller machines (ATMs) (see Table 2.1). As Table 2.1 illustrates, while Canada and the U.S. are similar in terms of per capita banking (reflected in the number of people per branch and per ATM), Mexico is extremely 'underbanked' and is thus likely to be very attractive to foreign entry.

Several important structural reforms took place in Mexico's banking

Table 2.1 *The structure of the Mexican, Canadian, and U.S. banking industries*

	Mexico 1992	Canada 1991	U.S. 1992
Number of Banks	18	18	62
Domestic Banks	7[2]	11451	—
Total Assets (US$ million)	158,848	621,494[3]	3,505,961
Total Net Income (US$ million)		2,000[4]	32,255
Return on Assets	,1%[5]	0.32%	0.92%
Concentration ration[1]	80%	77%	19%
Number of Branches	4,447	18,270	4,057
People per branch	20,027	7,583	3,578
Number of ATMs	10,272	2,641	67,241
People per ATM	3,673	93,000[6]	2,656
Assets of 3 largest banks (US$ million)	91,885	379,540	415,915

Notes:
(1) Percent of total assets held by four largest commercial banks
(2) Schedule I banks - majority Canadian owned banks. With FTA (1989) American schedule II banks can act like schedule I banks (i.e. - lower restrictions on branching, assets, etc.)
(3) Ten largest Canadian banks, 1992
(4) Source: 'The Banker', July 1993; 'The Financial Post 500', 1993
(5) Preliminary result calculated from Mexican stock market data
(6) 1990 data

Sources:
MEXICO: Garrido, Celso, 'Revelant Information about Commercial Banks, Financial Groups, and Regional banks in Mexico,' Workshop presentation, September 1993
U.S.: Barth, James R., 'Challenges to NAFTA: The Southeast Banking Compact,' Seminar presentation, February 1994
CANADA: Canadian Bankers Association, 'Bank Facts 1992;'
'The Banker,' July 1993, p.147
'The Financial Post 500,' 1993

system beginning in the 1970s (cf. Garrido, 1993; Welch and Gruben, 1993). These included:

1. the transformation of the commercial banks in 1974 to multiple (multi-financial product) banks able to hold shares in non-financial sectors;
2. increasing sector concentration, from 139 banks in 1975 to 62 banks in 1982, and finally to 18 banks in 1993;
3. the nationalization of the banking system in 1982 and re-establishment of barriers between it and non-bank sectors;
4. the reversal of nationalization beginning in 1989 and subsequent moves to open-market banking with commercial bank re-privatization and deregulation of financial markets (e.g. removal of interest rate restrictions)[2];
5. the introduction of regulatory reforms, abolishment of exchange controls, and creation of new reserve requirements in 1991 beyond those established by the Basle accord; and, finally,
6. the advent of NAFTA in 1993, committing Mexico's financial markets to open themselves to American, Canadian and other international competition.

In recent changes to the financial sector, a principal reform has been the sub-nationalization or decentralization of the banking system to offset the heavy concentration of banks within Mexico City and its environs. The goal of such an effort has been to encourage activity in the rest of the country, which remains 'underbanked' in terms of branch structure and financial services, especially in the poorest regions (Natella *et al.*, 1992).

B. Canada

Canada has seven domestically chartered or Schedule 1 banks,[3] down from 14 in 1985. Although ownership is diverse (with no one shareholder holding more than 10 percent of the voting shares), the six largest banks hold approximately 90 percent of the total banking assets (Kintner, 1993: 236), while the three largest account for 61 percent. If the current trend towards regulatory liberalization and mergers and acquisitions continues, there is likely to be further consolidation and asset concentration unless the 55 Schedule 2 banks can succeed in introducing a variety of financial services and become conglomerates like Canada's 'Big Six'.[4]

Responding to the challenge of an emerging regional and global economy, Canada's banking structure first began to liberalize in 1980 when its parliament amended the Bank Act. This legislation not only allowed for the chartering of foreign banks, but also removed many of the 'firewalls' segregating the four pillars of financial services: chartered banks, securities, trust companies and the insurance industry. Subsequently, in June of 1987, federal and provincial governments amended the Bank and Securities Acts to permit banks and other financial enterprises mutual ownership, and financial regulation was streamlined under a single regulatory authority.[5] Further revisions in 1991 enabled banks and trust companies to retail their financial products either through the acquisition of a subsidiary or a network agreement. (Kintner, 1993: 233–235). Taken together, these measures amounted to internal integration or consolidation of the banking system.

Despite this overall shift towards liberalization, however, the government continued to adhere to its 'market restricting' or 'functional' approach to the banking sector, by setting standards which limited ownership stakes to 10 percent, and preventing self-dealing or credit transactions (e.g. loans) between a bank and its subsidiaries (Boreham, 1993: 9).[6] In this way, Canadian banking legislation continued to uphold its revealed preference in favor of widely-held ownership and against ownership linkages between financial and non-financial enterprises. The net effect of the Bank Act was thus two-fold. On the one hand, it discouraged banks from engaging in commerce and other non-bank sectors, but at the same time it also revised legislation enabling commercial banks to move into other financial products. From this financial base, they could then expand via holding companies or subsidiaries into certain non-financial sectors, such as information technology.[7]

This trend would seem to suggest that the formation of finance-based holding companies is the precursor of the non-bank financial conglomerate, as has been the case in Mexico and Brazil. This trend is already beginning in Canada, where among the top 30 financial institutions ranked by assets in 1992, seven were conglomerates. Inevitably, more will follow suit until they dominate that country's financial industry. For example, Quebec, one of the two dominant financial markets in Canada, initiated a conglomerate strategy of financial concentration and networking beginning in 1981, with legislation which permitted one shareholder to purchase the entire capital stock of a stock brokerage company. The Toronto Stock Exchange followed suit and rescinded its ownership regulations a few years later (Boreham, 1993: 14, 17). To compete globally, Canada's federal government has now taken steps to liberalize banking, and Ontario and Quebec—competing with each other and competing for a share in the world market—have relaxed their financial regulations. This stimulated parliamentary financial regulation reform in 1987 (Kintner, 1993: 239). The phenomenon of increased conglomeratization appears to be a fixture in the future of Canada's financial system.

A step toward cross-border integration was realized in Canada in 1989 as a result of the Canada-United States Free Trade Agreement (FTA), which permitted American financial subsidiaries to operate like Canadian chartered banks. By 1992, all foreign owned subsidiaries were licensed to operate throughout the country, although some provinces still limit foreign ownership of provincially chartered institutions. All of these renovations have led to efforts to consolidate the country's dual regulatory environments. Currently, the country has three financial systems: a chartered banking system exclusively regulated by the federal government, a securities investment system supervised exclusively by the ten provincial governments, and trust and insurance services supervised by whichever layer of government grants the charter. Given the move away from one-enterprise, one-function regulatory structure, several jurisdictional disputes between federal and provincial authorities will undoubtedly occur (Kintner, 1993:231, 241).

C. The United States

Compared to Canada, Mexico, or any other country in the Americas, the U.S. has numerous financial institutions. In 1992, there were 27,489 commercial banks representing 44 percent of the total, whose combined assets (including all U.S. branches and foreign banks), were 26 percent of the financial institution total (see Table 2.2). Despite these aggregate figures, however, America's commercial bank assets are not nearly as concentrated as those of Canada and Mexico. The largest 100 banks accounted for 51 percent of the market, and its total concentration ratio is 19 percent, compared to 80 and 77 percent in Mexico and Canada, respectively. Mainly because of branching prohibition, which until recently forbade the establishment of commercial branches across state lines, the U.S. has more banking institutions per capita than any other country in the world. Finally, while Canada and Mexico have one principal regulatory authority,[8] the U.S. has four federal authorities and at least one at each state level. While there is pending congressional legislation to consolidate financial regulation under one agency (the Federal Banking Commission—FBC), the complexity of the present banking system renders regulatory uniformity quite problematic.[9]

Several changes in the American banking industry also occurred. From 1989 to 1992 alone, many financial institutions have failed. Savings and loans have been the most notorious. Between 1980 and 1992, nearly five thousand federally-insured institutions with $665 billion in assets failed. Commercial banks have also seen their market share eclipsed by non-banks which in turn have been invigorated by the rapid advances in information technology and fewer regulations.

Table 2.2 *Percentage Distribution of U.S. Financial Assets Held by All Financial Service Firms, 1950-3rd Quarter 1993*

	1950	1960	1970	1980	1981	1982	1983	1984	1985	1986	1987	1988	1989	1990	1991	1992	3rd.Qtr. 1993
Depository Institutions (1)																	
Commerce et al Banks	51.2	36.2	38.6	34.3	34.0	32.8	31.8	32.0	30.4	29.0	28.5	28.0	27.5	27.7	26.0	25.8	25.1
U.S. Chartered	50.5	37.5	36.6	29.3	28.7	27.9	27.0	27.0	25.5	24.0	23.2	22.6	21.6	22.0	20.3	19.7	19.1
Foreign Officers in U.S.	0.4	0.6	0.7	2.3	2.6	2.0	1.8	2.0	1.8	2.0	2.4	2.5	3.0	3.0	3.3	3.5	3.3
Bank Holding Companies	0.0	0.0	1.1	2.4	2.4	2.0	2.6	3.0	2.8	2.7	2.7	2.7	2.9	2.5	2.3	2.4	2.5
Banks in U.S. Provinces	0.3	0.1	0.3	0.3	0.4	0.3	0.4	0.0	0.3	0.2	0.2	0.2	0.2	0.2	0.2	0.2	0.2
Savings Institutions	13.4	18.7	18.7	18.3	17.4	16.5	17.1	18.0	16.3	15.3	13.5	13.6	12.9	11.4	8.9	7.7	6.9
Savings and Loan	5.8	11.8	12.8	14.4	13.8	13.2	13.8	15.0	13.6	12.6	12.8	12.9	10.3	9.1	7.0	3.9	NA
Savings Banks	7.6	6.9	5.9	3.9	3.7	3.3	3.3	3.0	2.8	2.6	2.7	2.7	2.4	2.2	1.9	1.7	NA
Credit Unions	0.3	1.1	1.3	1.6	1.5	1.5	1.6	2.0	1.7	1.8	1.8	1.8	1.7	1.8	1.8	1.9	1.8
Contractual Intermediaries																	
Life Insurance Companies	21.3	19.4	15.0	10.7	10.7	10.7	10.7	10.0	10.2	10.0	10.3	10.7	10.7	11.4	11.4	11.4	11.6
Other Insurance Companies	4.0	4.4	3.7	4.2	4.1	4.0	4.0	4.0	3.8	3.9	4.2	4.3	4.3	4.4	4.4	4.2	4.1
Private Pension Funds (2)	2.4	6.4	8.4	11.7	11.2	12.5	13.5	13.0	14.0	14.3	14.1	13.5	14.5	13.6	15.6	15.8	15.7
State and Local Government Retirement Funds	1.7	3.3	4.5	4.5	4.7	4.9	5.2	5.0	5.1	5.1	5.2	5.7	6.1	6.1	6.5	6.8	6.8
Others																	
Finance Companies	3.2	4.6	4.8	4.7	4.9	4.6	4.6	5.0	4.7	4.7	5.0	5.1	4.9	5.1	4.8	4.5	4.2
Mortgage Companies	NA	NA	NA	0.4	0.3	0.4	0.3	0.0	0.3	0.4	0.2	0.2	0.2	0.1	0.2	0.2	0.2
Mutual Funds (3)	1.1	2.9	3.5	1.4	1.3	1.5	1.9	2.0	3.1	4.6	4.7	4.3	4.8	5.0	6.2	7.4	8.9
Money Market Mutual Funds	0.0	0.0	0.0	1.8	3.9	4.2	3.0	3.0	3.1	3.2	3.2	3.2	3.6	4.1	4.1	3.9	3.8
Closed-End Funds	NA	NA	NA	0.2	0.1	0.1	0.1	0.0	0.1	0.2	0.2	0.4	0.4	0.4	0.5	0.6	0.6
Security Brokers and Dealers	1.4	1.1	1.2	1.0	1.3	1.6	1.5	2.0	2.0	2.0	1.4	1.3	2.0	2.2	2.5	2.6	3.0
REITs (4)	0.1	0.1	0.1	0.1	0.0	0.1	0.1	0.1	0.1	0.1	0.1	0.1	0.1	0.1	0.1	0.1	0.1
Issuers of Asset Backed Securities	0.0	0.0	0.0	0.0	0.0	0.1	0.1	0.0	0.5	0.9	1.3	1.6	1.9	2.3	2.5	2.7	2.8
Bank Personal Trusts	NA	NA	NA	3.1	4.6	4.7	4.6	4.0	4.5	4.4	4.1	4.1	4.3	4.2	4.3	4.4	4.3
Total Assets ($ in US Billions)	294	397	1,340	3,910	4,754	5,281	3,928	6,716	7,803	9,017	9,727	10,548	11,756	12,017	13,206	14,112	15,065

1. Commercial Banks consist of U.S. chartered commercial bans, domestic affiliates, Edge Act corporations, agencies and branches of foreign banks, and banks in U.S. possession. Foreign banking office in U.S. Inche de Edge Act corporations and offices of foreign banks. IBFs are excluded from domestic banking and treated like branches in foreign countries. Savings and loan associations include all savings and loan associations and federal savings banks insured by the Savings Association Insurance Fund. Savings banks include all federal and mutual savings banks insured by the Bank Insurance Fund.
2. Private pension funds include Federal Employees' Retirement Thrift Savings Fund.
3. Mutual funds are open-end Investment companies (including most Investment trusts) that report to the Investment Company Institute.
4. REITs are real estate Investment trusts.
5. Bank personal trusts are assets of Individuals managed by bank trust departments and nondeposit trust companies.

Source: Flow of Funds Accounts, Board of Governors of the Federal Reserve System.

From 1950 to 1992, the commercial banks' market share in assets has declined from 51 percent to 20 percent, while in the same period mutual funds (pension, money market, and retirement funds) have increased their share from 1 percent to 12 percent, accounting for a larger share than savings and loans, savings banks, and credit unions combined. These less regulated non-banks are increasingly providing loans either directly to both businesses and consumers, or indirectly through the acquisition of commercial paper and high-yield debt. Even credit card loans that were an important source of banks' profits in the 1980s, are now being offered by a myriad of businesses such as transportation and communication (Barth and Jahera, 1993: 2–5).

At least compared with Canada and Mexico, the picture of the American banking industry is one of fragmentation. In Canada, the federal government still manages the chartered banks, and the provinces supervise securities. In United States, in contrast, in addition to the fragmented regulatory environment, there is diversity among states in ownership, taxation, and jurisdiction. Savings and loan companies can be owned by non-banks but not by banks; credit unions, unlike other financial institutions, do not pay taxes; in some states, state chartered banks are granted broader securities and insurance powers than federally chartered banks; and 13 states have virtually created a fiefdom, that is, they only permit interstate banking on a regionally reciprocal basis (Barth and Jahera, 1993: 9). Moves to harmonize this diversity are underway, as evidenced by recent congressional attempts to legislate nationwide banking but, as in neighboring Canada and Mexico, sub-national challenges to regional integration remain.

Challenges and Opportunities

With the passage of the NAFTA, the structure of the North American financial system will undergo great changes in the next few years. And yet, before it can become fully integrated, the financial system will need to contend with the multiple regulatory and sub-regional barriers existing in Mexico, Canada, and the United States today.

A. Mexico

The first potential challenge to regional integration for Mexico stems directly from the particular nature of its financial system. Dominating Mexico's financial industry are 18 privately-owned commercial banks, of which two Mexico City banks, Banamex and Bancomer, control about 60 percent of the market. Mexico's banking structure is similar to most other Latin American countries in that it forms part of a larger system of '*grupos financieros*', wherein the largest and most active banks are owned and controlled by a group of wealthy families or friends. These banks are usually at the core of multi-company enterprises which transact in different markets through holding companies, but which do so under common entrepreneurial and financial control. This structure persists in Mexico (cf. Garrido, 1993), and therefore the role of its commercial banks cannot be fully understood without reference to the financial groups to which they belong (Giron, 1993).

Faced with underdeveloped domestic capital markets and limited external financing, Mexican *grupos* have increasingly spread from financial into non-financial sectors in an attempt to maintain their family's economic well-being and integrity. In essence, they serve as the 'financial arms of kinship groups', raising capital for their members' diverse investments and providing them with a corporate base 'to survive and prosper long into the industrial era'. In the process of expanding to other sectors, these *grupos* continuously consolidate their control (Makler, 1993). They link a diversity of economic activities and thereby contribute to the continuation of family capitalism and the family itself in countries undergoing rapid economic transformation.

The extent to which family capitalism erodes regional integration is unknown. On the one hand, the persistence of family capitalism has been cast as limiting the development of capital markets, various forms of wealth accumulation, and even the growth of regional markets. Williamson, for example, sees family capitalism resulting in capital concentration, monopolistic practices, and the overall impairment of competition and economic development. Yet other scholars have argued that kinship group banks advance development by compensating for high levels of risk and the lack of organized markets which characterize pre-industrial societies. Moreover, this development is not necessarily accompanied by the concentration of market power and monopolistic practices if it is tempered by policies which allow for free entry into banking and prohibit any discriminatory lending practices that might exist.

Family capitalism thus presents a paradox for countries such as Mexico, where it dominates a principal economic sector such as banking. On the one hand, it appears to contribute to a country's economic growth and industrialization through the development of the financial sector. At the same time, it is still unclear whether the capital concentration and oligopolization which accompanies this process will benefit the competition in the financial sector anticipated under NAFTA.

There is another challenge to integration in Mexico: sub-national compacts. Although Mexican banks are permitted to operate throughout the country, only eight are nationwide, five focus their operations on several regions, and the remaining five operate exclusively in one region of the country. But similar to the banking sector arrangements which exist in the southeastern United States, industrial and commercially-based regional groups are beginning to consolidate their power in the peripheral regions of Guadalajara, Estado de Mexico, Monterrey, and Yucatan.

Through a series of activities in these regions, these sub-regional groups are attempting to compete with the large national banks by providing banking services to promising but still underbranched areas.[10] Some are allying or merging (e.g. Banco Unión and Banco Cremí, Bancrecer and Banoro), others are developing links with regional enterprises, and still others are creating new regional banks such as Bansur in Chiapas which can then be developed by, for example, Bancrecer (Garrido, 1994). Recognizing this trend, and drawing upon their already vast and well-established branch network, larger banks such as Banamex and Bancomer are attempting to respond to these challenges by increasing their market share in these and other regions throughout the country.[11] However, these larger banks could be hampered in their efforts to penetrate more peripheral areas by market-inherent barriers such as lack of reputation and switching costs similar to those found in Europe (cf. Hoschka, 1993).

In addition to increasing intersectoral and inter-regional competition, we must also address the foreign challenge to Mexico's financial system and its integration. Until NAFTA's debut, foreign banks were limited to minority ownership in banks and securities enterprises, and were not permitted to engage in retail banking.[12] They can and did conduct wholesale banking activities such as import-export financing, leasing, loan intermediation for Mexican corporations in international financial markets, and private banking services for selected clients. As a result of the Brady Plan, the larger Mexican banks also began to collaborate with large American banks (mainly New York headquartered), to finance Mexican corporations using American deposit receipts and the bond markets in the United States (Garrido, 1994).

NAFTA has changed all of this. To begin with, aside from the sorts of 'market-inherent' barriers mentioned above, there are no legal barriers to entry into Mexican markets. Indeed, NAFTA regulations permit a metered entry of foreign banks during the next 10 years.[13] Moreover, this process is well underway, demonstrated by the fact that more than 100 foreign banks already have offices in Mexico City. But will American and Canadian banks enter Mexico's financial market with the rapidity and intensity implied by increasing financial integration?

Not in the short run, unless there is more cross-border commercial and industrial investment. Despite the fact that Mexico remains woefully underbranched and rising income levels have triggered a greater demand for banking services, major barriers still exist. One major barrier to foreign bank entry are the minimum and maximum capital requirements which will route all but the wealthiest American and Canadian banks to regional retail markets where the 'entry fees' are lower. Mexican financial authorities stipulate that the initial minimum capital requirement for any new foreign or domestic bank wishing to enter Mexico's banking system is $20 million (or 0.5 percent of their total paid-up capital plus reserves), while the maximum allowed is $90 million (or 1.5 percent of the sum of total paid-up capital). Indeed, subsequently approved Mexican banks paid more than $40 million to join the market, suggesting that '. . . investments well above the published minimum are encouraged' (Gruben, 1993: 23; also 17–18).

This minimum has undoubtedly discouraged most U.S. border banks already familiar with retail banking opportunities, as well as potential lenders to small and medium size businesses in Mexico. Indeed, as of the 1992 year end, the $20 million minimum capital requirement exceeded 100 percent of the assets of 86 percent of the Texas banks bordering Mexico (Gruben, 1993: 24), suggesting that they are not likely to look across the border for clients any time in the near future. Given the existence of these minimum capital require-ments, together with the long phase-in period which NAFTA stipulates for foreign bank entry, the new sub-regional Mexican banks mentioned earlier—Del Sureste, Interacciones, and Quadram—are probably the best positioned to consolidate their markets in the short run, to the exclusion of smaller North American lending institutions (Natella *et al.*, 1992[14]).

Nor, for the time being, is the entry of even the wealthiest American or Canadian banks highly likely. In response to the Chiapas uprising, the Mexican government announced that it was going to sell some or all of its remaining shares in Bancomer, Serfín, and Prime-International, its three largest domestic banks (*Financial Times*, February 14, 1994), two of which (Bancomer and Serfín), belong to industrial family *grupos* from Monterrey (Garrido, 1994). The government has invited American and Canadian banks to apply for licenses to establish Mexican subsidiaries, and it is entirely possible that American and Canadian banks might purchase some of these shares.[15]

At best, the large American banks might be willing to merge with an established *grupo* in order to test the Mexican City retail market before establishing their own bank. This would be consistent with multinational investment patterns found elsewhere in Latin America (cf. Brazil: Makler, 1993). When investing in Mexico, American and Canadian banks are likely to form alliances (mergers and joint ventures) with prominent local (incumbent) capital or families in order to gain access to local markets. From the Mexican perspective, such alliances would not only perpetuate family capitalism or *grupos* at the domestic level, but in turn integrate these 'grupos' into international markets. In all likelihood, any alliances that do occur will probably take place between Mexico's new sub-regional banks and the smaller border banks such as the International Bank of Laredo, Texas, or with a bank that has broken with its region and is actively seeking investments outside, such as NationsBank of North Carolina.

Whether Mexican banks will ultimately be eclipsed by the entry of technologically superior American and Canadian banks remains to be seen. While Mexican banks are still lacking in technological sophistication, this deficiency is amply counterbalanced by their established links to local markets. Indeed, when compared to America and Canada, Mexico's financial system is less regulated, resulting in few, if any, firewalls between the financial services they offer. Through their networks, these conglomerates are thus able to reach out and permeate a local population by offering a wide variety of financial services, ranging from commercial banking, brokerage, real estate, and insurance, to a variety of clienteles. This capacity for ready diffusion of numerous financial serves into local populations offers them a significant comparative advantage over their foreign competitors.

Moreover, the onset of NAFTA and foreign competition has also served as an impetus for existing banks to correct whatever technological and administrative weaknesses from which they may currently suffer, so as to effectively compete in the financial services market. Indeed, one can observe how the larger and more established Mexican banks (Banamex, Bancomer and Serfín) are attempting to reduce overhead and employment costs, to improve their information services and data bases, to 'liberalize' several of their financial services such as mortgage loans and credit card terms, and to develop marketing strategies which compete for diverse clienteles (Garrido, 1994). For all of these reasons, even if foreign banks do enter the Mexican market, they will undoubtedly face stiffened local competition.[16]

A final challenge to the current Mexican banking system stems from reforms that have opened this market to new kinds of financial institutions like 'non-bank banks'. The great expansion of credit during the last three years, together with the economic recession, led to an increase in non-performing loans, especially among small depositors. To correct for these inefficiencies, the government raised bank capital ratios (the amount of deposits held by the Mexico's Central Bank) to approximate the Basle standard. Given that commercial banks have no choice but to comply with this requirement, smaller businesses or small borrowers have increasingly sought loans from non-bank banks and other informal financial markets, where interest rates are often very high and terms usurious. By circumventing the national regulatory environment, these smaller institutions will significantly challenge the role of commercial banks in Mexico in the near future, resulting in financial market segmentation.

B. Canada

The liberalization of Canada's financial industry has been explained by a variety of market and political factors. These include the globalization of financial services, the onset of technology and electronic transfers, a parliamentary political system which dilutes the impact of public opinion and interest group activity on the legislative process, and Canadian federalism which encourages policy experimentation at the provincial level (Kintner, 1993: 232–235). Moreover, unlike the United States, where there are two financial systems in existence—the federal and the state—Canada's regulatory structure is much more pliable because there is only the federal system to reform.[17] Thus, Canada has been able to liberalize its financial system and to make substantial changes in its regulatory structure in a relatively short period of time.

As in the American and Mexican cases, there are compacts and sub-regional forces which challenge integration. In competing to deregulate and to build their advantage in global markets, the financial authorities of Canada's largest provinces—Ontario and Quebec— relaxed limitations on shareholding in the capital market's stock-brokering enterprises, believing that this would encourage financial institutions to self-deal. Ontario, for example, has no ownership limits, although it maintains strict self-dealing provisions.[18]

Sub-national initiatives have not only occurred in Canadian capital markets, but also in its banking sector. A merger produced Quebec's National Bank and an acquisition produced British Columbia's new foreign entrant, the Hong Kong and Shanghai Bank. Both are committed to local development, and both are now vigorously competing with the nation's six larger national banks for market share within their provinces, and throughout the country as a whole. Again, these trends signal new hurdles which Canadian authorities will have to confront as the process of regional integration continues.

C. The United States

In the discussion of challenges to Mexico, I examined the evolving role of both incumbent and foreign banks in the larger integration dynamic. In examining the American context, the focus will also be on cross-border entry or out-of-state entry by banks. This issue touches directly on the complex nature of the United States' regulatory system, which differs substantially from Mexico's and Canada's essentially singular systems.

In the U.S., there are both state and federal regulators of banks and other financial services, each with different degrees of authority over the activities of these services. As a result, the system is quite fragmented, with direct implications for both jurisdiction and reform. On the one hand, America's 'states rights' heritage and distrust of large enterprises has meant that state banking regulations are often at odds with federal regulations, not to mention the fact that the country's principal federal authorities are constantly in dispute with one another (cf. *New York Times*, January 25, 1994). In addition, reform in this two-tiered system has been exceptionally slow, as demonstrated by the fact that even the smallest changes in the Glass-Steagall and McFadden Acts have languished in Congress (Kintner, 1993: 234).

The story of state-level dominance over interstate banking began with the 1927 McFadden-Pepper Act. This act extended the scope of branch banking by enabling federally-chartered banks to branch within cities in which they were headquartered, but *only* if state-chartered banks enjoyed the same privilege.[19] The 1933 Banking Act further empowered states over federal authorities, by establishing a state sovereignty principle wherein both federal and state-chartered banks would be under state jurisdiction. This act remained in effect for over twenty years until a new, though still uncertain, regulatory era began in 1956, which placed bank holding companies under the supervision of the Federal Reserve (with the Bank Holding Company Act).[20] While the 'Fed' had the right to approve any interstate acquisition by a bank holding company within one year, the 1957 Douglas Amendment prohibited a holding company from acquiring banks in more than one state, unless approved by the state in which they also planned to establish banks. As this brief history of banking legislation demonstrates, state regulatory authorities had considerable leverage as compared with their federal counterparts.

Not until 1975 did the states actually begin to liberalize their rules on out-of-state banking, and even then, the laws favored state and regional banking to national banking. In that year, Maine was the first state to establish reciprocal banking; i.e. an out-of-state bank could acquire a domestic bank or establish a new (de novo) bank if a Maine bank were permitted the same access in the entering bank's home state.[21] New York and Massachusetts were the next states to legislate reciprocity. Massachusetts was the first state to start a sub-compact or sub-national form of integration, by extending reciprocity *exclusively* to six other New England states in order to exclude the large (mainly

New York), money-centered banks. For the next ten years (1975–85), all but 14 states erected some sort of similar barriers to entry.

As a result, in 1994, the 11,000 commercial banks in the United States were limited in their ability to operate across state lines. In 1985, the partial lifting of interstate banking regulations caused the number of interstate acquisitions to increase dramatically relative to the previous years, although the overall number of interstate acquisitions has remained low. Indeed, except for some 'mega-mergers' (e.g. Bank of America with Security Pacific, Manufacturers Hanover with Chemical), there has been little nationwide consolidation or integration between the smaller and medium size commercial banks (Hoschka, 1993: 271). Thus, while the regulations have been relaxed and interstate banking has increased, interstate branching is still only permitted in seven states (Montana, Nevada, New York, Oregon, Rhode Island, Utah and Virginia).

In the vast majority of cases, then, a significant amount of local regulation continues to preclude the existence of one national banking market in the United States. Intra- and interstate mergers and acquisitions have occurred, and some of these have been large scale. Moreover, given the onset of regional integration and the imminent collapse of interstate branching barriers, even more mergers and acquisitions are likely to occur in the future. But even with the passage of a bill that would permit nationwide branching, significant barriers remain that exceed even those of the European Community. (Hoschka, 1993: 272, 282) As a result, although the U.S. Congress is likely to soon enact interstate branching into law, this legislation will probably be challenged by states who will seek to counteract it by vigorously applying rules and/or establishing high 'entrance fees' along the lines of what the Mexicans have done.

At the same time, there also exists a type of financial integration which is likely to persist, and indeed, *resist* national integration.[22] It is sub-regional in form, and has occurred where banks and their state regulators have successfully used regulations to attract or contain out-of-state (foreign) banks. For example, Delaware and South Dakota—to mention but two examples of 'soliciting' states—have successfully wooed out-of-state banks by becoming a haven for credit card operations. As a result, these states have earned a significant increase in tax revenues and banking employment in a relatively short period of time. (Hoschka, 1993: 272–279).

In contrast, most sub-national units have repulsed suitors. A particularly striking case is the southeastern United States, where state legislation has restricted 'foreign' bank entry. Under this arrangement, non-regional U.S. banks cannot participate within the compact region, and while foreign banks are permitted *de novo* entry, there are severe restrictions on their expansion. Although new federal banking regulations are scheduled to break the branching barrier, others remain that will discourage entry, at least by larger banks. One of these is a federally imposed restriction that will prohibit any 'foreign' bank from acquiring more than 25 percent of the total deposits in the targeted state. Another respects each state's right to establish its own restriction on deposit capitation. Given that the southeast U.S. and other sub-national units have experienced remarkable economic growth in a relatively short period of time, one wonders if there is something to be said about the virtues of consolidated sub-regional banking structures, or for that matter, family compacts (*grupos*), as a wise means to achieve overall regional growth and development (cf. *Business Week*, September 27, 1993; *New York Times*, November 27, 1993).

Other regions within the United States may also initiate regulatory strategies to control cross-border entry. For example, in its struggle to overcome its recession, California—potentially the wealthiest sub-region in North America—is working to maintain investment and build business within its borders. But permissive banking policies which have resulted in increased foreign market share could lead to a backlash of protectionism, or at least to an increase in the advocacy for stronger local (intrastate) reinvestment regulations.

Another challenge to the American banking structure is isomorphic. While the Glass-Steagall Act currently prohibits U.S. commercial banks from providing investment and other financial services, Canadian and Mexican banks already provide such services. With NAFTA's debut and the inevitable integration of financial services, American commercial banks are thus increasingly likely to lobby U.S. regulatory authorities to eliminate this restriction.

Some Conclusions

This chapter has been descriptive and exploratory, touching upon the relations among institutions and markets within the financial sector. Numerous changes are occurring in finance in the Americas, and they are occurring more rapidly than in any other industry. Moreover, all of these changes have implications for regional integration.

We can see the impact of integration at all levels of the financial industry. In fact, what occurs at one level is mirrored at the others. Because of the liberalization or relaxation of regulatory environments within national boundaries, there is increasing integration *within* enterprises as they diversify their products and become more conglomerate in form. In turn, there is integration *among* companies as ownership rules are relaxed and they take on an increasingly conglomerate form, incorporating other financial and non-financial products into their realms. Third, there is integration in the financial industry *within* its sub-national compacts, and there is integration too *across borders*, as banks reach into new territories to form alliances and mergers with domestic incumbents.

In one form or another, all of this will mean increasing financial and economic concentration, the growth and welfare outcomes of which have not even begun to be predicted. The Mexicans are very familiar with economic concentration and conglomeration in industry and finance. It remains the dominant form of their economy. So are the Canadians, at least in finance, but there is more coming. But in the United States this form is new, or at least it has not been evident for several decades. 'Bigness' and nationwide networking—what some refer to as 'the financial highway'—is going to require some adjustment. This not only applies to the banks, but to their regulators, as they become larger and more centralized. Bigger might mean greater efficiency. It certainly will mean a greater concentration of power within the NAFTA compact. It is hard to say yet whether it means better. We should now devote more of our efforts to finding out.

References

American Banker, October 5, 1993.

Asociacion Mexicana de Bancos and Evans (1979)

BARTH, J. R. and JAHERA, J. S. (1993) 'The U.S. Banking Industry in Transition: Domestic and International Developments,' paper presented at the International Conference on Financial Institutions in Transition, Universidad Nacional Autónoma de Mexico and Universidad Autonoma Metropolitana-Azcapotzalco, May 27–28.

BOREHAM, G. F. (1993) 'The Banking-Commerce Question in Both a Canadian and Global Context,' paper presented at the International Conference on Financial Institutions in Transition, Universidad Nacional Autonoma de Mexico and Universidad Autonoma Metropolitana-Azcapotzalco, May 27–28.

CARSTENS, C. M. (1994) 'Improving Financial Services For The Poor', Mexico: Instituto Tecnológico Autónomo (ITAM), unpublished manuscript, February 14.

GARRIDO N., CELSO (1994) 'Los Grupos Privados Nacionales en Mexico', Mexico: Universidad Autonoma Metropolitana-Azcapotzalco (UAM), Azcapotzalco, Mexico, October.

GARRIDO N., CELSO (1994) 'The Internationalization of Financial Markets: The Mexican Case,' unpublished paper presented at Rockefeller Foundation Conference and Study Center, Bellagio, Italy, May 10.

GARRIDO N., CELSO (1994) 'Evolucion Reciente de los Grupos Economicos en Mexico,' *Revista de la Cepal*, Santiago, Chile, Agosto.

GIRON G., ALICIA (1993) 'La Banca Comercial en Canada, Estados Unidos y Mexico,'

Instituto de Investigaciones Económicas, Universidad Nacional Autonoma de Mexico (UNAM), unpublished paper.

GRUBEN, W. C. (1993) 'U.S. Banks, Competition, and the Mexican Banking System: How Much Will NAFTA Matter?,' *Financial Industry Studies,* Federal Reserve Bank of Dallas, October, 1993.

HOSHKA, T. (1993) *Cross Border Entry in European Retail Financial Services,* New York: St. Martins Press, Chapter 4.

KINTNER, E. (1993) 'Politics and Deregulation in the Canadian Banking Industry,' *American Review of Canadian Studies,* Summer, 231–246.

MAKLER, H. M. (1993) 'Brazilian Financial Conglomerates: Family Capitalism, Diversification and Implications for Hemispheric Integration,' paper presented at the International Conference on Financial Institutions in Transition, Universidad Nacional Autonoma de Mexico and Universidad Autonoma Metropolitana-Azcapotzalco, May 27–28.

NATELLA, S. *et al.* (1992) *The Mexican Banking System,* New York: CS First Boston.

New York Times, January 25, 1994.

SCOTT K. E. (1980) 'The Patchwork Quilt: State and Federal Roles in Bank Regulation,' *Stanford Law Review,* Vol. 32, 687–742.

WELCH, J. H. and GRUBEN, W. C. (1993) 'A Brief History of the Mexican Financial System,' *Financial Industry Studies,* Federal Reserve Bank of Dallas, October.

Notes

1. For example, several European countries have formed the European Community (EC). In addition, Argentina, Brazil, Paraguay, and Uruguay have formed a market in the southern hemisphere (MERCOSUR), and in early 1994, Canada, Mexico, and the United States signed the North American Free Trade Agreement (NAFTA).

2. These steps were also accompanied by a return to universal banking, and the reauthorization of financial groups, with some restrictions. Specifically, commercial banks are now able to hold equity positions in non-financial enterprises, but their holdings are limited to 5 percent of an enterprise's paid-in capital, while loans to principal bank shareholders, executives, or to the enterprises they own are limited to 20 percent of a bank's loan portfolio (Welch and Gruben, 1993: 8).

3. There are two types of banks in Canada: Schedule 1, or 'widely held' banks, where no shareholder hold more than 10 percent of the voting shares, and Schedule II, or 'closely held' banks, where one shareholder can hold in excess of 10 percent of the voting shares. While non-U.S. owned banks are subject to limitations on branching and asset size, American owned banks are exempt (Boreham, 1993: 7–9).

4. This should not be particularly difficult, given that several of the Schedule 2 banks can now legally operate like Schedule 1 banks. For example, the Hong Kong Bank of Canada has recently acquired three other Schedule 2 banks, and CT Financial, a financial holding company owned by a Montreal commercial conglomerate (Imasco Ltd.), acquired Canada Trust and Mortgage, the country's second largest trust company (Boreham, 1993: 16).

5. In other words, banks could own and operate insurance, trust, brokerage, leasing, loan and securities companies, and in turn, other financial enterprises such as

trust and insurance companies were also allowed to own banks (Kintner, 1993).

6. Self dealing refers to transactions between a bank, its subsidiaries, and 'related parties', e.g. officers of the bank and any companies in which they have substantial investments (Boreham, 1993: 9).

7. Coincidentally, this same process occurred in Brazil two decades ago (Makler, 1993).

8. While in Canada, the federal government instituted the Office of the Super-intendent of Financial Institutions (OSFI) to supervise and coordinate financial regulations, the regulation of securities activities remains a provincial responsibility.

9. Banking institutions are chartered, insured, or regulated by one or more of the following: Office of the Comptroller of the Currency (OCC) for national banks, the Office of Thrift Supervision (OTS) for savings and loans, the National Credit Union Administration (NCUA) for credit unions, the Federal Deposit Insurance Corporation (FDIC) for banks and savings and loans, the Federal Reserve for member banks and bank holding companies, and the individual state banking authorities, which regulate all state-chartered institutions (Barth and Jahera, 1993: 8). The U.S. Senate Banking Committee conducted hearings in early March 1994 on the consolidation of federal and state regulatory agencies.

10. The new multi-regional banks are attempting to develop a network of regional federation of banks rather than a national bank (Garrido, 1993).

11. The growth of regional banks was a result of the government's bank reprivatization and liberalization program that began in the mid-1980s. Mexican commercial banks located in the 'core' (Mexico City) began to increase their deposits and loans to the private sector, and reaped large profits because of large spreads (10 to 15 percent between passive and active rates of interest). When several non-financial and financial enterprises protested the cost of credits and the level of banks' profits, the government defused the conflict by authorizing the establishment of several industry-linked credit unions and nine new private banks, most of which are located in the 'periphery' of other regions (Garrido, 1993).

12. The exception here is, of course, the long established Citibank, which manages a branch under special agreement.

13. According to the NAFTA agreement, American and Canadian-based banks are collectively allowed up to 8 percent of total banking capital in 1994, with the limit gradually increasing during the next six years (the year 2000) when it is scheduled to disappear.

14. Source: an interview with Roberto Hernandez, President, Asociación Mexicana de Bancos, conducted by Celso Garrido N., 1993. Hernandez is also president of the Banamex group.

15. For example, the J. P. Morgan bank has already sought approval from the Federal Reserve to open a subsidiary in Mexico, and plans to operate through a bank and brokerage house. Foreign brokerage and insurance companies will be limited to 10 percent of the Mexican market (*Financial Times*, February 14, 1994).

16. Regardless of their efforts to penetrate the Mexican market, however, both foreign and domestic banks ultimately face a limit to their expansion, because neither foreign nor domestic banks will ever be able to compete with state institutions such as the Nafinsa public credit union (Natella *et al.*, 1992), or the myriad of informal financial services such as pawnshops, *cajas de ahorro*, and government

programs such as the *Patronato del Ahorro Nacional* whose clients are largely Mexico's poor (Mansell Carstens, 1994).

17. In point of fact, while banks are under federal jurisdiction, securities enterprises are under provincial jurisdiction, creating a disjuncture for regulatory authorities.

18. On the other hand, fueled by public opinion fears of foreign (principally American) acquisition of a major chartered bank or trust company, federal authorities are moving toward stringent ownership regulation, and are raising the standards through which an enterprise becomes licensed to participate in any area of financial activity (Chant, 1988: 132 as cited in Kintner, 1993: 240–241).

19. Much of the material for this brief summary of the evolution of American banking was gathered from a recent monograph on European cross-border entry (Hoschka, 1993: 269–270).

20. Kenneth Scott would argue that federal authorities (e.g. the Federal Reserve Board) dominate banking regulation. (Kenneth Scott, 'The Patchwork Quilt: State and Federal Roles in Bank Regulation,' *Stanford Law Review*, 32, 1980: 687–742).

21. Nine years later, in February, 1994, Maine reversed this law and allowed nationwide or non-reciprocal banking.

22. Compacts might not exist forever. Currently, NationsBank of North Carolina cannot expand further outside of its compact region because the compact requires that 80 percent of a member bank's deposits originate within the region. In its quest to expand throughout the United States, NationsBank is lobbying to modify this legislation.

3

NAFTA and Financial Services: Implications for Banks

STEPHEN LANDE, MANUEL MINDREAU AND MICHAEL LANDE

Introduction

This chapter will examine the effects of NAFTA on North American commercial banking by comparing the banking systems of the United States, Canada and Mexico and the consequences of the NAFTA treaty on these systems. We start by comparing the provisions of the U.S.-Canada Free Trade Agreement (FTA) dealing with commercial banking to provisions of NAFTA in this same area. Then we analyze the impact of both NAFTA and the 1994 peso devaluation crisis on the Mexican banking system and its implications for the other NAFTA member countries.

The U.S. banking industry is diverse and fragmented with concurrent federal and state chartering and supervision. Two important pieces of legislation that distinguish the U.S. banking system from its neighbors are the McFadden Act of 1927, which establishes state sovereignty on banking activities and prohibits interstate branching, and the Glass-Steagall Act of 1933, which separates commercial from investment banking. During the last two decades certain relaxation in the enforcement of the McFadden provisions took place. For instance, in 1975, contravening the McFadden Act, Maine was the first state to establish reciprocal banking for out-of-state institutions. By 1991, Hawaii and Montana were the only states to continue to deny entrance to banks from all other states (Bordo *et al.*, 1994, 327). However, although little nationwide consolidation occurred, sub-national forms of integration—mainly in the southeast and New England—did occur. Only very recently, in 1994, the McFadden Act was modified, giving state banks a two-year time frame to choose whether to abide by it or to establish mechanisms to allow out-of-state banks to fully operate in their states.

Regarding the operation of foreign banks in the U.S., the International Banking Act of 1978 brought the domestic agencies, branches and commercial affiliates of foreign-owned banks under federal supervision and regulation. Foreign banks had to obey branching prohibitions similar to those of the McFadden Act, enjoying essentially the same privileges and restrictions as U.S. banks (Binhammer, 1988).

On the other hand, the Canadian banking system is characterized by a few very large banks and a number of smaller ones. Nationwide branching is permitted, and the federal government has almost complete regulatory control of the commercial banking system. The shares of Schedule A banks (the largest domestic banks) are widely held—no investor can own more than 10 percent, and no group of non-resident investors can own more than 25 percent of the shares (Libby, 1994, 502). It should be noted that, although widely held, the Canadian banking industry is highly concentrated. The six largest banks (Canadian Imperial Bank of Commerce, the Royal Bank of Canada, Scotiabank, the Bank of Montreal, the Toronto Dominion Bank and the National Bank of Canada) hold over 90 percent of the banking assets, the three biggest of them representing 61 percent.

The Canadian banking sector started to liberalize in the early 1980s when new legislation was introduced allowing for the chartering of foreign banks and harmonizing federal and provincial legislation. The 1980 Bank Act also created a single regulatory authority and removed regulatory barriers that separated chartered banks, securities, trusts and insurance companies. Furthermore, since June 1987 Canadian banks were allowed into the securities business, a liberty denied by the Glass-Steagall Act to all but a few U.S. banks. Canadian banks were allowed to underwrite and distribute corporate securities and invest their surplus funds in government and corporate securities. At the same time, provincial governments relaxed their financial regulations and allowed banks to conduct non-bank activities—Ontario and Quebec took the lead in this. The right to sell private banking and asset management services followed in 1990. In addition, Canada has no equivalent of the U.S.'s Community Reinvestment Act, which requires banks to put money back into the community (they actually have to make loans where they take deposits) where they do business. However, limitations on ownership stakes still revealed Canada's preference for widely-held ownership against ownership linkages between financial and non-financial institutions. More recently, four new pieces of legislation passed in 1992 were introduced allowing

Canadian commercial banks to enter the trust business and granting them limited powers to sell insurance—Canadian banks were allowed to retail these financial products through the acquisition of subsidiaries and not through their approximately 6000 branches.

It should also be noted that in Canada political pressures do not seem as important in influencing monetary policy as in the United States. Since the early 1980s the Bank of Canada has used a wide variety of indicators such as open market operations, withdrawal and deposit of government funds from/to chartered banks, daily clearing balances for checks, and the use of primary and secondary reserves to aid in the formulation of monetary policy.[1] However, one goal that does seem more important in Canada than in the U.S. is foreign exchange stability, especially with respect to the U.S. dollar (Joyce, 1989).

Finally, regarding the activities of foreign banks in Canada, the 1980 Bank Act permitted foreign banks to operate subsidiaries in Canada as a special class of banks (Schedule B banks). However, the combined assets of these banks could not exceed 16 percent of total domestic assets of the Canadian banking system (Libby, 1994: 503). Furthermore, their size was controlled through regulatory guaranteed approval of their capital bases, and their right to establish branches was not automatic. In a word, before the signing of the U.S.-Canada FTA, foreign-controlled banks in Canada were relegated to a special status and limited in growth.

The 1989 U.S.-Canada FTA altered the above described picture by fueling cross-border integration. First of all, the agreement allowed U.S. financial subsidiaries to operate like Canadian chartered banks throughout the country. In addition, Canada agreed not to restrict U.S. ownership of various financial institutions. U.S. subsidiaries were exempted from the Bank Act provisions (namely the 16 percent restriction imposed on total foreign-controlled banks assets in Canada), and were allowed to open branches without having to apply to Minister of Finance. On the other hand, under the FTA, the U.S. allowed both Canadian and U.S. banks to underwrite Canadian government securities in the U.S., while allowing Canadian-controlled institutions the same treatment as U.S. banks with respect to any future amendments to the Glass-Steagall Act. Furthermore, both countries agreed to continue to provide the financial institutions of the other with the rights and privileges they now enjoy subject to normal regulatory considerations (Libby, 1994: 504).

The FTA basically confirmed the *status quo* for Canadian banks in the U.S. and guaranteed their future equal treatment with U.S. banks, while opening the Canadian market for U.S. banks. Given that at the time of the agreement the Canadian financial services industry was less restrictive, U.S. banks gained immediate access to a rapidly deregulating market and a wider range of operations. Moreover, U.S. banks were able to use their Canadian subsidiaries to circumvent provisions of the Glass-Steagall Act and other regulatory statues. The hope for Canadians was that this would lead to increased pressure for more deregulation in the U.S.

Contrary to some of the concerns expressed when the FTA was enacted, in the initial stage, Canadian banks expanded into the U.S. more than the reverse. This occurred because Canadian banks had reached expansion limits at home; they were in better financial condition than U.S banks; and they followed their customers to the U.S. (Farnsworth, 1992). For instance, in October 1994, Bank of Montreal became the first Canadian bank to be listed on the New York Stock Exchange. This listing underscored the bank's corporate strategy of expansion below the Canadian border. Bank of Montreal said it expected to triple earnings from its U.S. businesses by 2002 as part of an aggressive $700 million expansion plan—in 1994 businesses in the U.S. accounted for about 25 percent of the bank's net income, which according to Tony Comper, President of the bank, was expected to represent 50 percent by the end of the century.[2]

However, with the whole new range of opportunities opened for foreign banks in Canada under the 1992 amendments to the 1980 Banking Act, the Canadian banking market has been made more attractive for U.S. banks. New amendments to the Bank Act have expanded further the role of foreign banks, granting them access to the tightly controlled electronic banking network (the automatic teller system would be opened to retailers and brokerages), and into Canada's $9 billion auto leasing business[3] (Fennell, 1996: 34–5).

Nevertheless, in our opinion, the FTA while formalizing the overall trade relationship with the U.S., failed to redress problems related to bank affiliations with securities firms and insurance companies, interstate branching, and the extraterritorial application of U.S. law. The only principle embodied in the FTA financial service chapter was the *de jure* national treatment. In the absence of a measure of reciprocity, the national treatment principle put the country with the more open market—in this case Canada—at a definite disadvantage. American banks in Canada benefit from wider powers granted under the 1980 Bank Act and its subsequent amendments, as compared to U.S. legislation.

The FTA was also a one shot deal, which did not encourage future liberalization of the U.S. financial markets. As mentioned before, except for the provision regarding possible changes to the Glass-Steagall Act, the agreement only required the parties to continue to provide rights and privileges in place at the time of the agreement's signing. Therefore, although Canadian banks' branches, agencies and subsidiaries in the U.S. were grandfathered at their 1987 level, there was no specific commitment to automatically extend to Canadian banks any changes relating to interstate branching.

However, the financial sector aspects of the FTA must be judged on its own terms. In contrast to the provisions of the Banking Directive of the European Common Market, Chapter 17 of the FTA was not directed toward the integration of financial markets through harmonization in regulation. Nonetheless, the most striking feature of Canadian and U.S. financial markets has been the substantial integration that had been achieved despite the very different approaches toward regulation. The commitments taken by Canada and the U.S. reflect the differing objectives of the two parties.

The U.S. efforts in the FTA negotiation were directed at removing the features of the Canadian regulatory system that discriminated against its banks. On the other hand, the benefits received by Canada can be best viewed as 'defensive.' For the Canadian financial sector, maintenance of the status quo in the U.S. was desirable because overall, U.S. financial regulation gave equal, if not favorable, treatment to Canadian institutions. Moreover, the status quo was being disturbed by regulatory changes that jeopardized the position of Canadian institutions in the U.S. The removal of the restriction on bank ownership of securities firms in Canada, and the subsequent purchase of major firms by banks, placed the U.S. operations of the firms at risk in terms of the Glass-Steagall Act prohibitions on combining investment and commercial banking.

Similarly, though the International Banking Act in the U.S. gave Canadian banks a temporary exemption from a ban on interstate branching and subsidiaries, the exemption was scheduled to run out in 1988. The Canadian authorities thus acted defensively in the FTA financial sector negotiations. The exemption of securities of Canadian governments from the Glass-Steagall restrictions preserved the ability of securities firms associated with banks to underwrite and deal in these securities, a power that was threatened by their becoming owned by banks. Similarly, the extension of interstate banking powers allowed the Canadian banks to maintain the U.S. operations intact.

In conclusion, FTA provided that financial institutions of the other country be governed by the same regulatory rules as comparable domestic institutions. The deal was highly asymmetrical, as U.S. banks received powers in Canada, that Canadian banks did not receive in the U.S. because of the Glass-Steagall and McFadden Acts on investment and interstate banking. However, these agreements brought about strategic implications for Canadian banks:

1. move to a North American strategy,
2. move to fee-based services,
3. consolidation of domestic and retail strategies.

Increased price competition went hand-in-hand with this new focus on productivity.

NAFTA: Consolidating U.S.-Canadian Integration and Promoting Mexican Involvement

Regarding the integration of financial services between the U.S. and Canada, in essence, NAFTA built on the existing U.S.-Canada FTA provisions, although it did not significantly affect the powers of either U.S. or Canadian banks. However, the objective of making up for the shortcoming of the FTA in terms of immediate market access to the U.S. was not fulfilled by the NAFTA. For instance, there was no significant movement to eliminate the U.S. barriers left untouched by the FTA—although this changed in 1994 with the modifications introduced to the McFadden Act.[4] Nor was there a significant improvement to the FTA in terms of structuring the NAFTA around specific trade principles which were developed within the Uruguay Round of the General Agreement on Tariffs and Trade (GATT) and should provide greater certainty for existing and future Canadian bank operations in the United States. For instance, under NAFTA, the principle of national treatment was widened substantially to include the concept of 'equal competitive opportunities'. This broader principle will ensure that foreign banks in NAFTA countries will not be disadvantaged in their ability to provide financial services relative to domestic banks. The principle also ensures foreign banks will be extended the same rights and privileges as domestic institutions as laws change. It will guarantee, for example, that Canadian and Mexican banks will benefit from future changes to all U.S. banking legislation, including the Glass-Steagall Act. In this way, it goes much beyond what was accomplished under the FTA (Neufeld, 1994).

In addition, under NAFTA, subnational governments (U.S. and Mexican states and Canadian provinces) must abide by the terms of the deal—something not accomplished by the FTA. The NAFTA also contains a panel-type tripartite dispute settlement mechanism which may be used to address financial service disputes. The FTA provided only for consultations between governments but did not cover the settlement of financial disputes.

NAFTA provisions also ensured that the 'most favored nation' (MFN) principle apply to North-American trade, including the financial service industry. Provisions in Chapter 14 of the NAFTA provided for MFN with regard to:

1. the establishment of financial institutions,
2. investors of another party and investment of such investors, and
3. cross-border trade in financial services.

The significance of these provisions was that U.S. and Canadian commercial banks could establish subsidiaries in Mexico. MFN status is defined as each party according a financial services provider of the MFN party, the highest level of treatment offered to any foreign financial services provider, regardless of country of origin, with respect to establishment, acquisition, expansion, management, conduct, operation, and sale within its territory. Mexico has also agreed to extend NAFTA benefits to all financial services providers operating, and organized, under the laws of another NAFTA party. This meant that subsidiaries of Japanese or European banks operating in the U.S. would have access to Mexico to the same degree as an American owned bank operating in the United States (Kapiloff, 1994).

And lastly, the principle of transparency contained in NAFTA requires publication of legislative changes and ensures the ability of foreign banks to obtain clear information about application and licensing procedures and decisions. Transparency means that all parties to NAFTA must provide, wherever possible, advanced notice to all interested persons of any measure of general application that the party proposes to adopt, and then allow an opportunity for such persons to comment. In addition, there must be easy access to information concerning any required application, information needed for the completion of such an application and the status of such applications. All parties to NAFTA must also establish one or more inquiry point(s) which will be able to answer any questions regarding financial services measures. In sum, it is expected that the application of these specific trade principles to the financial services industry provides greater certainty for existing and future bank operations in the North America.

NAFTA confirmed the right of Mexican banks (already granted under legislation passed prior to the enactment of NAFTA) to operate in the United States NAFTA also extended the benefits that U.S. banks obtained from Canadian authorities through the FTA to Mexican banks. Specifically, Mexican investors are now allowed to establish subsidiary institutions in Canada which were exempted from restrictive ownership rules and investors do not have to ask for permission from the Canadian Ministry of Finance to open additional branches.

In terms of what was accomplished under the NAFTA, the changes regarding the Mexican banking system and its opening up for foreign investment are much more significant for the future integration of financial services in North America. Most importantly, with the signing of NAFTA, U.S. and Canadian investors were allowed to own 100 percent of Mexican banks. Nevertheless, under Article 1410 of NAFTA, Mexico was allowed several exceptions with regard to foreign investment and participation in its financial services sector. Almost all of these exceptions apply only during the transition period, which is defined as the period beginning with the entry into force of NAFTA (January 1, 1994) and ending on January 1, 2000 or six years from the date of entry into force.

The transition period was designed to allow Mexico's recently privatized industry time to adjust to the full brunt of competition from American and Canadian financial giants. Yet, even before the privatized banking system was able to gain the needed experience and before the transition period allowed full competition from foreign institutions, the newly-privatized banking sector was subject to unexpected challenges. For instance, for banks where Mexican ownership was present, the legislation limited foreign shareholders to C shares which could only represent 30 percent of the ordinary capital of individual banks. Foreigners could not own more than the percentage of shares allowed in the C category unless they owned 99 percent of an individual bank. However, they were subject to both individual and aggregate (or collective) capital caps. The individual capital limits established by Mexican law is a minimum of 0.12 percent and a maximum of 1.5 percent of the total capital of Mexican commercial banks during the transition period, after which they would be limited to 4 percent of the market share (Libby, 1994: 506). This stipulation was designed to protect Mexico's largest banks from foreign take-overs. Individual investors from Canada and the U.S. could expand beyond this 4 percent limit, but only through internal growth. The aggregate limit for such institutions was set at 8 percent of the system's total capital at the date of entry into the agreement, and is scheduled to increase, in equal yearly increments, to 15 percent by the end of the transition period.

NAFTA also provided that Mexico would reserve the right to freeze U.S. and Canadian investment, if foreign aggregate capital exceeds 25 percent of the Mexican banking industry at any time within four years of the end of the transition period. This 25 percent freeze could only last three years, and any further restrictions beyond this transition period would require the approval of U.S. and Canadian officials (Smith, 1993: 84).

However, some restrictions were permanent, meaning not limited to the transition period. Mexico (under its part B schedule) may require that any foreign financial services provider of another party must be engaged in providing the same financial services in the territory of that party. It is thus required by Mexican law that a foreign financial affiliate can only provide those services which it is licensed to perform in its own country. This is designed to balance the American restrictions against multipurpose financial institutions. Unlike full service Mexican banks, American banks cannot engage in such varied operations as brokerage, insurance, etc. Mexico reserved the right to review, and, if deemed necessary for the protection of its banking system, to reject any acquisition of an existing commercial bank, or any of the capital or assets of an existing commercial bank. Mexico was not obligated to approve any acquisition when the total capital of the acquired bank, plus the capital of all other banks owned by the investor, exceeds 4 percent of the total capital of all the commercial banks in Mexico.

Therefore, while the provisions of NAFTA focus on open access, member governments still reserve the right to adopt and maintain 'reasonable measures for prudential reasons.' It allows governments to impose those measures it deems necessary to provide for the protection of its investors, depositors, financial market participants, policy-holders, policy-claimants, or persons to whom a fiduciary duty is owed by a cross-border financial service provider. Thus NAFTA does not interfere with the fiduciary responsibilities of any of the governments to safeguard the security of the banking system.

Within this context, the Canadian banking industry largely achieved its objective of gaining entry into the Mexican financial markets. Canadian banks had maintained offices in Mexico since the turn of the century, but representative offices status—coupled with severe constraints in their operations in that country—precluded them from competing head to head with domestic players. Under NAFTA, Canadian and U.S. subsidiaries in Mexico receive national treatment and therefore are allowed to provide all the services that Mexican banks already provide. However, U.S. and Canadian banks operating outside of Mexico are still restricted to providing offshore services only (Karnin, 1992).

In the initial stage, trade finance business was expected to be the area of most rapid growth for Canadian and U.S. banks doing business in Mexico. In the second stage, the areas of corporate finance and capital markets will attract direct involvement by U.S. and Canadian banks. However, Canadian and U.S. banks are also targeting top-tier Mexican companies and correspondent banking partnerships to service their home-based clients, and joint ventures and acquisitions are already taking place. For instance, Banco Central Hispano already owns 20 percent of the financial group that controls Banco Internacional. In 1992, the Bank of Nova Scotia (Scotiabank) purchased 5 percent stake of Grupo Inverlat, the fifth largest Mexican bank (previously known as Comermex). However, the transaction was expanded and only perfected in February 1996. This arrangement allows Scotiabank to expand its trade finance and corporate banking business in Mexico. More importantly, over the longer term, it will allow the Canadian bank to participate in the growth opportunities in Mexican retail and small business banking. In this regard, the most interesting component of the deal is that both parties will be able to capitalize on Scotiabank's expertise and experience in running a nationwide, fully integrated network (in terms of system design and product development and marketing). More recently, in February 1996, Bank of Montreal purchased a 16 percent stake in Grupo Financiero Bancomer, the parent company of Mexico's second largest bank.[5] This has been signaled as a vote of confidence following the peso's December 1994 devaluation (Torres, 1996).

Similarly, the main benefit of NAFTA for U.S. banks will be through their relationships with U.S. companies that will prosper because of NAFTA, and only secondly through their participation in the Mexican banking system. U.S. banks will probably be aggressive in entering the Mexican retail banking sector; however, their involvement early on will be minimal: increased competition and opportunities will be the result of the gradual opening of the Mexican financial market (Thomas, 1994). In general terms, the extent of the movement of Canadian and U.S. banks into Mexico will depend on several factors. One is the health of the financial sector in the home country. At the present time, U.S. banks are consolidating operations in response to large outstanding loans and higher capital requirements and are not likely to expand rapidly into the Mexican market. However, as Canadian and U.S. businesses move into Mexico, then their banks will probably follow them there (Libby, 1994: 507).

Some analysts have the feeling that Canadian banks will do especially well in Mexico since they have more experience in a completely federally-supervised system (Jordan, 1993). Similarly, it is expected that U.S. banks will continue to ask for less regulation and broadened powers in the U.S. in order to compete with Canadian banks in Canada and Mexico. Within the NAFTA framework, the separation of investment banking from commercial banking provision of the Glass-Steagall Act will be the most likely target for reform.

NAFTA Provisions Solidified Privatization and Began Gradual Internationalization of Mexican Banking System

NAFTA was negotiated as a tool for gradually opening the Mexican market for North American banking. As described earlier, the provisions were carefully drafted to allow limited North American penetration into the market during a ten-year transition period which could be extended for an additional three years if the penetration was moving too quickly. The reason for the gradual opening was to protect the recently-privatized Mexican banking system from being taken over by North American banks before the new banks had developed sufficiently deep roots to protect themselves.

However, the newly-privatized Mexican banks were threatened soon after NAFTA implementation, not by competition from banks in its NAFTA partners, but by a general dislocation in the Mexican economy. Although some of the disruption in Mexican banking system came in the aftermath of the peso devaluation, part of it was due to the worldwide adjustment to changing financial situations which affected Japanese and American institutions as well. The financial stability of Mexican banks was seriously threatened by the number of non-performing loans held by the privatized banks and the shrinking profit margins of a number of banks. The Mexican Government devised a number of creative steps to tide the banks over the problem period. Ironically, one of the ways to assist Mexican financial entities to solve their capitalization problems and to promote strategic alliances between Mexican and foreign bankers was to accelerate and even go beyond Mexican liberalization obligations under NAFTA. This would both contribute to financing some of the non-performing loans held in the portfolios of the banking institutions and to improving the efficiency of their operations. In the short term, there has been little effect from this initiative. However, as the Mexican economy recovers, one expects that foreign banks—particularly U.S. and Canadian banks—will take advantage of the openings in the new law, resulting in an acceleration of the integration of the North American financial services industry.

Over the course of the past seven years, the Mexican banking system has undergone drastic changes. Some have been institutional: Mexico's banking system has gone from being a nationalized industry to a private one, open not only to domestic participation but to foreign competition as well. However, a common misperception is that the massive institutional changes stem only from the implementation of NAFTA. The Mexican Government began to privatize and introduce market forces into the operation of its financial sector well before NAFTA implementation. In fact, the same motivations which led to the privatization in 1992 of state-owned banks were responsible for Mexico's decision to open its banking system to North American participation under NAFTA.

The Mexican banking industry was nationalized in 1982 during the height of Mexico's foreign debt crisis. At that time, Mexico, after having suffered a massive devaluation, found the private banks a convenient scapegoat for the problem. However, the intervention of the state, not only in taking over the banks but in economic areas as well, probably aggravated the situation. It is worth noting that the period of recovery lasted for about 30 months, much longer than one expects Mexico to need to recover from the current situation.

In July 1990, more than three years before NAFTA went into effect, the Mexican Congress passed the Credit Institutions bill which can be viewed as the first step in reversing the 1982 nationalization law. The law provided for the privatization of the Mexican commercial banking sector. It provided for controlling interests only to be purchased by Mexican nationals. Foreigners could participate in the ownership of the newly privatized banks, but only as a minority shareholders—the only exception was Citibank whose existing operations were grandfathered. This outcome was guaranteed by the development of three categories of shares: domestic investors were given exclusive access to 51 percent of A-shares of Mexican banks; 19 percent of the remaining stocks were open to foreign residents of Mexico (B-shares); non-resident foreigners were given access to only the remaining 30 percent C-shares which carried no voting rights. Other than Citibank, the only U.S. banks which invested in the banking system were the Bank of Boston and American Express (see Table 3.1). At this point, U.S. banks did not seem to have the confidence to invest in situations where they did not exercise full control.

The actual privatization occurred at a time when economic prospects in Mexico were very promising. During the period of privatization between 1990 and 1992, economists were predicting economic growth in Mexico to be as high as 5 percent per year through the end of the decade. Bank earnings were expected to rise by as much as 12 percent per year during the same period. This optimistic outlook was responsible for Mexico's 16 commercial banks being privatized for a total cash flow of $12.4 billion. This is estimated to have been about three times their value on paper and 40 times their average yearly earnings. Privatized banks are usually valued at about 14 times earnings. Optimism about the future of Mexico continued to grow particularly after the initial negotiations for the North American Free Trade

TABLE 3.1 *U.S. Banks With Licenses to Operate in Mexico*

Citicorp (only foreign bank able to carry out retail operations)
Bankamerica Corp.
Bankers Trust New York Corp.
Chase Chemical Banking Corp.
J.P. Morgan & Corp.
Nationsbanks Corp.

Agreement (NAFTA) concluded in late 1992. A second spurt of enthusiasm occurred in late 1993 when the U.S. Congress finally approved NAFTA after a viscious Congressional debate.

Evolution of the Privatized Mexican Banking System

Consistent with expectations of growth from the market opening measures of the Mexican Government and from implementation of NAFTA, Mexico's monetary authorities pursued an expansionist fiscal policy. Less than two years after the banks were privatized and less than one year after NAFTA began to be implemented, a currency crisis resulted in a serious run on, and loss in value of, the peso. Reactions to political events in Mexico (the Chiapas uprising and the assassination of a presidential candidate) and changes in interest rates, had led to sudden declines in foreign exchange reserves as foreign investors started to pull out their portfolio investment. During the course of the year, Mexico's reserves dropped by more than $19 billion to fall below $6 billion by December 1994. With reserves so low, Mexico was unable to intervene effectively when the crisis hit in late 1994. The immediate problem was the decision of foreign investors to redeem their government debt in the form of *tesobonos*—a short-term treasury note indexed to the U.S. dollar. During 1994, *tesobono* debt increased by $26 billion, which far exceeded the $6 billion worth of foreign exchange held by the Central Bank of Mexico at the end of the year.

However, instead of turning its back on market reforms and resorting to balance of payments restrictions to protect its currency, Mexico was true to its NAFTA obligations and to its own commitments to opening its markets. Instead of restricting imports it continued to liberalize its markets for its most important trading partners. Domestic interest rates rose while economic activity contracted. The results were that the banks found themselves holding large loan portfolios at a time when repayment was difficult (see Table 3.2). Banks were forced to contract their outstanding portfolios as they struggled to maintain their financial position.

With the devaluation of the peso starting on December 20, 1994, Mexico's newly-privatized financial services sector was hit hard. However, the problem of the commercial banking sector may have predated this problem. The banks had engaged in liberal lending policies for the previous three years due to financial optimism, the need to meet a pent up desire for consumer credit and the desire to accumulate profits as soon as possible to offset the cost of purchasing the banks. Therefore, between 1992 and 1994, loans to the private sector increased by 220 percent, or more than 30 times the growth in the economy. On the other hand, coincidental with the privatization was an explosion of consumer credit. In 1991 and 1992, credit grew by an estimated 33 and 26 percent, respectively. Overdue loans increased from 0.71 percent of the total at the end of 1991 to 7.26 percent by December 1994. Thus, even before the December 1994 devaluation, some claimed that the growth was too fast. A Moody Corporation analyst argued that the system's ability to adjust to a liberalized banking environment had been hindered by a lack of experienced management, poor borrower disclosures, the absence of a strong credit culture, the paucity of credit bureaus and close links with concentrated industrial sectors (Crawford, 1995).

Given the positive outlook for growth in Mexico, the burgeoning credit appeared to be a situation that could be handled. It was hoped that an unwinding of excessive credit—especially consumer credit— could occur in the context of a growing economy without disruption. However, there was no chance to contain the problem after the December 1994 crisis. The rise in interest rates, and contraction of domestic economic activities resulted in the number of defaulted loans sky-rocketing. Fortunately, for the long-term growth of the Mexican economy, the Mexican Government did not pull back from economic liberalization, but continued to implement its NAFTA obligations to liberalize. This policy seems to be working as the duration of

TABLE 3.2 *Mexican Banks and Overdue Loans (1994)*

	Million pesos
Banamex	9189
Bancomer	8162
Serfin	7137
Inverlat (Comermex)	2975
Internacional	3025
Mexicano	2093
Atlantico	2036
M. Probursa	1085
Bancen	648
Promex	643
M. Norte	789
Confia	984
Banoro	864
Banpais	1.680
Bancrecer	1.219
Obrero	481
Cremi	n/a
Union	n/a

the current dislocation appears to be much shorter than similar situations.

In the financial sector, Mexico actually impelled the liberalization process by accelerating the pace of removal of its transitional restrictions beyond what was required under NAFTA. At the same time, Mexico provided improved access to third party financial institutions and investors not covered by NAFTA. Within this context, the February 1995 amendments to the 'Law to Regulate Financial Groups,' the 'Law of Credit Institutions,' and the 'Law of the Stock Market' gave foreign capital more of an opportunity to own a controlling interest in joint ventures with Mexican banks. As mentioned before, a bank's ordinary capital was constituted by three types of shares (A, B, and C). The reform consisted in eliminating C-shares, while permitting foreigners to own B-shares, thus allowing foreigners to own up to 49 percent of a Mexican owned bank.

However, the most significant change regarded foreign affiliates. The minimum requirement of capital to be owned by a foreign entity in its Mexican affiliate was reduced from 99 percent to 51 percent. Furthermore, to facilitate NAFTA intermediaries' participation in Mexican financial entities that need capital, an exception was made to some of the overall caps covering foreign participation in the banking sector. Subject to approval by the Ministry of Finance, this had the effect of raising the NAFTA interim aggregate capital limits on foreign investment from 8 to 25 percent. The new provisions also permit any foreign investor immediately to hold up to 6 percent of the total capital of commercial banks compared to a previous permanent limitation of 4 percent during the transition period. Furthermore, this percentage applies only to the capital of the acquired bank, whereas under the NAFTA provision, the authorities calculating the now-defunct 4 percent ceiling would have had to take into account the capital of other financial institutions controlled by the investor. The new rules also allowed foreign investors to acquire control of Mexican banking institutions through either direct investment or the establishment of holding companies in Mexico. Holding companies also do not need special authorization as long as they provide the same financial services which they provide in their country of origin. These amendments also further liberalized several laws such as existing requirements that bank directors must be Mexican nationals or Mexican residents.

Financing the bank's ability to deal with the increased number of non-performing loans was the immediate situation to be addressed. Unfortunately, there was a little influx of foreign capital following the February 1995 liberalization. Thus, the main burden to refinance fell on the Mexican Government. Past due loans exceeded $17 billion—or

18 percent of the system's net assets—despite the Mexican Government expenditure of $15 billion to bail out the banks (which is about equivalent, taking inflation into account, what the government earned from privatization). Bank bailouts were estimated to eventually cost the Mexican Government from $15 billion to $20 billion, an amount equivalent to 7 to 10 percent of the annual Mexican GDP. Fortunately, the bailout could be financed over time and thus the budgetary burden could be postponed. In addition, shareholders were expected to increase their investments in their banks by about $7 billion.

Future Prospects for North-American Investment in the Mexican Banking System

To encourage foreign investment in Mexican banks, the Mexican government has been pursuing a policy of helping the banks to recapitalize themselves by buying defaulted loans and encouraging foreign investment. The process has been fairly straight forward. A government-run Bank Insurance Fund, known as FOBAPROA, takes over a portion of the non-performing loans with appropriate restitution to the banks. In exchange, the parent companies of the bank or its other shareholders agree to add more capital into the bank—this involves selling convertible or subordinated debt securities. Thus, in a number of cases, foreign banks would make investments under more liberalized procedures than required under NAFTA.

The objective of these operations was to improve the bank's capitalization ratios or the ratio of overdue loans to capital reserves. For the moment, Mexico has very liberal rules for calculating bank loans overdue and, thus, the 17 to 20 percent overdue ratio probably understates the gravity of the situation.[6] In June of 1995, it was estimated that if the total amount of the overdue loans were to be correctly calculated, 40 percent of total outstanding Mexican banking loans would be non-performing, or overdue.

An example of how this process works can be found by examining the refinancing of some of Banamex's debt which took place in December 1995. FOBAPROA took over $2.6 billion of Banamex's non-performing loans, or about 12 percent of its portfolio. In return for this assistance, the bank's parent company, Grupo Financiero Banamex-Accival (Bannaci), agreed to boost the bank's capital by $1.1 billion before the end of 1996. In general, private shareholders were asked to make capital infusions into their banks equivalent to about 50 percent of the non-performing loans bought by FOBAPROA. Thus, for example, the third largest Mexican bank, Serfin, received an injection of $350 million into the bank in return for being allowed to off-load $750 million of overdue loans to the government.

A less desirable form of intervention occurs when the government must take over control of a bank due to its financial situation. So far, seven of the 18 banks originally privatized have been taken over by the government for liquidation, or for restructuring and sale to new owners. These banks include Banca Cremi, Banco Union, Banpais, Banco Obrero, Banco Interestatal, Banco del Oriente and Grupo Financiero Inverlat. However, three of the banks may have been placed there as a result of malfeasance—Cremi, Union and Banpais—and thus their status is not reflective of the peso crisis.[7]

The reforms also allowed foreign banks to take control of any of the banks which found themselves in financial trouble. Under the modified rules, only the three largest banks—Banamex, Bancomer and Serfin—were protected against such a takeover since they represented more than 6 percent of the outstanding capital of commercial banks. As of 1996, the only complete takeover occurred when Banco Bilbao Vizcaya of Spain brought 70 percent of the twelfth largest Mexican bank (Mercantil Probursa). As mentioned before, the Canadian Bank of Nova Scotia also bought a stake in Grupo Financiero Inverlat (GFI). FOBAPROA played a significant role when the transaction was completed in February of 1996 by acquiring 100 percent share of GFI and then selling 16 percent of those shares to the Canadian institutions for $50 million. In addition to the purchase of the 16 percent share, Bank of Nova Scotia acquired $125 million in eight-year bonds that can be converted into another 39 percent share in March of 2001. That will raise its total stake in Inverlat to 55 percent. Until that date, however, Inverlat will officially remain in the hands of FOBAPROA (Latin American Institute, 1996). In any case, although the future of the smaller banks is still in question, opportunities for cooperative ventures between them and regional U.S. banks offer the best chance for their survival in the near future.

However, in spite of these continuing problems, the outlook for the banking sector is increasingly positive. Within this context, larger Mexican banks should provide better opportunities for cooperation with North American financial institutions. Not only are these banks now allowed to buy any percentage of a Mexican bank up to 49 percent without being limited to C-shares—as did Bank of Montreal in February of 1996 when it bought 16 percent of the shares of Bancomer and J.P. Morgan when it invested in Serfin, Mexico's second and third largest banks respectively—but they can also develop joint products with their Mexican counterparts. It is evident that for the time being, U.S. and Canadian banks are not interested in acquiring Mexican banking retail operations. However, they can work with Mexican banks to market their new programs for consumer services. For instance, Mexican banks need technical assistance in such areas as credit card processing, bill paying, mortgage assessment and management techniques. Cooperative arrangements of this kind would allow banks in Mexico to reduce costs and increase their profit margin on banking operations. In this regard, the two largest Mexican banks, Banamex and Bancomer, are already showing signs of turning the corner towards full economic recovery. They both control 39 percent of the Mexican banking sector between them, and Mexican authorities simply cannot run the risk that their financial position deteriorates. Actually, the outlook for these banks materially improved once they began taking advantage of government assistance programs. Furthermore, ING Barings has recommended a number of Mexican banks for investment due to their improving asset quality, diversified sources of income and experienced management, citing Banamex, Bancomer and Inbursa as the best positioned to take advantage of the expected Mexican economic recovery.

The current top performer appears to be Bancomer. During the January–March period of 1996, Bancomer became the first Mexican banking group to set aside provisions which met international require-ments for covering bad loans—Bancomer created a loss reserve of Ps2.76 billion against non-performing loans. In 1996, Bancomer registers non-performing loans of around 9.2 percent of its total loan portfolio. On the other hand, Banamex, Mexico's largest private financial institution, recorded a 34 percent increase in operating profits for the first quarter of 1996. Growth of the bank's past due loans slowed to 6 percent down from 33 percent during the first quarter of 1995. In addition, FOBAPROA was able to contribute Ps750 million which allowed the bank's capital to cover 12.6 percent of weighted risk assets valued at about $15 billion. Total deposits in 1996 represent 54.4 percent of assets compared to 49.5 percent in December 1995.

In addition, Mexico is beginning to implement fiduciary and operational investment provisions similar to those which exist in the U.S. and Canada. This should facilitate the flow of North American investments and funds. Mexico is also expected to adopt the U.S.'s generally accepted accounting principles (GAAP) for banking by January 1, 1997, which should allow banks to satisfy stricter accounting standards on non-performing loans. Furthermore, improved use of data exchange will facilitate business dealings, while the introduction of U.S. management techniques should reduce costs, as well as increasing profit margins, in Mexican banking. In the same vein, the Mexican Government announced plans to establish a trust that groups together the assets of any of the nationalized banks not returned to the private sector and the loans purchased by FOBAPROA from the commercial banks. The trust is modeled after the Resolution Trust

Corporation set up in the U.S. to deal with failed savings and loan institutions. This new Mexican trust establishes a secondary market where distressed debt can be bought and sold, helping to lift the financial constraints on banks and the country's highly leveraged corporate sector.

On the other hand, there is probably no better indication of the return of confidence in Mexico than the acceptance of Mexican financial instruments on the international financial market. In January of 1996, Mexico successfully marketed a $1 billion seven-year Eurobond issue which helped Mexico pay back $2 billion of the money it borrowed from the U.S. plus $750 million in interests. Furthermore, in mid-April of 1995, the Mexican Government launched an offer to swap U.S.-backed Brady bonds for uncollateralized 30-year bonds. The Mexican Government offered to exchange between $1 billion and $2.5 billion of outstanding Brady bonds for a new dollar denominated global bond. The new issue lengthens the maturity of part of Mexico's sovereign debt and its servicing costs. Even though it represents a restructuring of only a small part of Mexico's $100 billion foreign debt and is being sold with a coupon more than 450 basis points above the yield on 30-year U.S. Treasury bonds, the fact that they are being sold without U.S. guarantees sends a signal that Mexico is emerging from its recent financial problem.

All the above mentioned events send clear signals that as the expected Mexican recovery takes hold, integration of Mexican financial services with their North American counterparts will proceed at an even faster pace than had been expected under the original NAFTA provisions. The implementation of the new regulations and amendments to Mexican laws by consolidating, accelerating and even going beyond NAFTA provisions guarantee this. From now on, what is most needed for this integration to take place is to create a more profitable business climate for banking in Mexico. This, in turn, is most dependent on increased and sustained economic activities which require banking services. Once the current economic crisis is over, opportunities for strategic alliances will again be fully explored. Thus, the aftermath of the banking crisis will result in a stronger banking system for Mexico, and a more integrated North American market.

References

BINHAMMER, H. (1988) *Money, Banking and the Canadian Financial System*. Nelson, Canada: Scarborough.

BORDO, M.D., ROCKOFF, H. and REDISH, A. (1994) 'The U.S. Banking System From a Northern Exposure: Stability versus Efficiency.' *The Journal of Economic History*, Vol. 54, No. 2, June, pp. 327–38.

CRAWFORD, L. (1995) *Financial Times*, 12 July.

FARNSWORTH, C. (1992) 'Canada's Mighty Banking March to the South.' *New York Times*, 8 April, p. 6.

FENNELL, T. (1996) 'New Rules for the Big Six.' *MacLean's*, 8 April, pp. 34–5.

JORDAN, C. (1993) 'Financial Services under NAFTA: The View from Canada.' *The Review of Banking and Financial Services*, Vol. 9, No. 6, 24 March, p. 45.

JOYCE, J. (1989) 'An Investigation of Government Preference Functions: The Case of Canada 1970–1981.' *Journal of Macroeconomics* (Spring) pp. 217–32.

KAPILOFF, H. (1994) 'Big Banks Are Seen Growing Despite Drop in Profitability.' *American Banker*, 27 May, p. 7.

KARNIN, D. (1992) 'Financial Services in Mexico and the North American Free Trade Agreement.' *CRS Report for Congress*, August 21, ERS2-CRS10.

LATIN AMERICAN INSTITUTE (1996) *Economic News and Analysis on Mexico.* University of New Mexico. February 21.

LIBBY, B. (1994) 'The Impact of the North American Free Trade Agreement on Commercial Banking.' *Journal of Economic Issues*, Vol. 28, No. 2, June, pp. 501–8.

NEUFELD, E. P. (1994) 'NAFTA changes the Game: A Canadian Perspective.' *Bank Management*, May/June.

SMITH, G. (1993) 'The Gringo Banks are Drooling: They're ready to swoop into Mexico once NAFTA is approved.' *Business Week*, 13 September, p. 84.

THOMAS, R. L. (1994) 'NAFTA Changes the Game.' *Bank Management*, May/June, pp. 55–59.

TORRES, C. (1996) 'Bank of Montreal Investment Helps Mexican Stock Market.' *The Wall Street Journal*, 28 February, p. C1.

Notes

1. In the U.S., the Federal Reserve utilizes changes in reserve requirements, changes in discount rates, and most importantly, open market operations.
2. 'Canada bank has big plans for U.S.' *The Miami Herald*, 27 October 1994, p. 8C.
3. Eighty percent of car leasing is already in the hands of American-owned firms such as General Electric Capital Leasing and General Motors Acceptance Corporation. *The Economist*, 4 May 1996, p. 73.
4. Canadian banks tried to use NAFTA's Article 1403 to press for relaxation of the U.S. prohibition on interstate banking. According to this article, Canada will consider permitting direct cross-border branching of U.S. commercial banks into Canada only when the U.S. permits interstate branching (Libby, 1994: 507).
5. Bank of Montreal paid between $424 and $477 million for the transaction. According to sources close to the deal, the total investment will be determined by the ultimate cost per share, which will be based on the value of the Mexican peso versus the U.S. dollar at the time the transaction is finalized (Latin American Institute, 1996).
6. Only the amount overdue is included in the calculation of the non-performing loan—in developed countries, the total amount of the overdue loans is included in the calculation. It is expected that as the program continues and banks rid themselves of more non-performing loans, the banks will introduce stricter criteria for estimating the value of non-performing loans. The Mexican government is utilizing assistance from the World Bank (IBRD) and the Inter-American

Development Bank (IDB) to help finance the purchase of non-performing loans from the banks.

7. Mexico also developed special programs for types of debtors with serious problems. One category of debtor has been those who construct and operate toll roads. The failure of these operations to generate the expected revenues from traffic tolls, resulted in most of them being in trouble. They jointly owe $3.8 billion. The government is treating them as a special case, promising to take over 50 to 70 percent of the interest charges on their debts, as well as to allow increases in toll charges.

4

The U.S. Banking Industry in Transition

JAMES R. BARTH, RAY CHOU AND JOHN S. JAHERA, JR

Introduction

The U.S. banking industry has undergone significant change and turmoil during the past fifteen years. The most widely reported and discussed developments have been the failure of several thousand federally insured banking institutions (commercial and savings banks, savings and loans, and credit unions) and the huge costs to resolve these failures. Indeed, in the case of savings and loans, taxpayers have been required to help cover the unprecedented failure resolution costs. Yet, other important developments that have received less attention have also occurred. In particular, while the combined financial assets of all financial service firms have grown throughout the post-World War II period, banking institutions have seen their share of this expanding pool of assets decline by nearly half. Increasingly, the products and services traditionally offered by banks are available elsewhere on more acceptable terms to both businesses and consumers. Advances in computer and telecommunication technology have reduced the costs of collecting, processing and transmitting information to facilitate this shift away from banks. But so have restrictive laws and regulations that impose burdensome costs on banks and prevent them from more freely adapting to an increasingly competitive and changing financial marketplace.

Developments in computer technology together with modern finance theory have also dramatically improved the ability to identify, measure, and thus price, risk. This has led to a much wider menu of financial products and services, including various derivative instruments, being made available in the marketplace in recent years which enables one to better manage risk. Banks are not only able to use these newer instruments to control their own exposure to various risks but also to generate fee income by developing and marketing them to others. Today, the total notational amount of derivatives of commercial banks alone is nearly three times their on-balance sheet assets.

The recent and continuing developments in informational technologies facilitate the integration of capital markets around the world. As incomes increase and wealth accumulates in an increasingly larger number of countries pursuing more market-oriented policies, cross-border trade and finance will continue to grow. This development is reflected in the fact that the U.S. share of world gross domestic product (GDP) has declined from 35 percent in 1965 to 24 percent in 1992 and its share of world population has remained relatively constant at about 5 percent. Of course, this international growth and integration will be strongly affected by the extent to which nations maintain barriers that impede the free flow of labor, products and services, and capital across borders.

The remainder of this chapter will discuss the transition the U.S. banking industry is currently undergoing in view of these developments. The chapter will also discuss the way in which geographical and other restrictions on banking operations in the U.S. affect the integration of banking markets, both domestically and globally.

Unprecedented Banking Institution Failures and Resolution Costs

U.S. banking institutions have suffered more in the 1980s and early 1990s than at any time since the Great Depression in the 1930s. As Table 4.1 shows, 4,695 federally-insured institutions with $665 billion in assets failed from 1980 through 1992 and were resolved at an estimated present-value cost of $165 billion. The savings and loan industry suffered the most. The federal insurance fund for savings and loans—the Federal Savings and Loan Insurance Corporation (FSLIC)—reported severe insolvency in the second half of the 1980s and taxpayers were notified by President Bush in February of 1989 that they would be required to help pay to clean up the mess. Indeed, a new agency, the Resolution Trust Corporation (RTC), was established in August of 1989 to resolve all savings and loans that had failed and were seized by the regulatory authorities through September of 1995. At the same time, the FSLIC was abolished and a new federal insurance fund for the remaining solvent savings and loan institutions was established, the Savings Association Insurance Fund (SAIF). Although the federal insurance fund for banks—the Bank Insurance Fund

TABLE 4.1 *Failed Federally Insured Depository Institutions: 1980–1993 Number, Assets, and Resolution Costs*

Year	Failed commercial and savings banks			Failed savings and loans			Failed credit unions		
	Number	Assets ($ millions)	Costs ($ millions)	Number	Assets ($ millions)	Costs ($ millions)	Number	Shares ($ millions)	Costs ($ millions)
1980	10	237	30	11	1,458	166	NA	NA	NA
1981	10	4,859	589	28	13,908	760	349	NA	NA
1982	42	11,632	1,271	63	17,662	806	327	NA	NA
1983	48	7,207	1,521	36	4,631	275	253	NA	NA
1984	79	3,276	2,292	22	5,080	743	130	208	20
1985	120	8,337	850	31	5,601	1,026	94	47	12
1986	145	6,830	1,732	46	12,455	3,066	94	116	29
1987	203	9,198	2,017	47	10,660	3,704	88	327	52
1988	221	52,623	5,530	205	100,660	31,790	85	297	33
1989	207	29,538	5,998	37	11,019	5,914	114	285	74
1990	169	15,365	3,042	315	108,896	37,302	189	485	49
1991	127	63,338	7,393	232	75,947	34,506	173	298	77
1992	122	46,158	4,700	69	35,338	6,715	154	773	107
Total	1,503	258,597	37,325	1,142	403,315	126,773	2,050	2,836	452

Source: James R. Barth and R. Dan Brumbaugh, Jr., 'The Role of Deposit Insurance: Financial Stability and Moral Hazard,' Seminar on Current Legal Issues Affecting Central Banks, International Monetary Fund, Washington, D.C., May 1994.

(BIF)—reported insolvency for both 1991 and 1992, it returned to solvency in 1993. Consequently, no direct taxpayer funds were needed to resolve troubled commercial and savings banks. Despite a large number of failures, only the federal insurance fund for credit unions—the National Credit Union Share Insurance Fund (NCUSIF)—survived the 1980s and into the 1990s without posing any serious threat to taxpayers throughout the entire period. It was, however, recapitalized by the credit unions themselves in 1985 with a 1 percent levy on their insured shares or deposits.

The problems encountered by banking institutions in the 1980s gave rise to five major pieces of banking legislation. The two laws enacted in the early 1980s—the Depository Institutions Deregulation and Monetary Control Act and the Depository Institutions Act—broadened the powers of institutions and eliminated interest rate ceilings on deposits. Although the deregulation came too late to prevent the devastation of the savings and loan industry, the overall effect was to blur the distinctions among the four different types of banking institutions. The three laws enacted in the late 1980s and early 1990s—the Competitive Equality Banking Act, the Financial Institutions Reform, Recovery and Enforcement Act, and the Federal Deposit Insurance Corporation Improvement Act—reimposed selective restrictions on the powers of banking institutions and curtailed the formation of 'nonbank' banks—financial service firms that offer either demand deposits, or commercial and industrial loans, but not both. This latter legislation also established higher and risk-based federal deposit insurance premiums, raised capital requirements while adopting a stricter measure of capital, and required regulators to take prompt corrective action against troubled institutions. Yet, the similarities among the different types of banking institutions essentially remained intact and the encroachment by nonbank competitors continued unabated.

Banking Institutions Lose Market Share

One of the more notable developments that has occurred over a lengthy period of time in the U.S. has been the declining share of total financial assets of all financial service firms held by banking institutions. As Table 4.2 shows, these institutions accounted for 65 percent of total assets in 1950, but only 34 percent in 1993. The biggest losers in terms of market share have been the U.S.-chartered commercial banks, whose share declined from 51 percent to only 19 percent over the same period. Pension and retirement funds now account for a larger share of total financial assets than U.S.-chartered banks. The aging of the U.S. population and the establishment of an

TABLE 4.2 *Percentage Distribution of U.S. Financial Assets by All Financial Service Firms: 1950–1993*

	1950	1960	1970	1980	1990	1993
Depository Institutions (1)						
Commercial Banks	51.2	38.2	38.6	34.3	27.7	25.1
U.S.-Chartered	50.5	37.5	36.6	29.3	22.0	19.1
Foreign Offices in U.S.	0.4	0.6	0.7	2.3	3.0	3.4
Bank Holding Companies	0.0	0.0	1.1	2.4	2.5	2.5
Banks in U.S. Possessions	0.3	0.1	0.3	0.3	0.2	0.2
Savings Institutions	13.4	18.7	18.7	18.3	11.4	6.7
Savings and Loans	5.8	11.8	12.8	14.4	9.1	NA
Savings Banks	7.6	6.9	5.9	3.9	2.2	NA
Credit Unions	0.3	1.1	1.3	1.6	1.8	1.8
Contractual Intermediaries						
Life Insurance Companies	21.3	19.4	15.0	10.7	11.4	11.6
Other Insurance Companies	4.0	4.4	3.7	4.2	4.4	4.1
Private Pension Funds (2)	2.4	6.4	8.4	11.7	13.6	15.2
State and Local Government Retirement Funds	1.7	3.3	4.5	4.5	6.1	6.9
Others						
Finance Companies	3.2	4.6	4.8	4.7	5.1	4.3
Mortgage Companies	NA	NA	NA	0.4	0.1	0.2
Mutual Funds (3)	1.1	2.9	3.5	1.4	5.0	9.3
Money Market Mutual Funds	0.0	0.0	0.0	1.8	4.1	3.6
Closed-End Funds	NA	NA	NA	0.2	0.4	0.6
Security Brokers and Dealers	1.4	1.1	1.2	1.0	2.2	3.0
REITs (4)	0.1	0.1	0.1	0.1	0.1	0.1
Issuers of Asset Backed Securities	0.0	0.0	0.0	0.0	2.3	3.0
Bank Personal Trusts (5)	NA	NA	NA	5.1	4.2	4.3
Total Assets ($ billions)	294	597	1,340	5,910	12,017	15,387

1. Commercial Banks consist of U.S.-chartered commercial banks, domestic affiliates, agencies and offices in U.S., including Edge Act corporations and Offices of foreign banks. IBFs are excluded from domestic banking and include all savings and loan associations and federal savings banks insured by the Savings Association Insurance (Fund. Bank Insurance Fund).
2. Private pension funds also includes the Federal Employees' Retirement Thrift Savings Fund.
3. Mutual funds are open-end investment companies (including unit investment trusts) that report to the Investment Company Institute.
4. REITs are real estate investment trusts.
5. Bank personal trusts are assets of individuals managed by bank trust departments and nondeposit, noninsured trust companies.

Note: The Flow of Funds Accounts were restructured in the second quarter of 1993.
Source: Flow of Funds Accounts, Board of Governors of the Federal Reserve System.

ever larger number of pension and retirement plans is likely to reinforce this trend in the next decade.

The big gainers in market share are not only the pension and retirement funds, but also the money market and other mutual funds. These financial service firms have seen their share of total financial assets increase to nearly 13 percent in 1993 from only 1 percent in 1950. They now account for a far larger share than savings and loans, savings banks and credit unions combined. Although money market mutual funds are not federally insured, their assets are marked-to-market on a daily basis and the resulting net asset value has enabled shares to be effectively payable on demand at par. The inability of these funds to clear checks directly through the Federal Reserve System, however, has contributed to restrictions being placed on the size and frequency of checks that may be written on the shares. Otherwise, the money market mutual funds would pose an even greater competitive threat to banking institutions than they already do.

These dramatic shifts in market shares among the various types of financial service firms reflect an increasingly competitive financial marketplace. U.S.-chartered banks in particular are under attack on both sides of their balance sheets. Individuals are increasingly becoming more financially sophisticated, and therefore, more active investors. Whereas time and savings deposits accounted for 27 percent of the total financial assets of individuals in 1980, the figure has declined sharply to 17 percent in 1996. In contrast, the shares accounted for by money market and other mutual funds increased from only 2 percent to 9 percent over the same time period. Modern informational technology enables these funds to operate at a relatively low cost compared to banks with their elaborate branching networks. These cost savings can then be passed on to customers in the form of higher returns. The existence of this competitive product means deposits that are federally insured and still largely physically collected at local institutions are increasingly susceptible to losing value as 'core' deposits (i.e., deposits that are relatively insensitive to interest rates and thus quite stable). Indeed, only 55 percent of the assets of Bank Insurance Fund (BIF) and SAIF depository institutions were funded with federally insured deposits in 1993 and only 17 percent of the total assets of all financial service firms.

At the same time, many large and established businesses are increasingly able to bypass banks and borrow on more favorable terms directly through the issuance of commercial paper. Even the growth in the below-investment grade debt market has provided many mid-size and less well-established businesses with a way to obtain funds on better terms than through bank loans. Banks are therefore increasingly losing customers on both sides of their balance sheets as the financial marketplace continually evolves.

More generally, the less regulated nonbank financial service firms are increasingly providing loans, formerly made by banks, either directly to both businesses and consumers or indirectly through the acquisition of commercial paper and high-yield debt. Even credit card loans that became quite important for many banks in the 1980s are now available from telephone and automobile companies, in addition to the types of nonbank competitors listed in Table 4.2. New developments in multimedia technology will only generate still further competition for banks in the coming years.

Besides these developments, securitization has adversely affected the franchise value of many banking institutions. The securitization of whole mortgage loans and other loans (including automobile loans, credit card receivables and even commercial real estate mortgages) has narrowed the spread between the returns on the corresponding unsecuritized assets and their associated funding costs. As a result, only the lowest cost providers among the banking institutions are currently able to operate profitably by originating such assets, holding them in their portfolios and then servicing them. Securitization unbundles these three activities and thereby contributes to undermining the traditional role played by banking institutions.

To appreciate more fully the important role played by securitization, consider the following. In 1950, depository institutions accounted for 60 percent of the total home mortgage loans outstanding. In 1993, the figure had fallen to 35 percent. In contrast, the total amount of home mortgage loans outstanding that had been securitized increased from zero percent to 41 percent over the same time period.

Banking institutions have not been totally passive as these developments have unfolded. As Table 4.3 shows, commercial banks have moved more assets into all types of real estate loans to replace their lost commercial and industrial loans. In 1993, real estate loans accounted for 25 percent of total assets, up from 14 percent in 1980. Commercial and industrial loans, in contrast, declined to 15 percent from 21 percent over the same time period. Banks are also relying more heavily on fee income as compared to net interest income. Indeed, non-interest income as a percent of total assets of commercial banks rose from 0.17 percent in 1980 to 2.02 percent in 1993. In the process, banks are increasingly replacing lost on-balance sheet business with off-balance sheet activities, including greater involvement in foreign exchange and interest rate swaps and other derivative instruments. Indeed, off-balance sheet assets of commercial banks have increased to $9140 billion in 1993 from only $75 billion in 1984. Banks are also broadening their menu of products and services to include

TABLE 4.3 Selected Information on U.S. Commercial Banks: 1980–1993

	1980	1981	1982	1983	1984	1985	1986	1987	1988	1989	1990	1991	1992	1993
Number of Institutions	14,435	14,416	14,453	14,468	14,466	14,383	14,179	13,684	13,108	12,707	12,344	11,920	11,466	10,971
Number of ATMs	18,500	25,770	35,721	48,118	58,470	61,117	64,000	68,000	72,492	75,632	80,156	83,545	87,330	94,822
Number of Offices	51,538	53,073	54,493	55,392	56,306	57,337	58,116	58,711	59,967	61,322	63,438	63,558	63,015	n.a.
Number of Employees	1,486,030	1,498,051	1,498,807	1,509,812	1,526,343	1,561,792	1,561,473	1,544,500	1,526,428	1,531,499	1,517,540	1,487,194	1,478,705	1,494,560
Total Assets ($B)	1,856	2,029	2,194	2,342	2,508	2,729	2,938	2,999	3,130	3,299	3,389	3,431	3,507	3,707
Equity Capital to Assets	5.79	5.83	5.87	6.00	6.14	6.19	6.19	6.02	6.28	6.21	6.46	6.754	7.52	8.01
Net After-Tax Income to Assets	0.75	0.73	0.68	0.64	0.62	0.66	0.60	0.09	0.81	0.47	0.48	0.54	0.92	1.17
Loan Loss Provision to Assets	0.24	0.25	0.39	0.46	0.55	0.65	0.75	1.25	0.54	0.94	0.94	1.00	0.74	0.45
Loss Reserves to Assets	0.54	0.56	0.61	0.66	0.74	0.85	0.98	1.66	1.48	1.62	1.67	1.60	1.55	1.42
Real Estate Loans to Assets	14.49	14.35	14.04	14.38	15.38	16.07	17.53	20.01	21.57	23.09	24.47	24.81	24.76	24.89
Commercial & Industrial Loans to Assets	21.06	22.40	22.98	22.41	22.53	21.16	20.44	19.64	19.18	18.75	18.15	16.29	15.30	14.54
Loans to Individuals to Assets	10.10	9.51	9.08	9.59	10.64	11.32	11.42	11.71	12.08	12.16	11.90	11.42	11.00	11.33
Total Deposits	79.82	78.31	77.77	78.67	78.25	77.58	77.64	77.85	77.68	77.25	78.18	78.34	76.97	74.29
Domestic Office Deposits, total	63.97	62.61	63.79	65.50	65.58	65.78	66.96	66.46	67.61	67.80	69.52	69.46	68.79	65.39
Demand Deposits	23.25	18.94	16.91	16.63	16.50	16.50	17.34	15.19	14.64	13.95	13.68	13.24	14.58	14.56

Source: Office of the Comptroller of the Currency.

more mutual funds, annuities, and investment management and advisory services. Banks, in other words, are still attempting to fulfill their traditional role of intermediating between savers and borrowers, but increasingly by earning more fee income and correspondingly less spread income. They are also relying less heavily on branches in favor of automatic teller machines (ATMs) in distributing services (see Table 4.3).

The main stumbling block in adapting to the changing financial marketplace, however, remains restrictive laws and regulations. Banks cannot compete freely in the securities and insurance areas. Nor can they freely branch nationwide or be owned by nonbank firms. Some authority to engage in securities and insurance activities has been provided to state-chartered banks in selected states and to a few bank holding companies by the Federal Reserve in recent years, but such authority is still quite limited (see Tables 4.4 and 4.5). Most states have also now permitted greater branching and banking privileges, mainly through regional compacts, but usually there are limits on the share of deposits that may be acquired by a single institution, as will be discussed below (see Table 4.6). Furthermore, although the U.S. Congress is currently considering legislation that would permit nationwide banking, such legislation, if enacted, is likely to permit states to opt out and to permit entry into states by banks only through the acquisition of existing institutions. The states would still completely control *de novo* branching. In addition, limits would be placed on the percentage of deposits that could be acquired by out-of-state banks, both within individual host states and nationwide.

The process of adaption, therefore, has been slow and incomplete. The important point remains that banks are the most heavily regulated financial service firms in the United States. They are unable to compete freely with the nonbank financial service firms that are increasingly engaged in what were once considered to be traditional banking activities. Indeed, the term 'bank' is defined legally today to be a financial institution that accepts demand deposits, makes commercial and industrial loans, and is insured by the BIF, which along with the SAIF, are administered by the Federal Deposit Insurance Corporation (FDIC). It is primarily this legal definition that enables one to distinguish between banks and nonbanks today, not simply the functions that the different types of financial service firms perform. It increasingly is only this definition that enables one to understand the reason for the categories into which the various financial service firms are placed in Table 4.2. Yet, as Table 4.3 shows, demand deposits of commercial banks only fund 15 percent of their assets, while commercial and industrial loans of these institutions only account for 15 percent of total assets.

TABLE 4.4 *Restrictions on Bank's Activities or Powers*

National banks	Banks in holding companies	State-chartered banks
	Insurance	
National banks in towns of 5,000 or less have been permitted to sell insurance	Bank Holding Company Act (BHCA) says that insurance is not permitted as a 'closely related to banking activity' for bank holding companies (bhcs).	Several states permit state-chartered banks to sell or to underwrite insurance or to do both.
Comptroller of Currency (OCC) has allowed national banks as incidental powers of banking to: **sell fixed and variable-rate annuities; **sell credit life insurance.	Federal Reserve Board (FRB) recently permitted a bhc to continue to sell insurance through two state-chartered banks that it was acquiring in Indiana. In another ruling FRB refused to grant Citicorp the same power through a Delaware state-chartered bank.	
	Securities	
Glass-Steagall Act (G-S) prohibits national banks from selling, underwriting, or affiliating with securities businesses but allows banks to deal with certain 'bank-eligible' securities, such as Treasury issuances, and to buy and sell on order for bank customers. Activities authorized by the Comptroller of the Currency for National banks: **discount brokerage; **investment company advice; **collective investment fund management (IRAs); **placing securities privately; **commercial sales **general obligation bond underwriting.	G-S prohibits banks from affiliating with entities in the securities business. BHCA forbids bhcs and their affiliates or subsidiaries from engaging in businesses other than banking or those 'closely related as to be a proper incident thereto.' FRB has authorized: **sale and underwriting of corporate debt securities; **underwriting commercial paper; **underwriting commercial revenue bonds; **underwriting consumer-related receivables and mortgage-backed securities; **providing investment advice; **brokerage services; **underwriting and dealing in money market instruments; and **providing foreign exchange advisory and transactional services.	G-S theoretically forbids all banks from directly engaging in investment banking. The following activities are permitted by at least several states to their state-chartered banks: **equity investment; **underwriting general obligations and revenue bonds; **offering full service and discount brokerage.
	Real Estate	
National Bank Act limits national banks to explicit powers and 'incidental powers as shall be necessary to carry on the business.' National banks may lease bank property that devolves upon them through loan default.	BHCA limits bhcs to banking and activities so closely related as to be a proper incident thereto. FRB has ruled the following activities to be 'closely related' to banking: **leasing personal or real property; **community development; **real estate and personal property and appraising; and, **arranging commercial real estate equity financing.	Various states authorize real estate development, equity participation, and brokerage activities for state-chartered banks.

Source: James R. Barth and R. Dan Brumbaugh, Jr., 'The Changing World of Banking: Setting the Regulatory Agenda,' Public Policy Brief, The Jerome Levy Economics Institute of Bard College, No. 8, 1993.

TABLE 4.5 *State Authorization of Selected Expanded Activities for State-Chartered Banks (a) March 1992*

Securities brokerage (discount and/or full)	General securities underwriting	Real estate equity participation	Real estate development	Real estate brokerage	Insurance underwriting	Insurance brokerage
Alabama (b)	Arizona (b)	Arizona (b)	Arizona (b)	Alabama (b)	Delaware	Alabama (b)
Arizona (b)	California (c)	Arkansas	Arkansas	Arizona (b)	Massachusetts (d)	California
Arkansas	Connecticut (b)	California	California	California (d)	New Jersey (e)	Delaware
California (c)	Delaware	Colorado	Colorado	Connecticut (b)	N. Carolina (d)	Idaho
Connecticut (b)	Florida	Connecticut (e)	Connecticut (e)	Florida	South Dakota	Indiana (g)
Delaware	Iowa (b)	Florida (b)	Delaware	Georgia	Utah (f)	Iowa
Florida (c)	Maine (b)	Georgia	Florida (b)	Idaho		Massachusetts (d)
Georgia	Massachusetts (d)	Iowa	Georgia	Massachusetts (d)		Minnesota
Hawaii (c)	Montana	Kentucky	Kentucky	Minnesota (b)		Nebraska (h)
Idaho (c)	New Jersey (e)	Maine	Maine	Nebraska		New Jersey (e)
Illinois	New York (b)	Massachusetts (d)	Massachusetts (d)	New Jersey (e)		North Carolina
Indiana	North Carolina (d)	Missouri (b)	Michigan	N. Carolina (d)		Oregon
Iowa (b)	Rhode Island	Nevada	Minnesota	Rhode Island		South Dakota
Kansas (b)	Tennessee	N. Hampshire (b)	Missouri (b)	Utah		Utah (f)
Kentucky	Texas (b)	New Jersey (e)	Nevada	Wisconsin		Virginia
Louisiana		N. Carolina (d)	N. Hampshire (b)			
Maine		Ohio	New Jersey (e)			
Maryland		Oregon	N. Carolina (d)			
Massachusetts (d)		Pennsylvania	Ohio			
Michigan		Rhode Island	Oregon (b)			
Minnesota (b)		South Dakota	Pennsylvania			
Missouri (b)		Tennessee (d)	Rhode Island			
Nebraska		Utah	Tennessee			
Nevada		Virginia	Utah			
N. Hampshire (c)		Washington	Washington			
New Jersey (e)						
New Mexico						

TABLE 4.5 *Continued*

Securities brokerage (discount and/or full)	General securities underwriting	Real estate equity participation	Real estate development	Real estate brokerage	Insurance underwriting	Insurance brokerage
New York						
N. Carolina (d)						
North Dakota						
Ohio						
Oklahoma						
Pennsylvania						
Rhode Island						
Tennessee						
Texas (b)						
Utah (b)						
Vermont						
Virginia (b)						
Washington (b)						
West Virginia (d)						
Wisconsin						

(a) Expanded activities above those permitted national banks and bank holding companies under the Bank Holding Company Act. Extent of practice unknown.

(b) Through a subsidiary.

(c) Laws are silent, but regulatory approval is possible.

(d) Possible through equity investment authority.

(e) Possible through leeway authority.

(f) Grandfathered institutions.

(g) Except for life insurance.

(h) Only in towns with less than 200,000 in population.

Source: James R. Barth and R. Dan Brumbaugh, Jr., 'The Changing World of Banking: Setting the Regulatory Agenda,' Public Policy Brief, The Jerome Levy Economics Institute of Bard College, No. 8, 1993.

TABLE 4.6 *Intrastate and Interstate Geographic Limitations on Banks Operating in the U.S.*

State	Intra	Inter	Date	Applicable states	Limitations	Previous inter restrictions
Alabama (AL)	S (90)	RR	September 88	AR,FL,GA,KY,LA,MD,MS,NC,SC,TN,TX,WV, & DC	5 years (i)	RR—July 87 excluding TX
Alaska (AK)	S (71)	NR	January 94	ALL	3 years	N—July 82
Arizona (AZ)	S (73)	N	July 92	ALL	NONE	—
Arkansas (AR)	L (till 99)	RR	January 89	AL,FL,GA,KS,LA,MS,MD,MO,NE,NC,OK,SC,TN,TX,VA,WV & DC	10 years, 25% (ii)	(RR—July 88 excluding GA, KS, WV, & DC)
California (CA)	S (06)	NR	January 91	ALL	NONE	RR—July 87
Colorado (CO)	L (till 97)	N	July 93	ALL	(iii)	RR—July 88
Connecticut (CT)	S (88)	NR	February 92	ALL	NONE	RR—June 83
Delaware (DE)	S (21)	NR	June 90	ALL	NONE	RR—January 88, restricted banking—June 86
Washington (DC)	S	RR	November 85	AL,FL,GA,LA,MD,MS,NC,SC,TN,VA, & WV	(iv)	—
Florida (FL)	S (88)	NR	May 95	ALL	5 years	RR—July 85
Georgia (GA)	L	NR	July 95	ALL	5 years (v)	RR—July 85 expanded March 87
Hawaii (HI)	S (86)	*	June 88	US TERR	(vi)	—
Idaho (ID)	S (33)	N	January 88	ALL	4 years	RR—July 85
Illinois (IL)	S (93)	NR	December 90	ALL	10 years	RR—July 86
Indiana (IN)	S (91)	NR	July 92	ALL	5 years, 12% (vii)	RR—January 86; expanded June 87 and July 90
Iowa (IA)	L	RR	January 91	IL,MN,MO,NE,SD, & WI	5 years (viii)	MN based Norwest Corp. permitted to acquire banks—72
Kansas (KS)	S (90)	RR	July 92	AR,CO,IA,MO,NE, & OK	15% (ix)	No Interstate Banking
Kentucky (KY)	L	NR	July 86	ALL	5 years 15% (x)	RR—July 84
Louisiana (LA)	S (88)	NR	January 89	ALL	5 years 25% (xi)	RR—July 87
Maine (ME)	S (75)	N	February 84	ALL	NONE	NR—January 78
Maryland (MD)	S	RR	July 87	AL,AR,DE,FL,GA,KY,LA,MS,NC,PA,SC,TN,VA,WV, & DC	3 years	RR with DE, DC, VA & WV only—July 85
Massachusetts (MA)	S (84)	NR	September 90	ALL	10% (xii)	RR—with New England states—July 83
Michigan (MI)	S (88)	NR	October 88	ALL	(xiii)	RR—January 86
Minnesota (MN)	L	RR	April 92	CO,IA,ID,IL,IN,KS,MI,MO,MT,ND,NE,OH,SD,WA,WI, & WV	30% (xiv)	RR—July 86; expanded August 88, August 90
Mississippi (MS)	S (89)	RR	July 90	AL,AR,FL,GA,KY,LA,MO,NC,SC,TN,TX,VA, & WV	5 years, 19% (xv)	RR with AL, AZ, LA, TN only—July 88

TABLE 4.6 *Continued*

State	Intra	Inter	Date	Applicable states	Limitations	Previous inter restrictions
Missouri (MO)	S (90)	RR	August 86	AR,IA,IL,KS,KY,NE,OK, & TN	13% (xvi)	—
Montana (MT)	L (90)	RR	October 93	CO,ID,MN,ND,SD,WI, & WY	6 years 22% (xvii)	No Interstate Banking
Nebraska (NE)	L	NR	January 91	ALL	14% (xviii)	RR—January 90, single bk. credit card operation—Aug. 83
Nevada (NV)	S	N	July 90	ALL	NONE	Restricted banking—April 84, RR—July 85
New Hampshire (NH)	S (87)	N	April 90	ALL	20% (xix)	RR—September 87
New Jersey (NJ)	S	NR	January 88	ALL	NONE	RR—August 86
New Mexico (NM)	S (91)	N	July 92	ALL	5 years, 40% (xx)	No Interstate Banking
New York (NY)	S	NR	June 82	ALL	NONE	—
North Carolina (NC)	S (21)	NR	July 96	ALL	NONE	RR—January 85 expanded October 88
North Dakota (ND)	L (87)	NR	June 91	ALL	19% (xxi)	No Interstate Banking
Ohio (OH)	S (89)	NR	October 88	ALL	20%	RR—October 85
Oklahoma (OK)	L (88)	N	July 87	ALL	5 years (xxii)	—
Oregon (OR)	S (85)	N	July 89	ALL	3 years	RR—July 86
Pennsylvania (PA)	S (90)	NR	March 90	ALL	NONE	RR—August 86
Rhode Island (RI)	S (56)	NR	January 88	ALL	NONE	RR—July 84
South Carolina (SC)	S	RR	January 86	AL,AR,FL,GA,KY,LA,MD,MS,NC,TN,VA,WV, & DC	5 years (xxiii)	—
South Dakota (SD)	S	NR	February 88	ALL	NONE	—
Tennessee (TN)	S (90)	NR	January 91	ALL	16.5% (xxiv)	RR—July 85 expanded April 88
Texas (TX)	S (88)	N	Jan 87 / Sept 01	ALL	5 years 25% (xxv)	—
Utah (UT)	S (81)	N	December 87	ALL	NONE	RR—April 84
Vermont (VT)	S (70)	NR	February 90	ALL	NONE	RR—January 88
Virginia (VA)	S (87)	NR	July 94	ALL	2 years	RR—July 85; Credit card operations—July 83
Washington (WA)	S (85)	NR	July 87	ALL	3 years	—
West Virginia (WV)	S (87)	NR	January 88	ALL	2 years 20% (xxvi)	Credit card & electronic data processing—June 86
Wisconsin (WI)	S (90)	RR	January 87	IA,IL,IN,KY,MI,MN,MO, & OH	5 years	—
Wyoming (WY)	L (88)	N	May 87	ALL	3 years (xxvii)	—

TABLE 4.6 Notes

Southeastern compact states are italicized; banks are generally required to obtain 80 percent of their deposits from within the region.

N = Nationwide Non-Reciprocal, NR = Nationwide Reciprocal, RR = Regional Reciprocal

* = HI, Interstate Banking allowed under certain conditions only (see note iv)

S = Statewide Branching

L = Limited Area Branching Only

Notes:

(i) Acquired banks in AL must be at least five years old and cannot branch across county lines for seven years after acquisition.

(ii) No BHC may control more than 25% of the deposits in AR; branching restricted to contiguous counties until January 1999.

(iii) Statewide branching in CO permitted by merger only until January 1997.

(iv) National Non-Reciprocal only if banks outside reciprocal region willing to invest in DC; acquired bank must have existed since December 85.

(v) Out-of-state holding companies may not establish new banks in GA.

(vi) Banks may be acquired in HI only if the acquiring organization has its headquarters in the U.S. Territories or the bank being acquired is failing.

(vii) No BHC may acquire more than (a) 25% of voting rights in an IN bank without permission; (b) 12% of total IN deposits.

(viii) BHCs cannot acquire more than 25% of any bank if the acquisition would give it over 10% of bank deposits; out-of-state BHC holdings may not exceed 35% of bank deposits in IA.

(ix) A BHC may not acquire any bank that would give the BHC control of over 15% of the total deposits of banks and thrifts in KS.

(x) Statewide branching by merger only; BHCs holdings may not exceed 15% of bank, thrift, and credit union deposits in KY.

(xi) No BHC can own or control more than 25% of the voting shares of a bank in LA.

(xii) State-wide branching in MA restricted to three bank acquisitions per year outside of home county; no BHCs holdings may exceed 15 % of bank deposits in MA.

(xiii) Out-of-state holding companies can not import their interest rates into MI.

(xiv) Out-of-state BHCs holdings may not exceed 30% of financial institution deposits in MN.

(xv) Statewide branching in MS subject to restrictions in small towns and cities and the deposit cap; BHCs may acquire any bank at least 5 years old or any failed bank.

(xvi) A BHC may not acquire any bank so that its holdings exceed 13% of bank, thrift, and credit union deposits in MO.

(xvii) Statewide branching in MT by merger; branching permitted in counties with no banks; out-of-state holdings may not exceed 22% of total deposits as of October 1997.

(xviii) Statewide branching by mergers except in bank's home city; out-of-state BHCs holding may not exceed 14% of deposits in NE.

(xix) A BHC in NH may not acquire any bank so that its holdings exceed 20% of total bank thrift, and credit union deposits in the state or more than 12 banks.

(xx) Statewide branching by mergers or in adjacent counties if no banks already exist; out-of-state BHCs holdings may not exceed 40% of financial institution deposits in NM.

(xxi) Out-of-state BHCs holdings cannot exceed 19% of total bank, thrift, and credit union deposits in ND.

(xxii) Statewide branching permitted by acquisition; BHCs must wait four years before entering into OK if their home state does not grant reciprocity, otherwise BHC may expand immediately.

(xxiii) Bill to enact national reciprocity is pending in SC legislature with an effective date of July 96.

(xxiv) Out-of-state BHCs holdings cannot exceed 16.5% of total TN deposits.

(xxv) Out-of-state BHCs holdings cannot exceed 25% of total TX deposits.

(xxvi) Out-of-state BHCs holdings cannot exceed 20% of total WV deposits.

(xxvii) Statewide branching in WY by merger or consolidation only.

U.S. Banking: Fragmented Regulatory Structure and Excess Capacity

The U.S. regulatory structure for banking institutions is quite fragmented. Table 4.7 presents information on the number and assets of the different types of federally insured depository institutions—and by implication their different state and federal regulators. As may be seen, despite all the turmoil during the past decade, there are still a substantial number of institutions—26,089 in 1993. Commercial banks, including U.S. branches and agencies of foreign banks, dominate in terms of assets, accounting for 77 percent of the total. In terms of number of institutions, they account for 44 percent of the total. Within the commercial banking industry, the largest 50 institutions accounted for 42 percent of total assets and the largest 100 institutions accounted for 54 percent at year end 1993. Largely because of the general prohibition against branching and banking within and across state lines until quite recently, the U.S. has fewer people per banking institution than most other countries of the world. Even within the U.S., moreover, the number of people per banking institution has varied over time. In 1920, for example, there were fewer than four thousand people per commercial bank whereas today there are more than twenty thousand.

Table 4.8 shows that the number of independent banks has declined sharply over the past fifteen years, while the importance of holding companies has increased, especially multi-state, multi-bank holding companies. More specifically, the number of independent banks declined from 9482 in 1980 to 2920 in 1993. At the same time, their share of total assets declined from 22 percent to 6 percent. The big gainers were the multi-state, multi-bank holding companies, whose share of assets rose from less than 5 percent in 1980 to nearly 70 percent in 1993. These developments reflect the banking turmoil in the 1980s and the changes in laws allowing greater intra- and interstate expansion of banking companies.

Banking institutions are chartered, insured and regulated by one or more of the following:

- the Office of the Comptroller of the Currency (OCC)—national banks;
- the Office of Thrift Supervision (OTS)—savings and loans and savings banks;
- the National Credit Union Administration (NCUA)—credit unions;
- the FDIC—commercial and savings banks and savings and loans;
- the Federal Reserve—member banks and bank holding companies; and
- the individual state banking authorities—all state-chartered institutions.

TABLE 4.7 *Assets and Number of U.S. Commercial Banks, Branches and Agencies of Foreign Banks, Insured Savings Institutions***, and Credit Unions—1980–1993*

| Year | Total | U.S. commercial banks | | | Branches & agencies of foreign banks | BIF insured savings banks** | SAIF insured institutions | | | | Credit unions | |
| | | National | State Member | State Nonmember | | | S&L associations | | Savings banks | | Federal charter | State charter |
							Federal charter	State charter	Federal charter	State charter		
NUMBER												
1980	36,435	12.15	2.74	24.73	0.92	0.89	5.45	5.51	0.00	0.00	34.14	13.48
1981	35,859	12.43	2.84	24.93	1.05	0.98	5.29	5.17	0.00	0.00	33.38	13.93
1982	35,127	13.04	2.96	25.14	1.19	0.90	4.82	4.54	0.00	0.00	33.11	14.30
1983	34,248	13.89	3.07	25.28	1.31	0.86	4.48	4.29	0.42	0.00	32.05	14.35
1984	33,554	14.59	3.15	25.37	1.39	0.87	4.35	4.31	0.68	0.00	31.44	13.84
1985	33,542	14.76	3.19	24.94	1.42	1.17	4.23	4.55	0.90	0.00	30.19	14.67
1986	33,062	14.71	3.31	24.87	1.51	1.43	4.07	4.44	1.21	0.03	29.51	14.93
1987*	32,079	14.39	3.40	24.86	1.59	1.26	4.02	4.24	1.50	0.06	29.31	15.38
1988*	30,943	14.04	3.42	24.90	1.67	1.59	3.63	3.89	1.93	0.08	29.47	15.38
1989*	29,686	14.06	3.38	25.26	1.80	1.70	3.02	3.28	2.26	0.19	29.71	15.33
1990*	28,583	13.92	3.53	25.74	1.93	1.70	2.45	2.91	2.77	0.06	29.78	15.22
1991	28,002	13.53	3.48	25.56	2.03	1.63	2.10	2.56	2.78	0.04	29.39	16.90
1992**	26,962	13.35	3.55	25.63	2.07	1.59	1.94	2.10	2.84	0.00	29.36	17.57
1993	26,089	12.73	3.71	25.61	2.08	1.81	1.82	1.59	2.93	0.00	29.50	17.71

TABLE 4.7 Continued

Year	U.S. commercial banks				Branches & agencies of foreign banks	BIF insured savings banks**	SAIF insured institutions					
							S&L associations		Savings banks		Credit unions	
	Total	National	State Member	State Nonmember			Federal charter	State charter	Federal charter	State charter	Federal charter	State charter
ASSETS ($B)												
1980	2,819	38.86	12.76	14.20	5.28	5.41	12.04	9.37	0.00	0.00	1.33	0.74
1981	3,060	39.27	12.66	14.39	5.66	5.09	13.11	7.80	0.00	0.00	1.28	0.74
1982	3,314	39.16	12.75	14.30	6.30	4.69	14.47	6.24	0.00	0.00	1.37	0.73
1983	3,639	38.32	11.76	14.29	6.31	4.70	13.65	6.94	1.77	0.00	1.50	0.76
1984	4,023	37.24	11.33	13.77	6.80	4.45	12.99	8.68	2.43	0.00	1.59	0.73
1985	4,438	36.76	11.17	13.77	7.05	4.62	12.34	8.64	2.95	0.00	1.76	0.94
1986	4,918	35.44	10.84	13.46	8.13	4.82	10.92	8.34	4.16	0.89	1.94	1.06
1987*	5,129	34.57	10.32	13.58	9.00	5.11	10.49	8.25	5.29	0.23	2.05	1.11
1988*	5,451	33.93	9.80	13.69	9.48	5.21	10.04	6.84	7.54	0.25	2.10	1.11
1989*	5,522	35.85	9.76	14.13	10.53	5.45	7.42	4.83	8.34	0.37	2.19	1.14
1990*	5,501	36.13	10.14	15.33	11.44	5.07	5.15	3.10	9.97	0.06	2.36	1.24
1991	5,491	36.15	10.80	15.52	12.79	4.65	3.75	2.51	9.67	0.02	2.62	1.51
1992**	5,515	36.39	11.57	15.62	12.97	4.30	3.01	1.85	9.55	0.00	2.95	1.79
1993	5,687	36.97	12.78	15.44	12.28	4.83	2.60	1.39	8.44	0.00	3.04	1.83

* For U.S. Commercial Banks, there is one bank with no assets that does not fit into any of the three categories.

**Data not available for BIF-insured savings banks versus SAIF-insured state chartered savings banks—data for both categories is under BIF-insured savings banks.

***Insured Savings Institutions equals BIF-insured savings banks plus all SAIF insured institutions.

Source: Office of the Comptroller of the Currency.

TABLE 4.8 *Organizational Structure of U.S. Commercial Banks: 1980–1993*

	1980	1981	1982	1983	1984	1985	1986	1987	1988	1989	1990	1991	1992	1993
Independent														
Number	9,482	8,708	7,693	6,646	5,703	5,094	4,589	4,230	3,969	3,746	3,545	3,358	3,182	2,920
Assets ($B)	405	383	330	281	247	225	212	203	201	209	204	229	240	215
Share of Total Assets (%)	21.82	18.89	15.08	12.02	9.87	8.28	7.26	6.84	6.53	6.43	6.11	6.77	6.94	5.86
OBHC														
Number	2,546	3,119	3,828	4,488	4,958	5,082	4,983	4,934	4,905	4,907	4,896	4,914	4,878	4,635
Assets ($B)	786	914	914	613	587	567	526	500	533	591	613	682	727	700
OSMBHC														
Number	324	355	418	518	671	806	856	837	807	783	764	722	673	630
Assets ($B)	580	523	671	714	658	667	543	442	385	348	415	328	287	257
Number of Banks	2,122	2,300	2,604	2,932	3,253	3,359	3,203	2,916	2,670	2,491	2,439	2,220	2,014	1,891
MSMBHC														
Number	16	18	21	33	53	65	100	132	143	160	171	174	177	190
Assets ($B)	85	208	273	729	1,010	1,259	1,639	1,824	1,960	2,103	2,109	2,144	2,205	2,495
Number of Banks	279	277	284	317	465	720	1,252	1,438	1,403	1,403	1,313	1,295	1,277	1,424

Notes: OBHC = One-Bank Holding Company; OSMBHC = One-State Multi-Bank Holding Company; MSMBHC = Multi-State Multi-Bank Holding Company.
Source: Daniel E. Nolle, 'Banking Industry Consolidation: Past Changes and Implications for the Future,' Office of the Comptroller of the Currency, Economic & Policy Analysis, Working Paper, May 1994.

With different regulators for different types of institutions, there is a lack of uniformity in regulation. For example, the OTS has granted permission to federally chartered savings and loans to branch nationwide, something banks cannot yet freely do. Savings and loans can also be owned by nonbank firms, something not permissible for banks. Credit unions, unlike the other banking institutions, do not pay taxes. State-chartered banks, in some states, are granted broader securities and insurance powers than national banks. More specifically, as Table 4.5 shows, 43 states authorize securities activities for state-chartered banks, with 42 allowing full or discount brokerage services and 15 permitting general underwriting. Also, 6 states permit insurance underwriting for banks and 25 states allow banks to sell insurance products. As Table 4.4 shows, some holding companies are also permitted to engage in securities activities. On May 19, 1993, for example, the Federal Reserve granted authority to Chemical Bank to underwrite corporate bonds, including below investment-grade bonds. The first such authority was granted to J.P. Morgan, Citicorp, and Bankers Trust in January of 1989. The Federal Reserve also granted authority to J.P. Morgan to underwrite equity securities in September of 1990.

The Chairman of the House Committee on Banking, Finance and Urban Affairs, Henry Gonzalez, introduced legislation in March of 1993 to provide for more uniform and consistent regulation. Under this legislation, which is consistent with proposed consolidation by the Clinton Administration, entitled the Regulatory Consolidation Act, a Federal Banking Commission (FBC) would be created. All regulatory functions of the OCC, OTS, FDIC, and Federal Reserve would then be transferred to the FBC. The OCC and OTS would be abolished, the Federal Reserve would focus exclusively on monetary policy and the FDIC would administer the federal deposit insurance funds. Only the NCUA and the insurance fund for credit unions would remain intact. If enacted, such a change in regulatory structure would facilitate a move towards emphasizing functions rather than institutions when financial laws and regulations are designed.

In view of the dominant asset size of the commercial banks among all U.S. banking institutions and their role in international banking, it is important to discuss their performance over the past four decades. This will enable one to understand better the current situation facing these banks. During the first three decades following World War II, both the rate-of-return on assets and the rate-of-return on equity capital for commercial banks increased. In the 1980s, however, both rates-of-return declined. At first glance, these data suggest that the recent problems within the banking industry are transitory. The data for the early 1990s would appear to support such a view. Indeed, the rate-of-return on assets in 1993 was 117 basis points and the rate-of-return on equity capital was 15.1 percent, both post-World War II highs for a single year.

A more thorough analysis of the data, however, reveals some fundamental problems. The strong performance in 1993 and the previous year was mainly due to an extremely steep yield curve, with short-term rates more than 300 basis points below long-term rates. Banks were paying relatively little on their deposits while earning substantially more on their assets. This situation is unlikely to persist given the current regulatory and competitive environment. Over the past 40 years, moreover, the differential between the rates-of-return on equity capital and U.S. Treasury securities has decreased every decade on average, even turning negative in the 1980s. At the same time, the ratio of net charge-offs-to-total-assets has steadily increased throughout the post-World War II period. The standard deviation of the return-on-equity capital has also tended to increase over the same time period. The fact that returns have declined while risk has increased within the banking industry is consistent with the existence of excess capacity. Interestingly enough, the Federal Reserve reported in 1932 that, 'The overbanked condition, which reached its peak after 1920, caused many banks to engage in high risk and marginal business, which contributed to the piling up of bank losses in the past decade.' With a flawed federal deposit insurance system and overly restrictive laws and regulations, such a situation exacerbated the costliness of institutions exiting the banking industry during the 1980s. In any event, based upon these and other developments described earlier, the U.S. banking industry is experiencing considerable restructuring and consolidation to improve its longer-term financial performance.

International Banking Operations

International banking operations have become increasingly important over time. As Table 4.2 shows, foreign banking offices in the U.S. accounted for 0.4 percent of the total financial assets of all financial service firms in 1950. This figure increased to 3.4 percent by 1993. More specifically, as Table 4.7 shows, U.S. branches and agencies of foreign banks accounted for 12 percent of the total assets of all depository institutions. Foreign banks have clearly established themselves as an important part of the U.S. banking industry. Indeed, they now account for more assets than the entire savings and loan industry (i.e., all SAIF-insured institutions).

At year end 1992, approximately 80 percent of all U.S. branches and agencies of foreign banks and 90 percent of the total assets held by such offices were state-chartered. This means that these offices are subject to regulation by the states in which they are chartered. The states most heavily involved in this regard are New York, California, Florida, Illinois, and Georgia.

The Foreign Bank Supervision Enhancement Act (FBSEA) of 1992, however, has granted new authority over state-chartered foreign banking offices to the Federal Reserve. More specifically, under this legislation the Federal Reserve is authorized to examine any office of a foreign bank in the United States. Each branch and agency of a foreign bank, moreover, must be examined at least once annually. In addition, the FBSEA applies the same financial, managerial, and operational standards to both foreign banks and U.S. banks. The federal regulators are also granted additional authority to terminate the U.S. activities of a foreign bank that is engaging in illegal, unsafe, or unsound practices. Lastly, entry into the U.S. by foreign banks is controlled by new requirements of home country supervision, on a consolidated basis, and by supervisory access to information regarding any foreign bank seeking to engage in business in the United States.

U.S. banks also engage in operations abroad. At year-end 1992, U.S. commercial banks had 217 foreign offices with $396 billion in assets. New York banks had 49 foreign offices with $292 billion in assets, while California banks had 18 foreign offices with $42 billion in assets. Banks in these two states therefore accounted for 84 percent of the total assets in foreign offices.

Regulating International Banking Operations

As banking markets become more fully integrated across national borders, a wider variety of financial products and services on more favorable terms will become available to both businesses and consumers. However, there currently are laws and regulations that may impede the transition towards greater banking integration.

Regarding the laws and regulations under which international banks operate, consider the case of cross-border banking in Canada, Mexico, and the United States. Despite their proximity to one another, the banking markets in these three countries are not highly integrated. However, recent actions have been taken to provide opportunities for greater integration. Canada and the U.S. enacted the U.S.-Canadian Free Trade Agreement (FTA) in 1988. Under this agreement, U.S. banks are now permitted to engage in securities activities on the same basis as Canadian banks. (However, the Federal Reserve, through Regulation K, does limit the absolute and relative size of certain nonbanking activities abroad, including securities underwriting and distribution.) U.S. banks also are exempt from the aggregate ceiling imposed on the asset holdings of all foreign banks. Furthermore, the

FTA removed many of the ownership restrictions on the acquisition of Canadian financial firms by U.S. investors. Canadian banks, in turn, are permitted to underwrite and to deal in their own government securities while operating in the United States. Those Canadian banks with interstate banking privileges in the U.S. prior to the enactment of the International Banking Act (IBA) of 1978, moreover, are indefinitely grandfathered.

The North American Free Trade Agreement (NAFTA), which became effective January 1, 1994, potentially provides a stimulus for greater banking integration in North America. The more general reasons center around Mexico's large population and potential for so much greater economic activity. In 1992, Mexico's population was 85 million and its GNP was only $295 billion. In comparison, Canada's population was 28 million and its GNP was $566 billion, while the U.S.'s population was 255 million and its GNP was $5905 billion. The recent economic reforms in Mexico and their positive effect on the economy thus far provide optimism regarding longer-term stability and growth. This situation should provide for greater cross-border trade and finance, especially between Mexico and the United States. However, the fact that Mexico's GNP is only 5 percent that of the U.S. means that the near-term effect on the U.S. economy is likely to be relatively small.

The more specific reason the NAFTA potentially provides a stimulus for greater banking integration is that it allowed U.S. and Canadian banks to acquire or to establish wholly-owned banking, insurance, and securities subsidiaries in Mexico since January 1, 1994. However, the combined assets of U.S. and Canadian banking subsidiaries are initially not permitted to exceed 8 percent of the Mexican banking industry's total capital. This ceiling rises gradually over time and then is completely eliminated shortly after the year 2000. The individual market shares of foreign banking subsidiaries will also be initially limited to a maximum of 1.5 percent of the industry's capital. This limit will also rise shortly after the year 2000—to 4 percent. These changes represent greater opportunities for Canadian and U.S. banks to enter Mexico because individual foreign ownership of Mexican banks is currently limited to a minority share of no more than 10 percent of the paid-up capital of an individual banking institution.

Although the FTA and the NAFTA potentially provide for greater regional banking integration, an important regulatory issue with respect to international banking is the range of activities in which a bank is permitted to engage in a foreign country. The current position of the U.S. is embodied in the IBA, which was enacted because of a concern that foreign banks operated in the U.S. with significant competitive advantages over U.S. banks. This legislation, for the first time, provided for comprehensive federal regulation of the U.S. operations of foreign banks. It embodies into law the principle of national treatment in the context of financial products and services. This means that domestic and foreign banking institutions are to be afforded equality of competitive opportunity. To implement the principle of national treatment, the competitive advantages of foreign banks over U.S. banks were ended. More specifically, the IBA no longer permitted foreign banks to establish full-service, deposit-taking branches wherever state laws allow and restricted the U.S. nonbanking activities of foreign banks, including underwriting securities.

Although the U.S. maintains a policy of national treatment, there are limited exceptions. The most notable one is that some states do not provide national treatment to foreign banks. On the other hand, the U.S. has also provided better than national treatment in some cases. For example, because the IBA grandfathered existing U.S. activities of foreign banks, 17 institutions were permitted to retain ownership of their securities affiliates in the United States.

While the U.S. standard of national treatment is unconditional, some industrialized countries have adopted a policy of reciprocal national treatment. This means that one country will grant national treatment to another only if its banks likewise receive national treatment in the other country. Interestingly enough, a major negotiating objective of the U.S. in the NAFTA negotiations was obtaining permission for its banks to branch into Canada and Mexico. This objective was not achieved, however, partly because Canada and Mexico perceive that their banks are not afforded equality of competitive opportunity in the U.S. financial services industry. As a result, the NAFTA provides each country the right to require that foreign banks operate through a subsidiary, which both Canada and Mexico do. (In June of 1992, branches and agencies accounted for over four-fifths of the total assets of all the U.S. offices of foreign banks. At the same time, branches and agencies accounted for about two-thirds of the total assets of all the foreign offices of U.S. banks. These data suggest that subsidiaries are not the preferred organizational form.)

In the U.S., the FBSEA now requires that retail deposit taking activities requiring deposit insurance protection be conducted by foreign banks only through an insured subsidiary. As a result, foreign banks cannot establish new insured branches to conduct such activities. Since the 52 existing insured branches that are grandfathered held only $4 billion in deposits in June of 1992, this requirement is likely to have little adverse effect on foreign banks.

The Second Banking Directive of the European Community (EC) establishes an EC-wide policy of reciprocal national treatment. In sharp contrast to the NAFTA, however, it also provides that member countries in general will have neither a role in the licensing or the day-to-day supervision of branches of banks from other member countries nor the ability to limit the number of branches that may be established. The directive also establishes a list of permissible activities that, once authorized by a bank's home country, may be offered anywhere in the EC, even when the host country does not permit its banks to engage in such activities. This degree of harmonization clearly goes well beyond any current or prospective agreements for international banking operations among countries in North America or elsewhere.

Geographic Barriers to Integration: State Branching and Banking Laws

The integration of banking markets across national borders is in large part dependent upon the ability of banks to operate wherever they choose. Yet, as mentioned above, NAFTA only permits U.S. banks to operate in both Canada and Mexico through subsidiaries, not branches, although there are no geographical limitations. Canadian and Mexican banks, in turn, may operate either through branches or subsidiaries, but confront significant geographical restrictions. The reason for the differences in geographical treatment is solely due to the current U.S. laws. In particular, the extent to which banks, both domestic and foreign, may operate within and across state lines in the U.S. is currently determined by state, not federal, law. And until quite recently, states have generally restricted geographical expansion by banks both intrastate and interstate. Even in those cases where states have permitted out-of-state banks to enter, entry has mainly been restricted to the acquisition of existing banks rather than through *de novo* banking or branching. The acquired banks must typically be operated as separate banks, with their own chief executive officers and boards of directors, rather than converted to branches of the acquiring banks. As a result of these restrictions on geographical expansion, integration of the U.S. banking market has been impeded. Until the U.S. moves to nationwide banking and branching, such geographical limitations will also impede the integration of banking markets throughout North America, despite NAFTA.

Table 4.6 presents the current intrastate and interstate geographic limitations on banks operating in the U.S. There are currently 13 states and the District of Columbia that permit only limited branching intrastate, while the remaining 37 states permit statewide branching. Most of the more liberal branching states only recently changed their laws, such as Texas, which was a unit banking state before 1988, in part because of a significant number of costly bank failures. (As an historical aside, U.S. President Grover Cleveland recommended branches for national banks in 1895, but smaller banks were opposed to this recommendation. As a compromise, in 1900 the minimum capital requirement for opening a national bank in small communities was reduced to $25,000 from $50,000. There were nine states, moreover, that permitted state-wide branching in 1909.)

Information about the limitations on interstate expansion also is presented in Table 4.6. At present, as already noted, such expansion can primarily be done through the acquisition and operation of separate banks, not through branches. There are 11 states that permit banks from other states to enter without restriction if they so choose, while 24 states permit entry but only on a reciprocal basis (i.e., banks may enter only if the states of the entering banks reciprocate for the banks of the states being entered). The remaining 14 states and the District of Columbia permit entry on a reciprocal basis, but only include banks from states in a specified regional area. As may be seen from the table, most of the liberalization in banking across state lines has occurred in recent years.

Focusing on those states that engage in regional reciprocal banking, the largest number belong to what is referred to as the 'Southeast Compact.' This compact consists of the 11 states and the District of Columbia (which are italicized in the table) that are located in the southeastern part of the United States. Banks in the southeastern states are permitted to operate throughout the region, while banks from outside the region are prevented from entering. The banks in the Southeast Compact accounted for 18 percent of the total assets of all banks in the U.S. in 1992.

The importance of the Southeast Compact is that it serves as an impediment to not only the integration of banking markets within the U.S., but also North America and elsewhere. The specific effect on foreign banks is due to the fact that banks in the states comprising the Southeast Compact are generally required to obtain 80 percent of their deposits from within the region. This means that Mexican or Canadian banks operating in Florida and desiring to expand into Georgia are precluded from doing so. The reason is that such banks obtain most of their deposits outside the region and this precludes them from satisfying the 80 percent requirement, which is based on all deposits, not simply U.S. deposits. As a result, they cannot expand their operations throughout the southeastern United States.

Table 4.6 also presents information indicating that there are restrictions on the degree to which out-of-state banks may control total statewide banking activities in various states. All of these types of legal restrictions, as well as social and cultural factors, will affect the integration of banking markets both within countries and across countries. Simply enacting treaties that liberalize financial activities across national borders may not lead to the degree of banking integration anticipated to the extent that regional compacts, such as the Southeast Compact, exist.

Conclusion

The bottom-line regulatory issue with respect to international banking activities is which legal and regulatory structure is the most appropriate to adequately contain the risk of severe disruptions in individual countries' credit and payments systems as global integration continually increases. This is a difficult and controversial issue to resolve. However, all of the accumulated evidence indicates that inadequately capitalized banking institutions have a proclivity to engage in excessively risky activities, particularly when those activities are funded with mispriced government insured deposits or other government provided subsidies. It is therefore incumbent upon regulators to require that institutions be adequately capitalized at all times. This means that both capital and risk must be properly measured. It also means that regulators must be willing to take prompt corrective action against troubled institutions. Furthermore, those banking institutions that are adequately capitalized should be allowed to adapt to changing market forces. This involves providing a 'level playing' field so that banking institutions can compete more freely in securities and insurance activities wherever and through whatever organizational form they consider most appropriate. Only when provided with the ability to pursue prudently all profitable opportunities can banking institutions be truly adequately capitalized. And only when these opportunities can be pursued without being impeded by regional compacts can risk be prudently reduced through greater geographical diversification.

Selected Bibliography

BARTH, J. R. (1991) *The Great Savings and Loan Debacle.* Washington, D.C.: The American Enterprise Institute, University Press of America.

BARTH, J. R. and BRUMBAUGH, R. D. Jr. (1993) 'The Changing World of Banking: Setting the Regulatory Agenda,' Public Policy Brief, The Jerome Levy Economics Institute of Bard College, Number 8.

BARTH, J. R. and BRUMBAUGH, R. D.Jr. (1994) 'The Role of Deposit Insurance: Financial Stability and Moral Hazard,' Seminar on Current Legal Issues Affecting Central Banks, International Monetary Fund, Washington, D.C., May.

BARTH, J. R., BRUMBAUGH, R. D. JR. and LITAN, R. E. (1992) *The Future of American Banking,* Armonk, N.Y.: M.E. Sharpe, Inc.

BENSTON, G. J. (1990) 'U.S. Banking in an Increasingly Integrated and Competitive World Economy,' *Journal of Financial Services Research,* Volume 4, Number 4, December: 311–339.

BRUMBAUGH, R. D. Jr. (1988) *Thrifts Under Siege*, Cambridge, MA.: Ballinger Publishing Company.

FRENCH, G. E. (1994) 'Banking in Transition,' Conference on The Financial System in the Decade Ahead: What Should Banks Do?, The Jerome Levy Institute of Bard College, April 14–16.

KANE, E. J. (1989) *The S&L Insurance Mess*, Washington, D.C.: The Urban Institute Press.

KANE, E. J. (1994) 'Financial Reform as a Market-Constrained Political Process,' Deakin University Working Paper Series, August.

KANE, E. J. and HENDERSHOTT, R. (1994) 'The Federal Deposit Insurance Fund That Didn't Bark in the Night,' Working Paper No. 4468, National Bureau of Economic Research, February.

KAUFMAN, G. G. and MOTE, L. R. (1994) 'Is Banking a Declining Industry? A Historical Perspective,' *Economic Perspectives*, Federal Reserve Bank of Chicago, May/June: 2–21.

NOLLE, D. E. (1994) 'Banking Industry Consolidation: Past Changes and Implications for the Future,' Office of the Comptroller of the Currency, Economic and Policy Analysis, Working Paper, May.

PARK, S. (1994) 'Explanations for the Increased Riskiness of Banks in the 1980s,' *Economic Review*, The Federal Reserve Bank of St. Louis, Volume 76, Number 4, July/August: 3–23.

SAUNDERS, A. and WALTER, I. (1994) *Universal Banking in the United States*, New York, New York: Oxford University Press.

SAVAGE, D. T. (1993) 'Interstate Banking: A Status Report,' *Federal Reserve Bulletin*, Volume 79, Number 12, December: 1075–1089.

U.S. GENERAL ACCOUNTING OFFICE (1993) *Interstate Banking: Benefits and Risks of Removing Regulatory Restrictions*, November.

WHEELOCK, D. C. (1993) 'Is the Banking Industry in Decline? Recent Trends and Future Prospects from a Historical Perspective,' *Economic Review*, Federal Reserve Bank of St. Louis, September/October: 3–22.

WHITE, L. J. 'Why Now? Change and Turmoil in U.S. Banking,' Occasional Paper Number 38, Group of Thirty, Washington, D.C.

5

Canadian Banking Strategy in North America

JAMES L. DARROCH

I. Introduction: Competing in a Regionalizing–Globalizing World

The 1980s saw significant changes to the Canadian banking industry which is captured by the movement from the term *banking* to *financial services* (see the Economic Council of Canada, 1989a; 1989b). Dramatic market opportunities for both geographic and product line extension simultaneously opened in both domestic and international markets. New threats arose at the same time. The fundamental challenge to Canadian bankers became to select appropriate opportunities and then to focus their considerable resources to win in these markets.

All six major Canadian banks—the Bank of Montreal, the Bank of Nova Scotia (Scotiabank), the Canadian Imperial Bank of Commerce (CIBC), the National Bank of Canada, the Royal Bank of Canada, and the Toronto Dominion Bank (TD)—are forging North American focused strategies (Darroch and Litvak, 1991; 1992c; 1994). Operations in Europe and Asia are still critical for the banks, but the strategic objectives for these operations are being redefined. Financial services networks are being realigned in order that global operations be focused to serve North American clients, including those with off-shore parents or subsidiaries. Existing and potential North American clients going abroad as well as foreign clients coming into North America are the targeted segments. Moreover, observers in Canada expect that recent and expected mergers in the U.S. will speed the Canadian invasion of the United States. (see Whyte, 1991: 3).

Canadian banks are not retreating from global markets, rather they are launching a major assault on the extended home market emerging from the Free Trade Act (FTA) and increasing western hemisphere co-operation and integration, such as NAFTA. This means that Canadian banks must develop strategies for competing in the U.S. and Mexican markets if they are to preserve their status in Canadian markets. It is important to realize that we are in the era of North American financial services, not Canadian banking. The North American strategies of the Canadian banks are a response to this new macro environment.

Success in a healthy home market is the key to global success. However, the notion of 'home market' has changed, as illustrated by the strategic changes undertaken by Deutsche Bank (see *The Economist*, 1991: 79–82). The Bank's future success is based upon competitiveness in the extended home market of Western Europe, not by asset rankings in banking league tables. Talk of regional dominance has replaced that of global ambition. Similar changes have taken place with the major Canadian banks.

Significant changes in regulation at both the provincial, national, regional, and international levels have created a new playing field. It is impossible to understand strategic changes at Canadian banks without recognizing how these regulatory forces combined with sweeping technological change to alter the bases of competition in what were once prime protected banking markets. Michael Porter in his *Competitive Advantage of Nations* (1990) makes a compelling case that the global competitiveness of firms is conditioned by the four forces that form the domestic diamond: firm strategy, structure and rivalry; demand conditions; factor conditions; and, related and supporting industries. (For applications to Canada, see Darroch and Litvak, 1992a; Rugman, 1992.) For that reason, our examination of the Canadian industry commences with the dramatic changes wrought by the two most recent Bank Acts of 1980 and 1991. It is essential to understand that the Bank Act, since its first passage in 1871 has been subject to review every 10 years in order to ensure that banking powers be in tune with changing market environments, and hence has a major impact on industry structure. Moreover, the Bank Act was designed to promote the chartered banks as powerful national financial institutions, not handicap them (Darroch, 1992, 1994).

Prior to this discussion, it is important to understand that while the Federal Government has power over the banking sector, the provincial governments have power over securities exchanges, investment banking and other key *financial services activities*. The movement from banking to financial services required efforts to harmonize the differing federal and provincial jurisdictions concerning the traditional *four pillars* of banking, investment banking, trust services, and insurance.

The same forces promoting globalization, i.e. new information technologies and new trade policies, opened up fissures between public policy makers at the federal and provincial levels, as it did at the international level. The desire of Quebecers to increase their power over their own affairs was an important factor in the unfolding of Canadian financial services policy (see Darroch and Litvak, 1992b). Since Jacques Parizeau was finance minister in the first Parti Quebecois government, Quebec had been the leading voice for change in financial services in Canada.

II. The Canadian Banking Landscape

A favourable regulatory framework noted by Salomon Brothers in an evaluation of The Royal Bank has made the six major federally chartered Schedule 1 institutions the dominant financial services players in Canada. The analysts at Salomon Brothers considered 'the regulatory framework for Canadian banks to be a significant positive compared with the conditions facing the U.S. industry' (*Globe and Mail,* 1991: B8). This has led to an industry that is highly concentrated, despite the entry of over fifty foreign banks following changes to the 1980 Bank Act. The six largest banks, the CIBC, the Royal , Scotiabank, the Bank of Montreal, the TD and the National Bank hold over 90 percent of the banking assets in Canada (Harris, 1994: 42). In 1993, the banks covered Canada with 7,744 branches, 12,160 automated banking machines (ABMs), and employed 172,776. In comparative terms, Canada is a world leader in branch coverage and second only to Japan in per capital coverage by ABMs (Canadian Bankers Association, 1994). A strong domestic base has always been key to the size and strength of the Canadian banks.

The 1994 Euromoney 500 presented a breakdown of the largest banks ranked by shareholders' equity in Canada, Mexico, and the U.S. There was also a retrospective on the first survey in 1981. In 1981, the top 100 included 3 banks from Canada, 1 from Mexico, and 21 from the United States. By 1993, Canada had 5, Mexico 1 and the U.S. 21 (Piggott, 1994a). While Canada seems to have made advances compared to the U.S., the more important 1994 ranking of the 100 Best Banks in the World by Euromoney, shown in Table 5.1, tells a different tale.

Two observations are obvious. First, the tremendous strength of the U.S banks, as signalled by the title of the poll, 'The Americans bounce back.' Thirty-nine of the 100 are U.S. banks. This is the result of a major recovery and restructuring by the U.S. industry (see Bird, 1994; McCoy *et al.,* 1994). In the first survey published in December 1990, only 17 U.S. banks made the rank. All five of the major Canadian banks also made the rank in both surveys, but many U.S. banks have

TABLE 5.1 *North America's Best Banks*

NA rank	1994 rank	1993 rank	Bank	S/H equity ($Bil)	Euromoney 500 ranking
1	1	1	JP Morgan	9.86	18
2	2	6	Banc One Corporation	7.03	38
3	5	1	Wachovia Corporation	3.02	98
4	6	6	Norwest Corp	3.57	83
5	10	—	Fifth Third Bancorp	1.20	227
6	12	9	BankAmerica Corp	17.14	5
7	14	—	Citicorp	13.95	11
8	16	14	Suntrust Banks	3.61	82
9	18	13	Bankers Trust New York	4.15	72
10	20	22	NBD Bancorp	3.25	95
11	22	17	Republic New York Corp	2.75	110
12	24	–	Northern Trust Corp	1.15	237
13	25	50	Keycorp	4.99	64
14	27	—	Huntington Bancshares	1.22	224
15	29	52	First Bank System	2.25	133
16	30	—	Firstar Corporation	1.16	235
17	32	94	Nationsbank	9.98	16
18	33	—	Golden West Financial Corp	2.07	142
19	35	—	Chemical Banking Corp	11.16	15
20	37	—	Wells Fargo & Co.	4.32	69
21	38	—	First Interstate	3.55	84
22	40	42	PNC Bank Corporation	4.33	67
23	42	61	Bank of Nova Scotia	4.43	62
24	43	84	First Union Corporation	5.21	53
25	47	29	Bank of Montreal	4.32	68
26	50	87	First Fidelity Bancorp	2.74	111
27	51	—	Bank of New York Company	4.07	75
28	53	—	Meridian Bancorp	1.19	231
29	55	—	Amsouth Bancorp	1.09	246
30	56	40	Corestates Bankcorp	2.03	146
31	60	58	National City Corp	2.76	108
32	61	—	SouthTrust Corporation	1.05	257
33	62	—	First Chicago Corp	4.26	71
34	63	—	State Street Boston Corp	1.10	242
35	64	56	Boatmen's Bancshares	2.13	140
36	66	—	Barnett Banks	2.87	104
37	68	—	Fleet Financial Group	3.64	80
38	71	41	Toronto-Dominion Bank	3.78	78
39	84	—	Chase Manhattan Corp	8.12	31
40	86	93	Mellon Bank Corp	3.31	92
41	89	—	Canadian Imperial Bank of Commerce	5.96	44
42	91	—	Crestar Financial Corp	1.06	252
43	94	51	US Bancorp	1.82	164
44	100	77	Royal Bank of Canada	5.94	45

Source: Charles Piggott, 'The Americans bounce back,' *Euromoney*, August 1994.

moved ahead. The point is made most obvious when we look at the expert rankings of the best 50. In 1990, 15 U.S. and 2 Canadian banks made the rank. Now, 26 U.S. banks make the cut, but no Canadian bank made it.

The obvious question is why have the Canadian banks been falling in the rankings? It is more than problems in real estate, which plagued all banks, or a reputed lack of internationalization of Canadian business (Nankivell, 1994: 9). The answer may lie in recent regulatory and market changes which led to an increased focus on the domestic market where weak competitors provided easy prey. This explains the move to a stronger Canadian asset base shown in Table 5.2. Changes in regulation were responsible for many of these expanded market opportunities.

III. Changing Regulatory Environments

The 1980 Bank Act reversed the legislation of 1967 that banned foreign banks from operating in Canada. Under the 1967 legislation, no shareholder could own more than 10 percent of a bank, nor could the aggregate of foreign shareholdings exceed 25 percent. Foreign banks were effectively prohibited entry into the Canadian market. This was in response to Citibank's acquisition of the Mercantile Bank. While the Mercantile was grandfathered, limits were placed upon future growth. By 1980, Canada recognized that previous protectionist policies were no longer appropriate and opened its borders to the great global, and other, banks of the world.

The complexities of the industry can be seen when it is recognized that the changes were in some ways designed in an effort to benefit the Canadian banks by forcing foreign banks to compete on a not

TABLE 5.2 *North American Assets as a Percentage of Total Assets*

	1983 % of N.A. Assets* Cda + U.S.	1983 $ Mil	1993 % of NA Assets* Cda + U.S.	1993 $ Mil	1983–93 $ Change as a %
Bank of Montreal	67 + 10 = 77	6,575	64 + 26 = 90	29,887	454%
Bank of Nova Scotia	49 + 14 = 63	7,065	59 + 19 = 78	19,500	276%
CIBC	70 + 10 = 80	6,609	72 + 12 = 84	17,454	264%
National Bank	74 + 4 = 78	688	82 + 10 = 92	4,206	611%
Royal Bank	63 + 8 = 71	5,800	81 + 6 = 87	9,664	166%
TD	66 + 12 = 78	4,714	77 + 17 = 94	14,339	304%

Source: Annual Reports of the Banks.

altogether level Canadian playing field (Friedman, 1981). Two categories of banks were established: the widely-held and Canadian-owned chartered banks known as Schedule A banks, and the new closely-held banks, mainly foreign, known as Schedule B banks. In order to gain entry, the applying bank had to convince the Minister of Finance that it would increase the competitiveness of the Canadian market and the bank's home government had to extend similar treatment to Canadian banks.

Various obstacles, including limits on size and forms of operation, made life difficult for the foreign banks. Schedule B banks were limited to lending 20 times their authorized capital. Moreover, the total market share of the Schedule Bs was limited initially to 8 percent of the market. In addition, they were required to obtain the permission of the Minister of Finance to open a branch office. The new banks were effectively limited to a segment of commercial lending. Yet, Canadian customers could now expect the banks to be operating in Canada.

In 1986, aggressive action by Quebec and Scotiabank sounded the death knell of the classic four pillars. Scotiabank took the opportunity to transform the Canadian banking industry when the Quebec Securities Commission granted Scotiabank a license to create a full service underwriter, Scotia Securities. The Ontario Government, responsible for Canada's largest capital markets, and the Federal Government were forced to follow. The 'Little Bang' of 1987 was the result. The separation between investment and commercial banking enshrined in Glass-Steagall in the U.S. was breached. Interestingly, Quebec is also home to the only Canadian-owned Schedule 2 bank, the Laurentian Bank, now controlled by the financial cooperative, the *Mouvement Desjardins* whose president, Claude Beland, is an advocate of Quebec separatism, although the cooperative is officially neutral.

A. American Express Becomes A Bank

Perhaps there is no greater indicator of the non-event nature of the entry of foreign banks, than by studying the one application for a bank license by a foreign firm that caused considerable furor among Canadian banks—American Express. American Express was not a traditional competitor and signalled significant changes to the Canadian retail market. Canadian bankers were outraged since they held that American Express was not regulated as a bank in its home country. The definition of 'financial institution' had to be stretched to include a 'financial corporation' and a foreign company would be allowed to enter into activities prohibited to Canadian banks, such as marketing of goods and travel services (see MacIntosh, 1991: 181–188.)

While Canadian banks were prepared to meet the challenge of other banks, the entry of this financial services retailer was met with howls of complaint over unfair competition. Complicating the application were rumours that American Express was receiving a benefit for supporting the Canada-U.S. Free Trade Act (FTA).

With the ratification of the FTA in January 1989, U.S. banks were released from the growth limitations which still govern other foreign banks, now known as Schedule 2s. The FTA provides that financial institutions of the other country are governed by the same regulatory rules as comparable domestic institutions. The application of national treatment means that U.S. financial services providers are accorded treatment no less favourable in like circumstances than Canadian providers receive with respect to government measures affecting the financial services sector. (See Industry, Science, Science and Technology, 1991: 6–7). While the Canadian banks were empowered to operate in the U.S., there were no essential gains. In fact, the deal was highly asymmetrical, as U.S. banks received powers in Canada that Canadian banks did not receive in the U.S., because of Glass-Steagall and the McFadden Acts on investment and interstate banking, respectively.

At the time of the free trade negotiations, some Canadian observers suggested that the concept of reciprocity rather than national treatment should govern the operations of U.S.-owned Schedule 2 banks because they were going to receive more immediate benefits under the FTA. This is not an altogether unique situation between Canada and the U.S., as a similar dispute involved the U.S. and the European Community (see Graham and Krugman, 1989: 117). Concerns over the competitiveness of national industries is an obstacle to the international harmonization of national regulations.

In 1990, American Express received its letters patent. The desire of American Express to be a bank in Canada merits some attention. In the U.S., the strategy had clearly been to become a full service provider—a financial supermarket—but not a bank. The issue concerns competitive advantage. Many commentators on the U.S. scene saw that regulation favoured 'non-bank banks' (Pierce, 1991). In Canada, regulation generally favoured the chartered banks (see Darroch, 1992).

The entry of American Express onto the Canadian scene heralded two important changes. Traditional Canadian retail banking had demanded an extensive branch network. The advent of electronic networks, such as Interac, which provided electronic banking access to all member banks (and all of the major banks are among the nine charter members), meant that this was no longer the case. In addition, there was a new emphasis on marketing. The bank of the future would use its distribution network to sell diverse financial services products and other products. The new entrant could optimize its business systems for the emerging environment without the handicap of historical attitudes and resource deployments. Given a Canadian view that banks are quasi-public utilities, the exit costs facing the traditional banks in certain retail markets is real. While the old providers would have to maintain service to all segments, the newcomers could cherry-pick.

The power of the Canadian banks may have been underestimated by American Express, at least in the short run. The Interac members set an entry fee that effectively blocked Amex from the major electronic banking network in Canada. New regulations did not destroy all barriers, but rather affected the costs of overcoming certain entry barriers. While the banks were losing some battles, they maintained control over other key aspects of the emerging distribution systems and payment networks. The question is for how long, given the rapid change in information technologies, such as Microsoft's interest in home banking, that affect the retail distribution system. In addition, public policy changes may force Interac to open up its network to new members (Partridge, 1994: B2).

B. The 1991 Bank Act

The 1991 Bank Act sought to remedy some of the obstacles to banks transforming themselves into financial services firms. Banks were allowed entry into the other pillars—they could now offer non-banking financial services such as trust or insurance through subsidiaries. In addition, they were allowed to establish 'networking' arrangements with other financial services providers. That is, they could now offer new services through their extensive retail branches. However, banks were prohibited from offering insurance services through their branches and were still prohibited from car leasing and selling life annuities.

Powers to offer new services to corporate customers were expanded so that the banks could deepen their relationships with their traditional customers by increasing the links made available by rapidly changing information technologies. While previously banks had offered some data processing related services, these powers were expanded to include: information processing; advisory services in the design, development and implementation of information management systems; and, design, development, manufacture and sale of ancillary computer hardware. Specialized financing services were also expanded as banks were allowed into a broader range of venture capital and merchant banking activities. In addition, banks were now permitted to hold, manage and develop land through their real property corporations and to own real estate brokerage firms.

At the retail level, banks were allowed to provide investment counselling, portfolio management and financial planning. With an aging population, this entry into asset management was fundamental if the banks were to remain the pre-eminent players in the Canadian market. Clearly the banks were powerful domestic players and were in a position to influence strongly, if not dominate the evolution of the Canadian financial services industry.

C. The North American Free Trade Agreement (NAFTA)

Under NAFTA, Mexico allowed Canadian and U.S. companies to establish banking, securities and/or insurance firms in Mexico in the form of either joint ventures or subsidiaries. Neither Canadian nor U.S. firms will be allowed to operate using a branch structure. There are limitations on market shares. During the transition period, the aggregate market share will increase from 8 percent to 15 percent for banks, and from 10 percent to 15 percent for securities firms. Individual firms will also be capped, but will see their ceiling go from 1.5 percent to 4 percent after the transition period. Securities firms will face a 4 percent cap.

Insurance firms also gain access to the market. Foreign firms were allowed to have 51 percent equity in a joint venture in 1998 and 100 percent by 2000. Initially, subsidiaries were limited to an aggregate market share of 6 percent. This increases to 12 percent by 1999 and is removed after January 1, 2000. Individually the subsidiaries face a share cap of 1.5 percent that will also be eliminated on January 1, 2000. Canadian and U.S. insurance firms that already have a presence in the Mexican market were allowed to increase their equity position to 100 percent in 1996.

Mexican commercial banks are exempted from the ownership rules on Canadian banks, which prohibit an individual from controlling more than 10 percent of a bank or a 25 percent restriction on foreign ownership. In addition, Mexican banks are exempt from the 12 percent foreign asset ceiling and from requiring the Minister of Finance's approval in establishing a subsidiary. In anticipation of increased Canadian-Mexican trade, Bancomer has already established a representative office in Toronto.

The key international regulatory change was the Basle Concordat developed at the Bank for International Settlements (BIS). This accord represented the attempt by regulators to level the playing field in international markets by creating common equity to asset ratios. By forcing banks to focus on the profitable allocation of capital to different activities, global banking markets were expected to return to appropriate risk-return parameters. International banking once again became an attractive market for those who had honed their skills in appropriate national arenas.

IV. Changing Bank Strategies

Taking North America as a region, the FTA and NAFTA did not significantly affect the powers of the Canadian banks. However, there have been significant strategic implications because of the effects on the customers of the banks. The following are the key strategic changes:

1. The move to a North American strategy;
2. Consolidation of domestic and retail strategies;
3. The move to fee-based services.

While the emergence of a North American strategy is of critical importance, following the logic of Porter (1990), the first move was to hone competitive advantages in the domestic market by taking advantage of new opportunities in retail markets. The shift to Canadian assets shown in Table 5.2 demonstrates this trend.

The focus on the domestic market can be seen in the behaviour of the banks and the investment banks. Since the 'Little Bang', all of the major Schedule 1 banks, with the notable exception of the TD (Toronto Dominion Bank), have purchased what were the major domestic investment banks. The acquisition of Burns Fry by the Bank of Montreal to form Nesbitt Burns extended the process. The weaker pillars were crumbling before the strong.

During the same period, the banks swallowed big chunks of the trust industry with the acquisition of Central Guaranty by TD in 1992, Royal Trust by Royal Bank in 1993, and Montreal Trust by Scotiabank in 1994. The significant troubles that surfaced at Central and Royal Trust had negatively affected public perceptions of the health of the industry and made individual firms easier pickings for the banks. Montreal Trust had been courted by CIBC before Scotiabank entered and won the fray. This battle was indicative of intensifying domestic competition.

The major remaining trust company, Canada Trust, which is owned by Imasco, is a formidable competitor both in retail and, now, in corporate markets. The innovative spirit of the trust companies, that has always acted as a pressure upon the banks to improve their service, is alive and well at Canada Trust. However, one wonders what the future holds for any closely-held Canadian firm.

Ironically, the involvement of the insurance industry with the trust industry may now be creating a similar situation in the insurance industry for the banks. The failure of Confederation Life can be, in part, traced to their trust subsidiary. While Confederation Life is only one firm, does this indicate that the insurance industry, which did not benefit from the regular examination of their industry that the banks did, is not as well prepared for the new world of financial services? Only time will tell, but it is clear that the major banks, with the exception of the Bank of Montreal, are targeting the insurance industry.

Table 5.3, which presents changes in the percentage of fee-based income as a component of revenues (net interest margins plus other income), reveals the success of the banks in moving away from being mere suppliers of deposit and credit services. One side effect of the new BIS agreement was to make credit more expensive and encourage this shift towards other revenue generating opportunities made possible by the changing regulatory environment. Ironically, this international agreement also made certain retail markets, especially home mortgages, more attractive because of favourable risk weighting on the assets.

The Bank of Montreal has signalled the importance it places upon the domestic market with its efforts to become the price leader with cuts to its prime rates. These moves further signal a new competitiveness in the Canadian market. The shift towards increased price competition went hand-in-hand with a new focus on productivity at all banks (Darroch, 1994: Ch. 6). However, even though the Bank of Montreal is not the low cost producer, excess liquidity in its asset portfolio made the price leadership strategy attractive.

A. North American Bank Strategies

Table 5.2 also shows the move towards greater weighting of the U.S. in their North American asset portfolios. With the exception of the Royal, all banks show a significant shift in percentage terms. In volume terms, all show a significant shift. Aftershocks from the LDC debt crisis make similar figures for Mexico meaningless.

TABLE 5.3 *Other Income as a Percentage of Revenue*

	1983	1993
Bank of Montreal	19	33
Bank of Nova Scotia	18	28
CIBC	21	33
National Bank	22	39
Royal Bank	21	32
TD	19	32

Source: Annual Reports of the Banks.

The Bank of Montreal, which owns the Harris Bank of Chicago, exemplifies the new aggressiveness of the Canadian banks in the U.S., especially since Matthew Barrett became Chairman of the Board in 1990. The bank expects to derive 50 percent of its income from the U.S. in the near future. In their 1990 Annual Report, Bank of Montreal management stated that:

> North America is our principal market place. Offshore, we will select regions of strategic importance for trade and investment flows affecting our North American customers.
>
> We will focus on three main customer groups:
> - The first priority is individuals and small and medium-size businesses in Canada and selected U.S. markets.
> - The second priority is selected segments among large national and multinational businesses across Canada and the U.S., including their international operations.
> - The third priority is individuals, corporations and institutions with investment interests in North America, located in selected offshore markets.

The bank clarified its North American strategy in its statement of 'Vision 2002.' Not surprisingly, given Harris as a strategic base, the bank has targeted eight mid-western states. This allows the bank to employ its knowledge of Canadian customers to advantage since the eight mid-western states account for 40 percent of Canadian exports. It is in these markets that the bank intends to profit from cross-border trade and investment flows. In 1994, the addition of Suburban Bankcorp to Harris gave substance to the words. The bank's strategy encompasses both growing its existing businesses and acquisitions.

The decision to become the first Canadian bank to list on the New York Stock Exchange lends further credibility to the North American ambitions of the bank. In the Euromoney Awards for Excellence 1994, analysts ranked the overall strategy highly and declared the Bank of Montreal to be the best bank in Canada.

Chairman Matthew Barrett has also been a champion for the expansion of NAFTA. There are actions to support the views. Nesbitt Burns signed an agreement with Mexico's second largest banking group, Casa de Bolsa Bancomer. Under the agreement the two will exchange research as well as sell securities. Previously, the bank had set up a NAFTA-oriented mutual fund in cooperation with Grupo Financiero Bancomer, SA. The bank will continue to extend its North American reach by leveraging its Canadian capabilities.

The strategic intent of the other major Canadian banks is also to capitalize upon the new opportunities and changing circumstances in North America. There are echoes of the statements by the Bank of

Montreal, especially in the post-FTA annual reports of the other major banks (see Darroch and Litvak, 1994).

CIBC Wood Gundy was cited as the best securities firm in Canada, in the same poll that selected the Bank of Montreal as the best bank. The choice reflects the overall commercial and investment banking activities of the bank since the recent reorganization developed by the bank with the assistance of McKinsey & Company continues the integration of Wood Gundy into the corporate bank. The bank is calling itself Canada's first global investment bank. The strategy is to reduce dependence upon corporate loans by focusing upon the origination of loans, and then packaging and selling these loans to investors.

The new strategy demands expertise in the sophisticated financial instruments used in financial engineering. Key to this is the $500 million committed to expansion in New York. A new commitment was demonstrated when CIBC Wood Gundy recruited five highly regarded derivative specialists from Lehman Brothers. Two months later, they were joined by six top traders from the same firm. Another indicator of success was Susan Storey, a senior derivatives trader and vice president, winning the merit award presented by the Women's Bond Club of New York. Ms. Storey became the first Canadian to win the award.

Royal Bank maintains a broad product portfolio for CFOs and has a substantial presence in the U.S., including the U.S. mid-west. But it has not really articulated a clear strategy for post-FTA expansion into the U.S. beyond Fortune 500 clients. However, the route seems to be one of cooperation or strategic alliances with U.S. players, if the arrangement for jointly delivering cash management services with Mellon Bank can be taken as a signal. It should also be noted that Royal has a solid reputation as a service provider with particular expertise in foreign exchange. In a survey of customers to determine their favourite bank for foreign exchange dealings, Royal moved from tenth in 1993 to a tie with JP Morgan for eighth (van Duyn, 1994). The only other Canadian bank to make the top 20 was the Bank of Montreal.

Scotiabank is in many ways the most global of all the Canadian banks and has set an expansion path for Latin America which is more aggressive than the other Canadian banks. Interestingly, while others were selling at distressed prices, Scotiabank held on firm to its Mexican loans, believing in Mexico's future. Scotiabank has forged a strategic alliance by taking a 5 percent ownership stake, with an option to go to 10 percent, in Grupo Financiero Inverlat in Mexico. There are two factors concerning this alliance that merit attention. First, it was the

Mexican banker, Agustin Legorreta, who appears to have initiated the search for a foreign partner. He found a cool reception among bankers who had been burned by Mexican debt. However, Cedric Ritchie, Chairman of Scotiabank, became interested and finalized the deal. Second, Scotiabank does not desire to place Mexican assets on its books, but it does recognize the need to service its international customers in Mexico, (*Financial Post*, 1993a: 13). The alliance provides Scotiabank with considerable capability.

The Mexican partner receives more than capital. Scotiabank and its investment banking arm, ScotiaMcLeod, will transfer technologies and products as part of the deal. The result of this cooperation is that several joint underwritings and participations in merger and acquisition activities are underway. It should further be noted that this move indicated a renewed interest in Latin America by Scotiabank which also has a 29 percent stake in Banco Sudamericano in Chile. The recent acquisition of 25 percent of Banco Quilmes, Argentina's seventh largest bank, offered further proof of the bank's commitment to Latin America.

It should also be noted that the bank has a significant presence in the United States. In 1992, the bank was in fifth in U.S. league tables in lending by full credit volume. The bank was the only foreign bank in the top ten. The rank reflects the strategic decision to be a strong player in the LBO and U.S. real estate markets. By 1990, Scotiabank had committed more than $8 billion to its LBO portfolio and $3.2 billion to real estate. This position in conjunction with the close relationship with Kohlberg, Kravis, Roberts & Co. that grew out of these activities provides solid base for future growth. Predictably, the bank will continue to be aggressive in U.S. markets.

The Toronto Dominion Bank (TD) has been the most affected by recession and economic sluggishness in Ontario. It shows one of the most dramatic portfolio adjustment towards North America. The changes in both the Canadian and U.S. percentages are striking. The bank is known to select industries where it can develop and leverage expertise. It is one of the leading experts in the cable television industry and augmented its position through its involvement in the acquisition of Mclean Hunter by Rogers Cable. TD has also expanded its New York operations and will continue to leverage its knowledge of selected industries.

The market opportunity may be the traditional one of bringing clients into Canada. The TD, which has limited both its national and international expansion, found that its lean operations were the model for global bank operations in the 1980s and 1990s (see Davis, 1985). Yet the core of its successful Japanese strategy was based upon superior knowledge of the Canadian market, rather than upon the competitiveness in the Japanese market. TD gave the following explanation as to why the bank was the top profit maker among 83 foreign banks in Japan for fiscal 1990:

> This was no fluke. If you go back to 1982, our strategy was entirely different from most foreign banks at the time. Other banks were lending at very low margins. We felt that Japan was a capital exporting country and that it would be like bringing coals to Newcastle if we were to try to lend money to Japanese companies. Our strategy was to assist the outflow of capital from Japan to Canada and other countries (Terry, 1990: B1).

It is worth noting that Canada Trust has also put in place a cross-border strategy and is improving its capability in sophisticated financial instruments. Any forecast of future industry evolution must take account of Canada Trust, increasingly sophisticated chief financial officers (CFOs), and non-traditional competitors, such as GE Capital which affect both corporate and retail markets through activities such as car leasing.

V. Are The Canadian Banks Competitive?

Table 5.4 by Canada's leading bank analyst, Hugh Brown of Nesbitt Burns, compares Canadian and U.S. banks on several key dimensions. Brown holds that changing the basis of comparison to the 50 largest U.S. banks would make no significant difference. The Canadian banks have been in a tough market environment which has forced them to become efficient, as the comparison between general overhead shows. The superior performance of the U.S. banks in terms of credit quality will diminish, especially as the recent severe recession in Ontario and Canada is replaced by growth. Historically, the two markets resemble each other more closely.

There are major differences in revenue streams. The question is whether the superior revenue streams are related to superior capabilities. It is difficult to see how different capabilities could lead to such a wide gap in interest rate margins, given that this is the result of differences between rates paid to depositors and borrowers. While better relationship management can reduce price sensitivity, the question is to what degree. In a study of U.S. supercommunity banks, variations between net interest margins between Super Community banks and more local traditional banks of 50 basis points were reported with extremes of 100 basis points (Bird, 1994: 24–26). However, it is difficult to see how the differences between Canadian and U.S. banks could be so extreme, given the population base, and why such a change between the two periods.

TABLE 5.4 *Profit Margin Analysis—Canadian versus U.S. Banks*

	1988	1988	1993	1993
	Canadian banks	All U.S. banks	Canadian banks	All U.S. banks
Net Revenue Spread	$ 3.09	$ 3.57	$ 2.88	$ 4.01
Fees	1.19	1.48	1.35	2.08
Total Net Revenues	$ 4.28	$ 5.05	$ 4.23	$ 6.09
General Overhead	(2.34)	(3.34)	(2.65)	(3.87)
Loan Loss Provision	(0.58)	(0.57)	(0.76)	(0.46)
Pre-Tax Income	$ 1.36	$ 1.14	$ 0.82	$ 1.76
Taxes and Preferred Dividends	0.67	0.35	0.43	0.60
After Tax Income	$ 0.69	$ 0.79	$ 0.39	$ 1.16
Other Data				
Common Equity Leverage	24.6X	16.9X	23.6X	13.8X
ROE	17.0%	13.3%	9.1%	16.0%
Total Avg. Assets ($ BIL)	$436	$3,035	$621	$3,605
Avg. ROE 1984 to 1993			9.8%	9.8%

Source: Hugh Brown, 'Chartered Banks—Stop Complaining and Start Buying,' Burns Fry Limited, May 25, 1994.

The increase may suggest a less competitive environment in the United States. Has consolidation in the U.S. market radically changed market conditions between 1988 and 1993? If competition has lessened, it could account for the higher fee income. In this scenario, the lower numbers of Canadian banks are the result of more demanding customers and tougher competition among roughly equal rivals.

It is also possible that the comparison is somewhat misleading because of differing product market strategies in the two populations. However, in this scenario, improved economic conditions as Ontario and Canada leave the recession behind should boost bank earnings and consequently return on equity (ROE) to U.S. levels. This market assessment suggests that the Canadian banks can be competitive, and a lower cost structure could be a significant advantage in some markets, especially ones dominated by transactional orientation.

A. New Opportunities

The opportunities for banks with North American capabilities vary with different market segments. For that reason, it is important to consider the following different markets in the light of NAFTA: export financing; multi-national corporations (MNCs); small and medium-sized corporations (SMEs); and retail banking.

B. Export

The increase in trade fostered by the FTA between Canada and the U.S. will be replicated by Canadian-Mexican and Mexican-U.S trade following the formal acceptance of NAFTA. The Canadian banks already have well-developed export financing capabilities and are now actively developing this capacity in Mexico via representative offices. Canadian banks will be drawn into Mexico in order to increase their share of Mexican exports to Canada. The Canadian banks will not be content with solely financing Canadian exports into Mexico.

C. MNCs

A major threat comes from the reorganization of MNCs. The experience of Canadian subsidiaries by Xerox and CIL (Imperial Chemicals) reveal that increasing competition promotes economic rationality in strategies which require centralized financial strategies. Key decisions affecting financial policies will increasingly be made at the head office—pulling Canadian banks into their North American orientation. Rather than seeing increased market opportunities to sell other services in a healthy relationship, opportunities will be decreased as MNCs use their home country banker. Trade liberalization moves this threat beyond the boundaries of the FTA and NAFTA. Changing financial strategies of MNCs will demand new globalization strategies from financial services firms. Alliances with other financial service firms, such as the one between Royal and Mellon, may be the wave of the future.

The vitality of the Mexican economy in conjunction with the evolving NAFTA environment can only increase the activities of Canadian MNCs in the Mexican environment. As Mexican economic development continues, there will be increased demands for goods and services in which Canadian companies are globally competitive. This is especially true as Mexico develops its infrastructure to improve its overall competitiveness. To compete against U.S. and Canadian firms, Mexico will have to develop its telecommunications network. Advanced telecommunications networks are key enablers for domestic firms in the global marketplace of the 1990s. Northern Telecom has much to offer. Systemhouse has publicly stated that it sees a big future in Mexican telecommunications (see *Financial Post*, 1993a: M7). In a similar vein, Canadian firms, such as Spar and Bombardier, with expertise in enabling industries, are finding attractive markets. As has always been the case for multi-national banks, Canadian banks will follow their clients into these new markets. The question is not whether, but how.

D. SMEs

From a banker's perspective, this segment will merit increased attention. MNCs with their access to credit, and CFOs with sophisticated knowledge of financial engineering, is a tough market for commercial banks. The future source of profitability for banks will be in meeting the increasingly sophisticated needs of this segment. It should further be noted that rationalization of many larger and disparate enterprises is continuing to create market opportunities for SMEs. The international expertise and experience of the Canadian banks can offer considerable assistance to entrepreneurial North American firms who seek to take advantage of new north-south opportunities. It is these smaller firms going North American who are most in need of the sophisticated information and financial engineering products of the banks. Servicing the Canadian market demands increased focus on the U.S. and Mexico.

The growth of intra-industry trade since the FTA has shown that firms that specialize can succeed. The success of Canadian firms in the specialized steels and specialized wood product markets demonstrate this trend. This specialization allows Canadian firms to use their knowledge assets to increase the value added of their products. Specialized firms serving growing markets will be key drivers of Canadian and Mexican economic development. As the Mexican market opens up, Canadian SMEs will find opportunities in previously protected segments such as the automotive and processed foods. The success of Connors Brothers, a New Brunswick sardine canning company, shows the future for Canadian companies. Connors believes that the Mexican market could easily be five times the size of the Canadian market and it is a staging area for the huge South American market (*Globe and Mail*, 1993: B4).

E. Retail

The emergence of strong regional and super-regional banks, as well as the value attributed to Citibank's Mexican networks, attests to the importance of retail banking and its linkages to SMEs. The question for Canadian banks is not whether to be international, but how to be international. Having always developed their strategies in a multinational or global context can provide competitive strength *vis-à-vis* purely regional competitors. Branches of Canadian banks will differ from local U.S. and Mexican banks just as the local television affiliates of NBC, CBS, ABC and PBS differ from their purely locally-based competitors. Foreign branches will cater to local differences, but provide immediate access to a much broader and international array of products and services via electronic networks. The experience of the Bank of Montreal suggests that retail banking is attractive and that the Canadian banks have strengths that can be exploited.

VI. Concluding Observations

The dramatic leap forward made by the Bank of Montreal after the appointment to CEO of 44-year-old Matthew Barrett clearly reveals the importance of leadership. Barrett has revitalized the bank and set it upon a new course, while some of his competitors were perceived to be holding back. However, we can expect to see some changes to this scenario as new blood is taking over at virtually all of the banks. And, all of the new leaders are aware of Barrett's success.

Despite this optimism for the changes that new leadership will bring, there are reasons for caution. First, the dynamism of U.S. regionals and super-regionals demonstrates a new style of retail banking. While Canadian banks compare well on the average, can they meet the challenge to match the numbers produced by the outstanding retail performers, such as Banc One? As retailers, how do the U.S. banks see the entry by Wal Mart into Canada? Traditionally, banks are followers. Perhaps most worrisome in this changing competitive scenario are the changes being wrought to both products and distribution by electronic media. While the banks are moving into more advanced telephone and other telecomputationally-based distribution, are they in the same league as their U.S. rivals?

Given the generally poor results posted by foreign banks in Canada, the banks have time to fortify their retail position. However, the lags and gaps between strategy formulation and implementation could create powerful entry points for competitors. We saw American Express lose the battle, but can they win the war? If they do, who and what will follow?

Perhaps the most interesting battle will be fought in the mid-market. For SMEs going into the U.S. and Mexico, who will provide better service, Canadian or U.S. banks? The Canadians have competed with success against money-centre banks for Fortune 500 accounts for years, but how will the expansion plans of U.S. regionals and super-regionals be affected by the FTA? The decision by the Bank of Montreal to target the mid-west is interesting in this regard. But what about its Canadian clients who are moving into other regions? Will other Canadian banks target the mid-west or other complementary regions? Since focus has its limits as well as its advantages, what scope of operations will be necessary to service North American oriented clients? The impact of the FTA on banking clients will have major impact on future banking strategies on both sides of the border.

The Canadian banks are formidable competitors and are gearing up for a challenging future. They recognize the challenge in both retail and corporate markets and have developed and implemented strategies to capitalize upon the changed market place. In the past, their reputation for stability has been a source of competitive strength. But this may be tied to a conservatism that will be severely challenged by more demanding customers in all segments. The new competition demands the benefits of conservatism be coupled with a new entrepreneurial spirit focused upon customer defined excellence as the *raison d'etre.*

References

BIRD, A. (1994) *Super Community Banking: A SuperStrategy for Success.* Probus: Chicago.

CANADIAN BANKERS ASSOCIATION (1994) *Bank Facts 1994.*

DARROCH, J. L. (1994) *CANADIAN BANKS AND GLOBAL COMPETITIVENESS.* MONTREAL & KINGSTON: MCGILL-QUEEN'S UNIVERSITY PRESS.

DARROCH, J. L. (1992) 'Global Competitiveness and Public Policy: The Case of Canadian Multinational Banks,' *Business History.* 34: 3 (July).

DARROCH, J. L. and LITVAK, I. A. (1991) 'Canadian Banks: New Strategic Initiatives,' *Business Quarterly.* 56: 2 (Fall).

DARROCH, J. L. and LITVAK, I. A. (1992a) 'Diamonds and Money,' *Business Quarterly,* 56:3 (Winter).

DARROCH, J. L. and LITVAK, I. A. (1992b) 'Gaps, Overlaps and Competition Among Jurisdictions: Evolving Canadian Financial Services Policies and Regulations,' *Journal of World Trade.* 26: 2 (April).

DARROCH, J. L. and LITVAK, I. A. (1992c) 'Strategies for Canada's New North American Banks,' *Multinational Business.* Spring.

DARROCH, J. L. and LITVAK, I. A. (1994) 'Los bancos canadienses, el ALC y el TLC: estrategias de competencia y cooperacion,' *Comercio exterior,* 44: 1 (enero).

DAVIS, S. I. (1985) *Excellence in Banking.* London: Macmillan.

ECONOMIC COUNCIL OF CANADA (1989a) *A New Frontier.* Ottawa: Ministry of Supply and Services.

ECONOMIC COUNCIL OF CANADA (1989b) *Globalization and Canada's Financial Markets.* Ottawa: Ministry of Supply and Services.

THE ECONOMIST (1991) 'New dreams at Deutsche Bank,' June 22, pp. 79–82.

EUROMONEY (1994) 'Awards for Excellence 1994,' July.

FINANCIAL POST (1993a) 'Modernizing Mexico's financial sector: Banking on new partnerships,' May 18, p. 13.

FINANCIAL POST (1993b) 'Systemhouse see big future in Mexican telecommunications,' Special Report, June 12, p. M7.

FRIEDMAN, K. J. (1981) 'The 1980 Canadian Banks and Banking Law Review Act: Competitive Stimulus or Protectionist Barrier?' *Law and Policy in International Business* 13.

GLOBE AND MAIL (1991) 'Investment News,' 'Report on Business,' May 16.

GLOBE AND MAIL (1993) 'N.B. processor fishes for sardine sales: Connors hopes for NAFTA stimulus,' Report on Business, September 20, p. B4.

GRAHAM, E. M. and KRUGMAN, P. R. (1989) *Foreign Direct Investment in the United States*. Washington, D.C.: Institute for International Economics.

HARRIS, C. (1994) 'Banking's Rankings,' *Canadian Banker*, November/December.

INDUSTRY, SCIENCE, SCIENCE AND TECHNOLOGY (1991) *Banking*. Ottawa: Ministry of Industry Science and Technology.

MACINTOSH, R. (1991) *Different Drummers: Banking and Politics in Canada*. Toronto: Macmillan.

McCOY, J. B., FRIEDER, L. A. and HEDGES, R. B. JR. (1994) *Bottomline Banking: Meeting the Challenges for Survival and Success*. Chicago: Probus Publishing.

NANKIVELL, N. (1994) 'Canada slips in competitiveness,' *Financial Post*, September 7.

PARTRIDGE, J. (1994) 'Competition watchdog nearing Interac solution,' Report on Business, *Globe and Mail*, July 13.

PIERCE, J. L. (1991) *The Future of Banking*. New Haven and London: Yale University Press.

PIGGOTT, C. (1994a) 'Euromoney 500: what a difference a decade makes,' *Euromoney* June.

PIGGOTT, C. (1994b) 'The Americans bounce back,' *Euromoney*. August 1994.

PORTER, M. E. (1990) *Competitive Advantage of Nations*. New York: The Free Press.

RUGMAN, A. M. (1992) 'Porter Takes the Wrong Turn,' *Business Quarterly*, 56: 3 (Winter).

TERRY, E. (1990) 'T-D Bank a surprise in Japan,' Report on Business, *Globe and Mail*, August 6, B1.

VAN DUYN, A. (1994) 'Working for their money,' *Euromoney* May.

WHYTE, H. D. (1991) 'Mergers of U.S. banks may speed Canadian invasion,' *Financial Post*, July 2, p. 3.

6

Internationalization of the Mexican Financial Market

IGNACIO PERROTINI AND LUIS MIGUEL GALINDO

Capital has the worldwide reputation of being timid like a deer and fast like a hare, but having a memory like an elephant. What can financial opening do to master such a beast? The answer is: nothing much in isolation, and beyond that the answer is not straightforward.
Helmut Reisen

Introduction

Since the devaluation of the peso in December 1994, the Mexican financial system has faced a substantial increase in its annual inflation rate, high nominal interest rates, a strong economic depression, a tight monetary policy, a fast growth of non-performing loans, and a new set of regulations. The current crisis defines an environment for commercial banks utterly different from that of 1994, the first year of the North American Free Trade Agreement (NAFTA) between Canada, the United States and Mexico.

The long-run consequences of the situation are still far from clear. However, empirical evidence indicates that Mexican banks are facing strong cash problems. The traditional illiquidity of the financial system, the availability of credits to Mexican banks contracted in foreign currency, and the increasing trend of past-due loans are pressing the already exhausted bank reserves. The government has taken measures accordingly, including special funds to provide liquidity, a proper regulation to create contingent reserves for non-performing loans, and new rules for the operation of foreign banks within the country. Under such new rules, foreign banks are allowed to hold 49 percent of Mexican banks' shares and will certainly be more free to operate nationwide. Furthermore, there is special interest in promoting mergers between Mexican and foreign banks as a way of cushioning the cash balance crisis, and to improve the productivity of the banking sector. The conditions for foreign financial firms to establish themselves in the territory—without the former restriction (accorded by NAFTA) of having to form subsidiaries—have been eased.

Our analysis basically focuses on the impact of Mexico's order of economic liberalization on the national banking sector. Several topics call our attention. First, while discussing the antinomies of financial liberalization, attention is paid to the timing and sequential steps of this process; second, regarding the antinomies of what we call the NAFTA framework, current empirical evidence suggests that gradualism might not have taken place yet and will not do so. Ironically, the actual financial crisis is suddenly liberalizing our financial system at a much faster pace. Third, a general framework to analyse the recent monetary policy, its economic logic and its possible weakness is also presented.

This chapter includes four sections. The first one is an assessment of some macroeconomic aspects of the current financial reform. In the second part, the NAFTA framework is discussed bearing in mind the latest financial phenomena. An analysis of recent monetary policies and their most likely effects is conducted in section three. The last part is the conclusion.

I. Macroeconomics of Financial Reform

Since 1988 Mexico has witnessed a dramatic revamping of its financial system, while policy-makers have been implementing market-oriented development strategies. A conspicuous component of this reform is a financial liberalization process, where privatization of the banking sector leading to oligopolistic financial groups is a major outcome.[1]

It seems that Mexican policy-makers assumed that some of the main (theoretical) benefits of financial opening was a higher capital inflow. The rationale behind goes as follows: countries that open their capital account should experience capital inflows, which, in a developing economy, are badly needed to finance investment at a lower cost as opposed to domestic savings. If this argument holds, then financial liberalization should at least serve two purposes. First, it would help to overcome financial repression and, second, would contribute to develop a more efficient and competitive banking industry. From the point of view of the Mexican government, the macroeconomic and long-term benefits arising from the latter purpose are manifold. By and large, the banking sector has a positive impact on more equitable income distribution when it operates within *complete* financial markets; financial institutions (particularly banks) enhance the effectiveness of countercyclical policies in that they buffer exogenous shocks to the economy (one must bear in mind that the Mexican economy has been consistently vulnerable to external financial and real shocks over the last two decades); as growth boils down to investment and investment calls for savings, banks play a major role in the allocation of savings into the most profitable economic activities (the current saving-investment gap in Mexico is negative in the order of 7 to 10 percent of gross domestic product (GDP)); in an open economy, financial markets organized around a high degree of internal rivalry contribute to price-level and exchange rate stability, thus preventing balance of payments crisis.

Under the influence of these tenets and given the essential role of financial markets for the overall viability of an economy, the Mexican government proceeded into a deep liberalization reform of the overregulated financial system towards the end of the 1980s. While financial repression was dismantled as quantitative credit controls, compulsory reserve requirements and fixed interest rates were abolished,[2] money and capital markets were developed more impetuously between 1988 and 1994. Under the impulse of the euphoria associated with more stable expectations after the debt renegotiation, the privatization of the commercial banking sector and the approval of NAFTA financial deepening, M4/GDP increased more than 50 percent between 1988 and 1994. Such an incremental upswing took place after a long period (September 1982–September 1988) of depressed financial intermediation, when the bulk of the banking sector's resources were dedicated to financing the huge fiscal deficits of the 1980s. Further, financial innovation, which often comes along with a liberalization process, gave birth to a multitude of new public and private securities, thus opening opportunities for national and foreign investors.[3]

According to Ronald McKinnon (1993) there is an 'optimal' sequential order to economic liberalization which should not be disturbed: 'How fiscal, monetary, and foreign exchange policies are *sequenced* is of critical importance' (McKinnon, 1993: 4). The details of the path of an economy submitted to a metamorphosis from a model of command and control (financial repression) to a truly and 'full-fledged market economy,' depend on the economy's initial conditions. Nonetheless, the so-called optimal order advises not to 'take all liberalizing measures simultaneously' (McKinnon, 1993). The first measure must be to attain balanced public finance with a small government debt-to-GNP ratio. The easing of inflation, thus obtained, should pave the way for the second step, namely the opening of the capital market. But this move may unleash financial panics and bank collapses. The key to averting them, adds McKinnon, hinges upon the government's previous 'achieving of overall macroeconomic stability' (McKinnon, 1993). Only after successful trade and finance opening have been achieved is it advisable to start the liberalization of foreign exchange markets because 'in the balance of international payments, transacting on current account is best liberalized much faster than international capital flows' (McKinnon, 1993: 7). Finally, provided the economy shows price-level stability and equilibrium in the money and exchange markets, the conditions are satisfied for freeing international capital mobility: 'Free foreign exchange convertibility on capital account is usually the *last* stage in the optimal order of economic liberalization' (McKinnon, 1993: 10).

In the case of Mexico's liberalization experience, the various stages of the aforementioned sequence are not clearcut in the course of time. Further, it seems that the anticipated and desired effects arising from each stage interfered with each other. Even worse, some other macroeconomic policy measures conflicted with such expected effects. For instance, the exchange rate policy used as an anchor for inflation. In the initial phase of trade liberalization, the real depreciation of the domestic currency that prevailed up to the beginning of 1988, eased the negative impact of import liberalization on domestic output, employment, and the current account. In contrast, during 1988–94 the observed low real exchange rate increased the macroeconomic costs of liberalization and forced massive capital inflows in order to maintain the weak internal and external balance (Ros, 1995). A balanced budget, lower inflation, privatization of banks and of other major previously owned-government assets, deregulation of financial markets, trade liberalization and, last but not least, the restructuring of foreign debt greatly contributed to Mexico's qualifying (again) as a viable investment place for funds available in the world financial markets.[4] Nonetheless, the bulk of inflows attracted via high nominal interest rates was short-term capital: in 1993–94 speculative investment roughly accounted for 75 percent of total capital movements, and a non-negligible share of the remainder was allocated in the non-tradables sector (franchises in the service sector), which allow no competitive edge in the new open environment. For this reason, in spite of the financial reform, Mexico remained vulnerable to quick capital reversal, in the event of a sudden external shock,[5] or to an unticipated change in investors' preferences due to, for instance, either an increased country risk (measured as the yield differential between Tesobono and that of U.S. Treasury bills) or an increased currency risk (the difference between Tesobono and CETES). In the end, portfolio foreign investments, along with the market structure (a set of oligopolistic groups created by the re-privatization of commercial banks) originated by the financial reform, inhibited efficient intermediation of investment and savings. This argument couples with official data of financial costs of capital, liquidity ratios at microeconomic levels, and the ratio of non-performing loans to total loan portfolio of the banking system as a whole.

Seemingly, even though the government stuck to McKinnon's optimal path during the first phase of the transition towards a liberalized economy, it is evident that Mexico's financial reform diverted from it afterwards. Hence the capital flights and the buildup of foreign indebtedness—mainly through institutional investments in Tesobono and CETES—observed especially during 1992–94. Hence, the ensuing speculative attacks against the peso—with its hindermost collapse—throughout 1994.

The financial reform set the stage for subsequent deregulation and reprivatization of commercial banks. Later on, during 1990–92, banks were sold at an income to price ratio of 10; the new owners had to pay three times their book value on average. The reforms of this period served three purposes; namely, the rescue of public finance, the refunding of private firms, and the attempt to create a sounder financial market. In so far as the commercial opening increased foreign rivalry, a ceiling was set for rising prices. Second, a long-run agreement was reached with regard foreign debt, which improved financial market expectations about the Mexican peso. Finally, the NAFTA negotiations established a new environment that, presumably, would pave the way for long-run investment.

The new bank owners bought businesses that had maintained high profit rates over the last few years, meaning steady income flows. As Alan Stoga (1990) pointed out, they purchased 'banking licenses more than bank assets'. However, the non-performing loan/assets ratio far exceeds the 10.4 percent rate of 1995, three times as big as the ceiling suggested by the Basle Accord. The dramatic increase in banks' vulnerability thenceforth is, indeed, related to the credit cycle expansion unleashed by deregulation and the elimination of the legal reserve requirements. Besides, a sounder public finance orchestrated by conservative fiscal policy and a faster growing economy in 1989–92, compared to 1982–88, prompted the banking system to engage in more dynamic and risk-taking business behavior.

The latest devaluation of the peso thoroughly changed Mexico's financial landscape. By and large, it was hoped that joint ventures, mergers, financial liberalization, foreign competition, new bank licenses issued in 1994, consolidation of financial groups, and fiscal discipline would improve financial rivalry. It is worth mentioning that Banamex, Bancomer, and Serfin, the three largest banks in the country, still hold over 60 percent of the market. Therefore, financial liberalization failed to break the nut of oligopolistic (inefficient) competition that prevailed prior to the financial reform.

II. The NAFTA Framework: Limits and Shortcomings

To a large extent, NAFTA set the framework within which the new Mexican financial system was supposed to develop for at least the next ten years. Nonetheless, under the new conditions defined by the current financial crisis, there seem to be good reasons to suspect that a great deal of such arrangement now seems obsolete. Let us try to substantiate this hypothesis.

In fact, the three fundamental asymmetries between the NAFTA members' financial systems (differential size in terms of assets and capital basis, regulation patterns and financial legislation, and difference in both quality and strength of the currencies involved) determined most of the content of NAFTA's Chapter 14, where the negotiated framework is condensed.[6] NAFTA is mainly based on types of financial intermediaries, presumably 'an approach that is more congruent with Mexico's regulatory and supervisory practices' (Trigueros, 1994). On the one hand, NAFTA allows foreign financial firms to operate in Mexico only through subsidiaries subject to both national treatment and a gradual liberalization process (upper limits to maximum capital values for foreign banks apply both individually and globally). On the other hand, it discourages and even prohibits cross-border financial transactions. This measure aims at assuring that Banco de México shall continuously control domestic monetary policy, which is an essential instrument for balance of payments stability when capital mobility prevails.[7] It was also believed that with this approach the economy would benefit in various respects: foreign banks' subsidiaries would bring about an improvement of the domestic regulatory scheme; a higher degree of oligopoly in the banking sector would be thus prevented; and the efficiency loss associated with the establishment of limited subsidiaries could be overcome by the gradual liberalization scheme with greater participation of foreign banks in the long-run. Obviously, it is too early to discard outcomes that have not yet materialized. However, as Trigueros (1994) has correctly pointed out, a harmonized regulatory pattern for financial services across NAFTA countries is not part of this story. Citicorp, for instance, is already taking advantage of the national treatment clause to consolidate a financial holding, a choice not allowed in the United States.

Since subsidiaries of foreign banks may not participate in the wholesale market, they have troubles in attaining economies of scale and in diversifying risks. This is why they prefer to operate in niches, whereby the reduction in the degree of oligopoly derived from their participating in an illiquid market turns out to be negligible. Corporative credit, dollar payments clearing and dollar liquidity supplying, repurchase and resale agreements rather than commercial loans are some examples of preferred operations conducted by the above-mentioned subsidiaries. Citicorp works with the 200 largest Mexican corporations, while Chemical Bank focuses on the 100 largest enterprises in the market, such as General Motors, Kimberly Clark, Celanese Mexicana. Unlike Mexican banks, foreign banks with business in Mexico neither have past-due loans problems nor—for this reason—have to face the claims of both El Barzón (an organization of highly indebted consumers, mid-size and small entrepreneurs) and the National Association of Credit Card holders against prevailing high financial margins and in favor of past-due loans restructuring. Further, oligopolistic tendencies have been reinforced: an overvalued domestic currency for over two years, and its drastic depreciation in December 1994, triggered a financial crisis with finance capital taking over big industries and smaller banks;[8] the increased capital provisions, imposed on banks by the government due to a high share of past-due loans, not only increases illiquidity in the economy but also puts half of the banking system on the brink; as loan defaults and liquidity constraints continue to plague various economic sectors, mergers and acquisitions start to appear as a solution to widespread bankruptcies and capital inadequacy.

In sum, the appealing and most celebrated financial liberalization strategy is in disarray. The government confronts three choices with regards the ongoing crisis in the banking sector:

1. let the banks with the highest risk rate fail and rescue the very big ones (Banamex and Bancomer) on the grounds that they are key to independent monetary policy;
2. bail out the banking system, and
3. accelerate the opening of the financial system in a greater scope and more drastic way than that negotiated in NAFTA.

The first choice is too costly politically speaking; the second pick is too costly economically (roughly $23 billion); the third one requires an active role on behalf of foreign banks. So far, the government is choosing a sort of combination of all three options, but this necessarily drives us beyond NAFTA.

III. Monetary Policy and Financial System

In order to face the crisis derived from the exchange rate collapse, the government has applied an adjustment policy since the beginning of 1995 called *Acuerdo de Unidad para Superar la Emergencia Económica (AUSEE)*. This program was supported by the *Programa de Acción para Reforzar el Acuerdo de Unidad para Superar la Emergencia Económica* (PARAUSEE) two months later.

TABLE 6.1 *Redemptions of Public Bonds*

	CETES	Tesobonos	Bondes	Ajustabono
February	7,532	17,916	1,688	149
March	10,968	17,437	955	181

Source: Carpeta de Indicadores del Banco de México.

The government has advocated to employ a tight monetary policy in order to control inflation and reduce the uncertainty in the domestic financial market. After the devaluation of the peso in December 1994, the main concern was threefold: control the panic in the financial market; confront the continuous capital outflows; and reduce the currency risk. In this scenario, there was special concern about the Tesobonos market. The government had increased the issuance of Tesobonos substantially during 1994 in order to stop capital outflows. Table 6.1 summarizes the holdings of Tesobonos and Cetes and their period of redemption during the first quarter of 1995. The general impression was that most of this money would leave the country at the end of the redemption period, thus generating another currency crisis.

The intention of a tight monetary policy was already evident when the Central Bank committed itself to a domestic credit ceiling of 10 billion new pesos for 1995. This ceiling represents around 17.5 percent of the total monetary base at the end of 1994. Moreover, there is empirical evidence which indicates that the monetary base decreased 12 percent in nominal terms and around 26 percent in real terms during the first three months of this year. This contraction is apparent in terms of real money balances, in particular in terms of M1 (Table 6.2).

TABLE 6.2 *Basic Macroeconomic Indicators. Billions of New Pesos*

	Jan	Feb	Mar	Apr	May	Jun
MB	51,200	49,790	48,806	47,553	46,208	
M1	138,874	132,267	124,207	121,707e		
M3	592,432	585,998	612,447	558,150e		
IPC	3.76	4.24	5.90	7.96	4.18	3.24
E	5.51	5.68	6.70	6.29	5.97	6.42
Deposit	13.0	5.3	4.0			
Credits	29.9	24.3	20.2			

MB = monetary base; Deposits = real rate of growth; IPC = inflation; E = exchange rate; Credits = real rate of growth; e = estimated.

The contraction in the monetary aggregates is not only a result of a tight monetary policy, but also an outcome of the main determinants of the demand for money in Mexico. The demand for money in Mexico is a stable function, which in the long run depends on income and on opportunity costs given by the nominal interest rate. However, during periods of macroeconomic instability the inflation rate and the currency substitution effect are certainly relevant factors. The empirical evidence can be summarized considering the following model (Cuthbertson and Galindo, 1994):

$$(m3 - p)t = -.75 + .24D4yt - .15DRt - .33DDpt - .01DCSt - 2$$
$$(-2.14)\ (2.73)\quad (-3.21)\quad (-2.28)\quad (-3.05)$$
$$-.18[(m3 - p) - 1.50yt + .36R]t - 4$$
$$(-2.53)\qquad\quad (3.78)\quad (-2.49) \tag{1}$$

NNLS. Sample 1978Q3–1990Q3, R2 = .66 SEE = 3.40%,
PAR(22,17) = .34, LM(4,34) = .56, RESET(1,37) = .62, JB = .03,
WHITE(1,47) = .41, ARCH(4,35) = 1.02, CHOW(11,27) = .96,
CUSUM: pass CUSUMQ: pass

where LM is the Lagrange multiplier test for autocorrelation, RESET is a test for functional form, JB is the Jarque-Bera test for normality, White and ARCH are tests for heteroscedasticity and CHOW, CUSUM and CUSUMQ are tests for structural change, m3t is the demand for M3, Rt is the nominal Mexican interest rate, p is the price index and CS is the currency substitution effect measured as:

$$CSt = R^* (\ t + (E[St + 1] - St)/St \tag{2}$$

where E is the expectations operator and lower case letters denote the logarithm of the series.

Equation (1) shows that money balances decrease sharply during periods of strong macroeconomic instability, economic depression, high inflation and expectations of continuous devaluations or insolvency risk. This equation indicates that a reduction in capital outflows is only possible by generating a reliable exchange rate (Equation (2)). Hence Mexican authorities are trying to control the expectations about the exchange rate through a tight monetary policy with high interest rates; they also allow the operation of the future exchange market.

The Banco de Mexico substantially increased the interest rate in the public bond market in the first quarter of 1995. In particular, Tesobonos and CETES have fluctuated sharply. The interest rate of Tesobono went up as high as 25 percent and, afterwards, down to 20 percent between January and February 14, when auctions were closed down. Simultaneously, the interest rate of CETES increased at an average of 68.32 percent in March. This trend is also shared by most interest rates, thus driving the TIIP (average inter-bank interest rate) upwards to its peak of over 109 percent by mid-March (Table 6.3). Such fluctuations in interest rates has produced a portfolio adjustment process. Banco de Mexico had to redeem around $15 billion in Tesobonos during the first quarter of the year, while the share of CETES held by foreigners had increased at the same time.

Despite the relatively smooth process of redemption shown so far by Tesobonos, capital outflows have not ceased in early 1995. Rough measures indicate that capital outflows during the first three months of 1995, consisted of around $7 billion. This capital outflow was financed by IMF borrowings, the U.S. Treasury facilities and Mexico's own international reserves. However, there are still outstanding foreign liabilities to be redeemed this year: $17 billion in Tesobonos and $18 billion in credits to Mexican commercial banks.

Mexican authorities have again allowed the existence of a futures exchange market, both in Mexico and at the Chicago Mercantile Exchange, beginning in March 1995. This measure aims at reducing the uncertainty about the future spot exchange rate and, therefore, at preventing more capital flights (equations 1 and 2). A futures market for the Mexican peso used to exist (between 1978 and 1985). There is empirical evidence of speculative attacks against the peso during that time. This can be observed considering the existence of a bias of the future exchange rate as a good predictor of the future spot exchange rate during that period. In formal terms, if the future exchange rate is an unbiased predictor of the future spot rate then:

$$st + 1 = b0 + b1ft + et \tag{3}$$

with $b0 = 0$ and $b1 = 1$. Where ft represents the future exchange rate evaluated at time t. Again, lower case letters represent the logarithms of the series. The empirical evidence for Mexico for the period 1978–1985, using the Johansen procedure (1988), can be summarized in the future market for one month (Galindo, 1994):

TABLE 6.3 *Nominal Interest Rates in Public Bonds. Monthly Average*

	December	January	February	March
CETES (28 days)	15.85	36.45	40.91	68.32
CETES (91 days)	16.92	38.34	40.97	69.64
Tesobonos (91 days)	7.91	17.87	16.78	
TIIP	24.77	45.22	53.10	85.23
CCP	16.95	29.87	35.98	56.82

$$sct + 1 = .0284 + .9876fvt \qquad (4a)$$

$$svt + 1 = .0300 + .9851fct \qquad (4b)$$

where sct + 1 represents the buyer market and svt + 1 the seller market. The results clearly indicate that the forward exchange rate was, in general, above the future spot exchange rate. This implies the presence of a continuous risk premium in favor of the future market. It is also worth mentioning that the risk premium tends to increases with the course of time of the contract (Galindo, 1994).

The tight monetary policy, as shown both in the reduction in money balances and in current high interest rates, also implies a drastic decline in liquidity. Banks had begun 1995 with a huge debt due to the process of reprivatization. In fact, the government sold commercial banks in the early 1990s at a price that is now considered too high by normal indicators. For example, Banamex, the largest bank in the country, was sold at 2.5 times the book value of earnings. This price was only reasonable considering two important factors: the possibility of high and fast profits of the new banking system, based on its oligopolistic structure and the general illiquidity of the Mexican banking system (Gutiérrez-Pérez and Perrotini, 1994; Garber and Weisbrod, 1993). This situation has only been possible due to several shortcomings: the regulatory framework and government supervision have been quite flexible and permissive; and the re-privatized banking sector has been isolated from the challenges involved in new instruments and investments in risky markets.

After the re-privatization of commercial banks, the Mexican financial system faced a strong restriction of funds. The Mexican economy can be defined as an illiquid market. This is due to the high level of risk and volatility in most financial assets; hence a high proportion of total wealth is invested in either illiquid assets such as land, real estate or foreign bank accounts. Moreover, transactions in Mexico depend more on bank deposits than on government securities *vis-à-vis*, for instance, the United States. Under these conditions, the traditional role of a financial system—the allocation of resources from surplus sectors to deficit ones—is partially broken (Garber and Weisbrod, 1993). As a combined result of macroeconomic policies (overvalued exchange rate with high interest rates) and endemic illiquid markets, Mexican banks were forced to seek foreign loans in order to supply the system with liquidity. It must be borne in mind that, during this period, the public bond market (one of the main sources of liquidity in recent years) had shrunk because of a decline in the public deficit. The public debt as a proportion of GDP reduced from 27.8 percent in 1988 to 13.2 percent at the end of 1994.

The recourse of foreign loans was certainly a possible option under a reliable exchange rate system. However, the credit boom of the last four years came to an end in an unfashionable way. The sharp increase in internal interest rates was not expected by most firms and consumers. Most of the credits contracted during 1989–94, on the basis of a stable economy with a slow but steady growth rate and a low inflation rate, look quite different today in a depressive economy with high inflation rates. The ratio between non-performing loans and total credit has steadily increased from 7.3 percent in December 1993 to 7.5 percent in December 1994 to almost 10.4 percent during the first three months of 1995. The deterioration in the quality of financial assets, due to the rise in non-performing loans and to the scarcity of funds, has led to an increase in intermediation margins of around 16 percent during the first semester of 1995, and to a substantial decrease in banks' profit.

During the first semester of 1995, most financial institutions came close to a disaster. Still, most financial groups (such as Serfin, Inverlat, Mexival, Cremi-Union) are running out of funds and need a continuous flow of funds in order to constitute reserves, pay for liabilities issued towards the purchasing of banking assets, repay foreign loans, and also to build up a compulsory 60 percent reserves for non-performing loans.

The PARAUSEE includes several measures to face the current emergency status of financial institutions. Among the most important of these measures are the *Programa de Capitalización Temporal* (PROCAPTE). On February 22 1995, the National Bank Commission ordered the banks to increase the cautionary reserves with either 60 percent of non-performing loans or 4 percent of total portfolio of credits. This measure, which should protect the solvency of the banking sector, has become an additional problem because of the liquidity constraints of banks themselves. The PROCAPTE is basically concerned with providing enough liquidity to commercial banks for them to accomplish reserve requirements.

Also, the government has introduced a unit of investment called UDI. This mechanism is a unit of account fixed in real terms with a daily adjustment to the inflation rate. In this sense, it represents a defence against high inflation rates. The main purpose of UDI is threefold: to reduce the pressure represented by an accelerated amortisation rate of credits during inflationary periods; to prevent a depreciation of bank deposits; and, therefore, to increase investors' confidence in domestic financial instruments. So far, several banks, such as Banamex, Bancomer, Banco Mexicano, Atlántico, and Internacional are already issuing deposits in UDI. Nonetheless, UDI involves a macroeconomic (fiscal) risk: with regards to UDI, the government invests in real terms and takes liabilities in nominal terms. If inflation goes out of control, we might see another fiscal crisis.

Additionally, over the last two decades the Mexican financial system has faced successive new sets of regulations and laws that have alternatively reduced and enhanced its performance without reducing its exposure to risk. At the beginning of the 1980s, the Banco de Mexico used to regulate credit flows through a complex system of differential reserve requirements, which varied according to the characteristics of the loan. Later, the change introduced in monetary policy in order to control both monetary aggregates and the increasing volatility of interest rates certainly made it an impossible task to operate this system (Baqueiro and Ghigliazza, 1983). Nowadays, the new monetary policy focuses on the control of the monetary base and on continuous auctions in the public bond market (open market operations). However, this system is not strong enough yet to confront the dimension of the actual financial crisis, and hence it failed to reduce the risk exposure of commercial banks.

On March 17 of 1995, Banco de Mexico introduced a new system of reserve requirements in order to have a better control of monetary aggregates. This system basically reduces the overdraft facilities of private banks with the Central Bank. Private banks are now forced to pay a compensation for their daily overdrafts. This measure, nevertheless, imposes additional constraints to an already illiquid banking system. The strict control of monetary aggregates on behalf of the Banco de Mexico, the illiquidity of the market and the risk positions taken by private banks during the overvalued exchange rate period, have led the entire financial system to a fragile scenario.

The Central Bank, in order to supply the economy with liquidity, has allowed new limits to foreign ownership in the Mexican banking sector. On 27 January 1995, the Congress approved modifications to the following laws: *Ley para Regular las Agrupaciones Financieras* (bill for the regulation of foreign financial groups), *Ley de Instituciones de Crédito* (Law of Loans Institutions) and *Ley del Mercado de Valores* (the Stock Market Law). These modifications are basically meant to increase the maximum limit for foreign investment in Mexican banks from 30 percent to 49 percent. Such measure are still in their early stages, but we can expect several mergers between Mexican and foreign banks, or even among Mexican banks. The first step was taken in May of 1995 by an initial agreement between PROBURSA Financial Group and Banco de Bilbao Viscaya, which intended to convert that Mexican financial institution into a branch of the Spanish bank.

The difficult economic position of the national financial system has also led to government interventions in the market. Grupo Financiero Havre, Cremi-Unión and Asemex-Banpaís are some examples. Further, Serfin, the third largest bank in the country, Inverlat, Bital, Bancen, Confia bank and Banorie are already using the facilities of the

PROCAPTE. In the same vein, the Fobaproa had given US$2 billion to commercial banks by May of 1995.

Basic indicators show the difficulties amongst financial institutions during the first semester of 1995. The rise in the non-performing loans to total credit ratio was already mentioned above. Also, the reserves to non-performing loans ratio and the reserves to total portfolio ratio were increased from December 1994 to March 1995 from 47.7 percent to 53.7 percent, and from 3.6 percent to 5.6 percent, respectively. Simultaneously, net profits have gone down from more than 3 billion new pesos to minus 300 hundred million new pesos during the first quarter of 1995 (see Tables 6.4 and 6.5). Some other banking indicators also show similar negative trends. For example, by the first quarter of 1995, all banks show a decreasing trend in their yield per share. In particular, Serfin and Banco Internacional reported a fall of around 18 percent. Few financial groups reported an increase in their yield per share. It seems that, under these circumstances, only the two largest banks in the country, Banamex and Bancomer, plus a few small ones, such as Banorte, are to some extent adequately facing the financial crisis.

IV. Conclusion

In this chapter we have argued that Mexico's banking sector is currently facing a financial crisis brought about by a contradictory process of financial liberalization. Such financial opening not only departed from the so-called 'optimal path', but also prompted the economy and banks to eagerly seek foreign loans. Between 1980 and 1987, the exchange rate policy (frequent strong currency devaluations) made it more appealing to contract loans in pesos than in the foreign market. However, during 1988–94 a quasi-fixed exchange rate and the macroeconomic policy in general, triggered a real appreciation of the peso and lowered the relative cost of loans in dollars. The result was a continuous and ever-increasing financial fragility of the economy, best represented by the amount of

TABLE 6.4 *Basic Indicators of the Banking System. March 1995*

Total Assets	Deposits	Utility	Past-due Loans	Total Credits
916360.7	473527.0	–329.0	65983.7	636473.3

Note: Values at the end of period in millions of new pesos. Own preliminary estimations based on information from Comisión Nacional Bancaria and banks' balance sheets.

TABLE 6.5 *Basic Ratios: March 1995*

Non-performing Loans to Total Credit			Reserves to Non-performing Loans		Reserves to Total Credit		
Dec 93	Dec 94	March 95	Dec 94	March 95	Dec 93	Dec 94	March 95
7.3	7.5	10.4	47.7	53.7	3.1	3.6	5.6

Source: Own estimations based on information from Comisión Nacional Bancaria and Bolsa Mexicana de Valores.

Tesobonos and other short-term capital issued in 1994, as well as by the successive speculative attacks against the domestic currency. Of course, once the government substituted a flexible exchange rate for the quasi-fixed regime the banking sector became vulnerable to financial shocks. Thus, a tight monetary policy has become an essential part of the adjustment program, since foreign investors are particularly sensitive to currency risks. Capital flows are still imposing additional constraints on Mexico's financial system. The fragility of Banco de México's international reserves is shown by the fact that they may not be sufficient to avert a panic in Tesobonos and that net international reserves (taking out reserve liabilities such as IMF drawings) might be negative.

We also contend that the most salient effect of the actual financial crisis is that the NAFTA framework for financial affairs has been surpassed. Therefore, the banking sector shall be subject to a much faster opening process starting in 1995. Ironically, this is the only choice for several commercial banks, if they are to stay in business.

References

ASPE, P. (1993) *El Camino Mexicano de la Transformación Económica*, Fondo de Cultura Económica, México.

BANCO DE MEXICO (1995) *Informe Anual 1994*, México, DF, pp. 332.

BAQUEIRO, A. and GHIGLIAZZA, S. (1983) 'La politica monetaria en México: el marco institucional. In GONZALEZ, H. E. (ed.), *El sistema económico mexicano. Un análisis sobre su situación*. México.

CUTHBERTSON, K. and GALINDO, L. M. (1994) The Demand for Money in Mexico and Currency Substitution', *Discussion Papers in Economics*, University of Newcastle, pp. 14.

GARBER, P. M. and WEISBROD, S. R. (1993) 'Opening the Financial Services Market in Mexico'. In GARBER, P. M. (ed.), *The Mexico-US Free Trade Agreement*, MIT Press, Cambridge.

GALINDO, L. M. (1994) *The Demand for Money, Interest Rates and the Exchange Rate in Mexico*, PhD thesis, University of Newcastle-Upon-Tyne, p. 400. Unpublished.

GUTIERREZ-PEREZ A. and PERROTINI, I. (1994) 'The New Banking System: Challenges and Perspectives'. In FATEMI, K. and SALVATORE, D. (eds) *North American Free Trade Agreement*, Pergamon Press, London.

HENDRY, D. F. and MIZON, G. E. (1990) *Evaluating Dynamic Econometric Models by Encompassing the VAR*, mimeo.

MANTEY DE ANGUIANO, G. (1995) *La liberalización financiera en México y su efecto en el ciclo económico*, unpublished paper presented at the Seminar on *Ciclos Económicos y Financieros y el Tratado de libre Comercio*, UNAM, p. 20.

McKINNON, R. (1993) *The Order of Economic Liberalization: Financial Control in the Transition to a Market Economy.* Johns Hopkins, Baltimore.

ROS, J. (1995) Trade liberalization with real appreciation and slow growth. In HELLEINER, G. K. (ed.), *Manufacturing for Export in the Developing World: Problems and Possibilities.* Forthcoming.

STOGA, A. (1990) 'La venta de los Bancos Mexicanos', in *El Financiero*, México.

TAYLOR, R. (1994) 'Revolution in Motion', in *The Banker*, August.

TRIGUEROS, I. (1994) 'The Mexican Financial System and NAFTA', in *Mexico and the North American Free Trade Agreement: Who will benefit?* BULMER THOMAS, V., CRASKE, N. and SERRANO, M. (eds), Macmillan London.

Notes

1. The great expectations that Mexico's banking reform has awaked in the mind of some financial analysts are best represented in the following candid statement to be found in a leading financial magazine: 'The industry which emerges from the "big bang" of 1994 will be leaner, more competitive and better prepared to meet rapidly growing domestic needs while coping with the challenges of closer regional integration' (Taylor, 1994: 31).

2. Control over the growth of domestic credit aggregates was achieved through these instruments between 1950 and 1988. In as much as financial repression recursively led to domestic credit rationing, it became an important factor in the determination of capital flights and private foreign borrowing episodes.

3. For instance, among public instruments are *Tesobono*, a Treasury note with one and three month maturities indexed to the dollar, and *Ajustabono*, with three- to five-year maturities and returns indexed to the inflation rate. *Obligaciones, Commercial Paper* and *Banker Acceptances* are different kinds of private securities popularized within this period.

4. With balanced budgets, two more advantages should follow: first, the policy-making process can stick to Mundell's rule with no troubles, i.e. fiscal policy can be assigned at maintaining internal balance, while monetary policy is in charge of external balance; second, the so-called Tanzi effect (hyperinflation reduces real tax revenues due to collection lags) tends to zero. Therefore, fiscal control must go along with the elimination of financial repression.

5. Unlike other Organization for Economic Cooperation and Development (OECD) countries, Mexico cannot spread or postpone the most dire effects of external shocks through time.

6. Cf. (Gutiérrez-Pérez and Perrotini, 1994) for a discussion of these asymmetries.

7. Paradoxically enough, when it comes to financial liberalization, it is cross-border transactions which benefits banks clients the most.
8. Banamex-Accival group and Bancomer took over Aeroméxico; Grupo SIDEK, from the construction industry, was forced into default. Early in 1995 Televisa and Telmex, the two largest firms of the communications industry, merged towards joint ventures in telecommunications.

7

The Globalization of Financial Services: Implications for Competition in the North American Market

CARLOS PALOMARES

Introduction

The financial services industry is currently amidst a drastic process of evolution—a process that has been ongoing for approximately the last 20 years. With technological innovation and the globalization of products and services as its tools, the scope and competitive forces driving the financial services industry have been altered significantly. Parameters both within and outside the industry, which have traditionally and somewhat rigidly defined lines of business and strategic action, have been substantially reconstructed. Within the industry, as technology advances and product lines expand, the distinction between banks and non-bank financial institutions is being blurred. No longer is the notion of universal banking a pipe dream in this era of technologically driven product design, delivery and innovation in what is now a virtually global marketplace.

Given these developments, the landscape of the financial services industry is akin to a new order. This chapter will, in some detail, attempt to define this new order in North America by fleshing out several of the current trends that are sure to mold the future playing ground of the financial services industry. With particular attention being devoted to North America, both the internal and external environments in which banks are existing will be examined thoroughly. At the core of this analysis, shaping the logistics of both the internal and external order in North America, is the North American Free Trade Agreement (NAFTA).

Within the context of this historic agreement, several major themes have emerged as tantamount to the course of future endeavors in the industry. Among these are:

- the impact of technology/information superhighway on banking;
- the redefinition of competitive forces;
- the overall consolidation of the industry.

Through the examination of the development of these trends in North America, the process by which the financial services industry's new order has taken shape will be delineated, and the eye toward the future can begin to take focus.

NAFTA's Shaping of Competition

It is abundantly clear that as of January 1, 1994, the face of the financial services market in North America changed dramatically. With the same magnitude of impact that the McFadden Act of 1927 and the Glass-Steagall Act of 1933 had on the banking sector in the United States, NAFTA's ratification and implementation has virtually eroded the borders between the United States, Canada, and Mexico to produce a single North American market for financial services of some 370 million consumers. This event is not only significant in that it represents a concrete sign of regional and hemispheric economic integration, but NAFTA also has particular repercussions for the financial services industry in North America. In the words of William S. Haraf, vice-president of policy analysis for Citicorp:

> It (NAFTA) is the most comprehensive trade agreement affecting financial services firms yet negotiated, and it establishes many useful precedents that could serve as a model for other bilateral and regional trade agreements.[1]

Among the key NAFTA provisions that can be labeled as pivotal to the future of the financial services industry in North America are the following:[2]

- U.S. and Canadian banks will be eligible to establish fully capitalized subsidiaries in Mexico without being bound by previously established foreign ownership restrictions. The only qualifications are that no U.S. or Canadian banks can capture more than 15 percent of the total bank capital in Mexico until January 1, 2000, and thereafter, no foreign share can exceed 30 percent of the total market until January 1, 2004.
- No U.S. or Canadian banks can acquire Mexico's largest financial institutions. After a transition period, this restriction is lessened to allow for up to a 4 percent ownership of shares in these institutions.

- Until January 1, 2000, U.S. and Canadian banks can acquire small and medium-sized banks, given that these acquisitions do not amount to more than 25 percent of Mexico's total bank capital.
- Any U.S., Canadian, or Mexican financial institution will be eligible for national treatment in any of the other NAFTA countries. Simply stated, this signifies that foreign financial institutions are eligible to engage in any lines of business in the other NAFTA countries that domestic financial institutions can do there. In Mexico, this stipulation includes foreign bank branching (given the reform of the U.S. interstate banking laws) and the formation of holding companies that can offer a wide range of financial products.
- Residents of any NAFTA country have unrestricted access to the financial services offered in any of the three NAFTA nations, with the exception of non-Mexicans providing short-term peso denominated instruments to Mexico or its residents.
- Compliance with NAFTA's stipulations and regulations will be monitored by a panel that deals exclusively with financial services dispute settlement.

The United States, Canada, and Mexico

These provisions are considered key because their sole common thread is ultimately the creation of a single market for financial services in North America. Consequently, the true significance of NAFTA lies more in the principle of creating this single mammoth market— possibly the first concrete step toward economic integration of all of the Americas—rather than the total impact of the agreement on the developed economies of both the United States and Canada. This fact is evidenced not only through the existing economic relationship between the two nations as each other's largest trading partner, but it also speaks to the specifics of the FTA signed in 1988 between the United States and Canada, which essentially allows for reciprocal treatment of the two nations in each other's markets (see Chapter 3 of this book). In short, NAFTA is something of a non-event as far as the economic dynamics between the United States and Canada is concerned. The focus is clearly on Mexico, and the opportunities that its opening markets could represent.

To further qualify this assertion, it is useful to compare the demographics and economic indicators of the three NAFTA nations. In terms of population, Canada has roughly one-third the population of Mexico, which in turn has approximately one-third the population of the United States. These figures taken out of context can be somewhat misleading, but when coupled with economic indicators such as gross national product (GNP) and GNP per capita—both good measures of a country's degree of development, economic sophistication, and level of investment—the total picture regarding NAFTA becomes substantially more clear. In 1994, the United States had an annual GNP figure of approximately $6.200 trillion with a per capita rate of $23,400, while Canada shows a figure of $569 billion in GNP and $19,600 per capita. Here, Mexico reveals the infancy of its economic development with figures in the $330 billion range for GNP with a per capita rate of approximately $3,600. This merely superficial comparison quite concretely reveals that the Mexican economy is approximately half the size of Canada's, and roughly 5 percent the size of that of the United States.[3] Thus, the conclusion to be drawn is that NAFTA's potential impact—especially on the economy of the United States—will be quite minimal in raw terms.

Nonetheless, and as has been proven already in NAFTA's short history, the aforementioned facts regarding NAFTA's potential impact are in no way an affirmation that the agreement does not have very significant implications for the expansion of the developing Mexican market. Viewing NAFTA in this broader context not only allows for prime strategic positioning as the process toward the creation of the world's largest economic and free trade zone begins, but it also allows participants to benefit from what promises to be substantial growth in the Mexican economy and market.

The Mexican Financial Landscape

This necessarily begs the questions regarding competition and those forces that will dictate the successful penetration of the Mexican market. Augmenting this complex equation is the fact that this entire process of hemispheric economic integration is a direct function of the current size, structure, and regulatory environment of the Mexican banking sector. Within this context, there are two main issues that must be addressed:

- the receptiveness and compatibility of the existing Mexican banking structure; and
- the opportunities that the Mexican market represents.

Mexico's current banking structure is the direct consequence of a series of reforms that began in the 1970s. The culmination of these efforts is a banking system that is currently characterized by concentrated ownership and focused distribution in and around Mexico City. The result is a Mexican banking universe whose structure is approximately 4 percent the size of the U.S. industry and 25 percent the size of Canada's. Moreover, the Mexican commercial banking universe is severely underbranched and consists of only 18 privately owned banks, two of which (Banamex and Bancomer) control approximately 60 percent of the market. Additionally, and as is the case in most Latin American nations, these banks are held closely and operated by groups of wealthy families and/or friends—'*grupos financieros*'—who operate them at the core of multi-faceted and extremely large holding companies that do business in several different markets. The grupo banks serve to raise capital, consolidate control, and provide a solid base or link for various investments, thus ensuring prosperity going forward. As a direct result of this orientation, the Mexican financial services market experiences what can be termed as considerable capital concentration and oligopolization. When compared to the U.S. market, whose three largest banks—Citicorp, Bank of America and Chemical Banking—hold only 12 percent (as of 1994) of the country's total banking assets, it is clear that there exists a very real and defined discrepancy in the size and structure of the two nations' financial services industries.[4]

Barriers to Entry

These facts notwithstanding, it is safe to assume that U.S. and Canadian banks, drawn by the lure of Mexico as the first step toward access to all of Latin America, will enter the Mexican financial services market in lieu of both of these rather formidable barriers to entry. Perhaps the most apparent barrier to entry that Mexico represents was spelled out quite clearly in anticipation of NAFTA's passage with the intent of scaring competition and aggrandizing national foreign direct investment levels. This stipulation centers on the minimum and maximum capital requirements to enter Mexico's financial service industry. Initial minimum capital requirements are in the $20 million range, with a maximum allowance of paid up capital in the amount of $90 million. These high levels of requisite initial investment are diverting all but the largest U.S. banks to Mexico's regional retail markets where initial levels of investment are substantially lower.[5] Even the larger U.S. banks are shying away from such substantial initial investment schedules, citing that Mexico essentially amounts to a new and untested market into which such levels of investment are not yet justified.

The result is that many U.S. financial services firms will plan to enter Mexico through a strategic alliance or a merger. Given the aforementioned restrictions on the foreign ownership and acquisition of Mexico's largest financial institutions stipulated under NAFTA, strategic alliance seems to be the next best alternative. Not only do such alliances give foreign banks the opportunity to test the Mexican market, but they also allow for the erosion of the Mexican *grupos'* source of competitive advantage over foreign entrants—access to established relationships and local markets. This is an invaluable resource in a relationship-driven service industry such as banking that intends to be based in a country like Mexico whose business culture is decidedly social in nature. From the Mexican perspective, such alliances expose the nation's banks to the wealth of experiences and resources that large foreign global banks possess.

Another repercussion of the risk and cost associated with entering the Mexican market is that many foreign banks will postpone their penetration into Mexican retail banking in favor of exploiting other areas where they have a decided comparative advantage. Within this context, areas of particular import are cross-border mergers and acquisitions, trade and equities.[6] With today's advances in modern technology that have virtually eroded traditional geographical boundaries and constructed in their place the global information superhighway, cross-border transactions among markets are almost second nature to the world's largest financial institutions. Moreover, national equity market activity already takes this fact into consideration with several analyses revealing that the Canadian, U.S., and Mexican stock markets all reacted favorably with positive returns in direct response to various announcements concerning NAFTA's formation and ratification. The Mexican market even reacted favorably in response to specific qualified endorsements of the agreement.[7] 'Not only does such cross-market activity provide for exposure in the previously restricted Mexican market, but it allows foreign entrants both to bypass the large expenditures and sunk costs associated with initial construction and equipment purchase, and to forego exorbitant office space rental rates in Mexico City, which currently hover in the range of double New York prices.'[8]

The Mexican Financial Services Market: A Good Opportunity

In lieu of the facts that have been presented regarding the various barriers to entry and the disjunction between the Mexican, Canadian, and U.S. financial services markets, in order to remain faithful to the aforementioned proper and broad view of NAFTA as a catalyst toward hemispheric economic integration, it only stands to reason that there is also significant support for the opening of the Mexican financial services market as a good strategic and potentially profitable opportunity. The first and foremost area of consideration under this umbrella of opportunity is the existing condition of the Mexican consumer market as severely underbanked. As of 1992, Mexico had approximately 4,500 bank branches to Canada's 7,500, and the United States' almost 68,000. This works out to a figure of about 18,500 people per bank branch, which is roughly six times more than the approximately 3,500 people per branch that has been customary in both the U.S. and Canada. Moreover, the data with reference to automatic teller machine (ATM) market penetration reflects a similar trend of underbanking in Mexico. The number of ATMs in Mexico is approximately 4,200, which shows a customer service base per ATM of an astounding 21,000. This compares extremely negligibly with figures in Canada that hover in the 10,500 range for ATMs and 2,700 people per ATM. The United States shows similar demographic numbers with virtually 95,000 ATMs and a figure of approximately one ATM for every 2,700 people.[9] These figures take on an added dimension when viewed within the context of NAFTA's stipulation for national treatment of all U.S. and Canadian financial services institutions that decide to enter the Mexican market. In short, this means that in light of the concentration of banking in and around Mexico City, foreign banks will be free to open branches in the rest of Mexico's drastically underbanked areas which are filled with eager and undeserved customers.

The second area of focus when referring to Mexico's banking opportunities is growth and profitability. This overwhelming sense of potential is reflected not only within the Mexican banking industry, but also in Mexico's national business forecast figures and economic outlook for 1995.[10] Among the figures that will have a direct impact on the health of the financial services industry are overall investment figures, which are up approximately 12 percent for the 1990s versus the 1980s, reflecting confidence in the path of Mexico's economic development. In addition, real GDP growth is up almost 3 percent for the 1990s with a corresponding 1 percent decrease in unemployment and a 3 percent increase in the national rate of consumption. Within the Mexican banking industry, the data is equally as encouraging. Not only is the Mexican financial services sector slighted for a 15 percent growth rate in the next year, but some of Mexico's largest financial/banking institutions have a history of outperforming their counterparts in the United States in some key profitability indexes. For example, in 1992, Banamex and Bancomer showed figures of 2.3 percent and 2.0 percent respectively in terms of return on average assets (ROA). This compared favorably with an average of large U.S. banks, which for the same year, showed a figure of only 0.9 percent ROA. In addition, numbers reflecting the return on average equity (ROE) for Banamex and Baricomer were in the 30 percent range, with large U.S. banks showing ROE figures hovering only around 14 percent.[11] When combined with the aforementioned reference to Mexico's current underbanked state, these figures not only reflect that there is a defined and undeserved target market in

Mexico, but that if administered properly, endeavors in Mexico's banking sector can be profitable and an added bonus to the financial performance of many of North America's largest banking institutions.

The last major area of opportunity that exists for foreign entrants into the Mexican market centers on the current practices of the existing Mexican banks. Of particular importance here are the pricing and fee structures that prevail in many of Mexico's banks. Due to the fact that the competitive situation can, at best, be termed an oligopoly that is serving an essentially captive market, participating banks basically have free reign in Mexico. This fact is reflected quite handsomely in their levels of bank prices and fees, which are astonishing compared to the prevailing prices and fees in the competitive U.S. market. For example, overdraft charges start at $75 per check, and if a customer is fortunate enough to be approved for a mortgage or automobile loan, interest costs exceed 30 percent per year range. Needless to say that these figures are substantially higher than their corresponding rates in the United States and Canada.

Moreover, there is a prevailing lack of emphasis on customer service as a priority in Mexico's banks. It is not uncommon to see long lines that snake out of bank branches with frustrated customers who wait sometimes for more than an hour for service. In addition, there exists what has been called a 'technology void' in Mexico with reference to banking services. The under penetration of ATMs that was mentioned previously is a perfectly viable case in point. Further supporting this fact is the precedent-setting $2 billion per year that has been allotted exclusively by the various Mexican banks to address this significant problem.[12]

This significant allocation of resources to technological development by the Mexican banks speaks to the crux of what lies ahead for the post-NAFTA Mexican financial services sector. In short, this response is a free acknowledgment of the fact that NAFTA changes the competitive landscape in which these large Mexican banks will do business. Not only will the deficiencies of the Mexican banks be exploited by adventurous foreign entrants, but the incumbent Mexican banks will seek to shape up and compete fiercely in response to threats on what has been the lifeblood of the *grupos financieros*' prosperity for decades. In this battle, the *grupos*' most valuable weapon will be their access to long-developed local relationships and markets that outsiders will be hard pressed to penetrate. The result will be that the previously protected Mexican financial services market will now be exposed to those forces that are dictating the future of the delivery of bank services in the rest of North America and most of the modern Western world. In short, previously unwitnessed competition will arrive abruptly and forcefully into the Mexican banking sector, with both U.S. and

Canadian financial services firms taking strategic aim at what is clearly viewed as the first step towards the penetration of Latin America and its financial services/banking needs.

Until this point, the objective has been to examine the external environment of the financial services industry in North America. By analyzing the current changes that are taking place in what promises to be a hotbed of new market activity in Mexico, the foundation for the most important market-based issue that faces North America's financial services institutions and banks has been delineated. Having done this, the next step is to examine the internal environment of the financial services industry in North America to determine what forces will simultaneously be at work in dictating the way in which North America's financial services institutions and banks pursue their market based strategy and penetration of Mexico, while they continue to compete with their traditional rivals in the rest of the continent.

Technology: the Key to Future Competitiveness

Among the factors that are dynamically affecting the financial services industry in North America, the one that most holds the key to future success is applied technology. Financial services information technology holds this distinction because in its applications are direct repercussions for both operational efficiency and quality of customer service—the two areas that single-handedly dictate how successfully a bank is able to attract revenue and achieve margins. In today's era of innovative global computer technology and acute emphasis on the control of information flow and the delivery of bank services, the degree to which an institution has a grasp on its IT applications will directly compromise or aggrandize the institution's level of efficiency and effectiveness in reaching both its operational and financial goals. With respect to Mexico, this assertion is enhanced by the fact that Mexican banking can be currently characterized as existing in the technology void referred to earlier. Mexican banks have only recently realized that the wave of the future in banking will be dictated by the pace of technological innovation. In short, the Mexican market is technologically underserved, and its banks are far behind their American and Canadian counterparts in the pursuit of applied technology. This will undoubtedly be the key competitive bargaining chip that foreign entrants into the Mexican market bring to the table.

With this knowledge in hand, virtually all North American banks are investing billions of dollars each year in attempts to utilize technology to its potential. Unfortunately, this is a more complex process than one might expect due to the pace at which innovation and change permeate the technology that they so covet. In other words, the pace and scope of technology is so dynamic that the know-how can be accessed by virtually anyone, but no one entity can ever completely dominate and monopolize it. The result is series of competitive maneuvers—some traditional, some extremely out of the industry's character—that seek as their objective the efficient and effective use of technology for banking purposes. This ongoing quest to be up to speed with the ever emerging technology curve has become so intense that many banks have added to their in-house information systems (IS) functional areas by hiring outside consultants to plan internal strategy for the pursuit and development of the technology that they plan to use as the key to their overall market strategy. Such actions not only reaffirm that technology is a very real priority atop today's banks, but that this same technology has pushed itself down the corporate ladder with a significant amount of the technology decision-making being made at the business unit and departmental levels. Examples of projects that have been diligently pursued by bank technology consulting leaders such as Andersen Consulting, and which are quite common in today's marketplace, include imaging strategies, workstation technology for investment banks, and mortgage banking applications.[13]

In response to this overwhelming trend within the banking industry, large technology and computer firms are also adjusting to allocate significant amounts of resources and strategic significance to bank technology. A case in point is IBM, who amidst their recent reorganization effort, formed a 2,000 employee product development unit devoted specifically to banking and financial services technology. This strategic unit sees as its focus beating competitors by speeding technology to banks that retain its services.[14] In short, IBM seeks to evolve its competitive advantage based on the other major component of the technology equation—time.

The injection of this time component has directly led to another significant development in the way in which banks will deliver services to customers and operate their businesses. This development stems from the acknowledgment of the dynamic and virtually incomprehensible rate of innovation in bank technology. The result of this acknowledgment has been the formation of strategic alliances whose objective is to share in the daunting pursuit of applicable banking technology. Perhaps the premier organization in this area is the Financial Services Technology Consortium—a banking research alliance organized by Citicorp in 1993. Members include among others, Citibank, Bank of America, Chemical Bank, Chase Manhattan Bank, NationsBank, AT&T, IBM, and Unisys. The founding philosophy behind alliances such as these is the realization by major banks in North America that they can accomplish more far quicker by cooperating rather than competing in critical areas of significant new banking technology. Projects of particular import at this juncture include check imaging and electronic payments. Not only does focusing on such projects through these strategic alliances provide for easier and more complete access to new technology applications, but 'coopetition'—the blurring together of cooperation and competition—has also afforded these banks the use of these applications as a source of competitive advantage against the many non-bank financial services institutions that are now venturing into what have traditionally been bank serviced product offerings.[15] In short, these bank technology alliances are allowing banks to serve customers in a faster, more complete, and more convenient manner. The words of author Kenichi Ohmae from his book *The Borderless World* very aptly capture the advantage and significance of such strategic alliances:

> In stable competitive environments, the alliance to loss of control exacts little penalty. But this is not the case in a changeable world of rapidly globalizing markets and industries—a world of converging consumer tastes, rapidly spreading technology, escalating fixed costs, and growing protectionism. Globalization mandates alliances, makes them absolutely essential to strategy.[16]

Applied Technology: The Future of Quality Bank Service Delivery

As was alluded to earlier, one of the main reasons for the aggressive pursuit of bank technology is to improve the quality of service delivery. Banking is a service industry in which success is measured wholly by the experience of the customer. Complicating matters more is the fact that customers' banking needs are constantly laden with demands for increased convenience, access to greater numbers of creative products, and faster service. In short, as is the case in most service driven industries, consumers have perfected the cry of 'more for less.'

Toward this end, banks have responded by utilizing technology as their greatest tool in satisfaction of today's more complex bank customer. This, undoubtedly, is a trend that will continue long into the future. The question then becomes what specific applications in today's marketplace are achieving customer satisfaction and bringing smiles to the faces of those with demanding banking needs. The following summarizes several of the areas that are currently being utilized and developed further in today's market. All will continue to be tantamount to the future of the North American banking sector and those who compete within its scope.

Consumer Access

Due to the aforementioned heightened customer sensitivity to convenience and speed in their bank services, access to accounts is an area that has gravitated to the fore. No longer are customers demanding the locational convenience of bank branches, now they want quick and easy access to all of their money, anytime. The response to this challenge has come in many forms, beginning with the advent of the ATM which has become an absolute fixture in today's banking world and is the cornerstone on which CATs (customer activated terminals) and other future out-of-home electronic delivery systems are being built. Currently, ATM transactions are growing at an annual rate of 12 percent—30 percent faster than branch transactions.[17] Nevertheless, technology has now evolved beyond the ATM to begin to erode the usefulness of the traditional brick and mortar branch that considered itself strategically well placed if it could serve its customers within a five to seven mile radius, referred to industry wide as a 'branch trading area.'

Upon the industry now, and sure to lead the next era of bank service delivery, is a new series of remote delivery options. Among these new applications are screen phones, smart phones, interactive television, and home personal computers through which financial services can be accessed and delivered. Speedier bank service is developing through internal data compression and multiplexing, as well as cellular network applications and digitalization that will make simultaneous voice and data transmissions possible.[18] As consumers begin to feel more comfortable with technology, and this degree of comfort continues to alter consumer behavior to produce demands that outpace current product offerings, customers will be inundated with new, more powerful tools which will make their ride down the 'information superhighway' as smooth as possible.

The reality of the matter is that this transformation has already begun to take place. Today, one third of bank customers utilize their bank's automated telephone service to access their accounts and receive account information. This particular application is capable of breaking down geopolitical boundaries that have traditionally compromised a consumer's banking capabilities on the basis of physical location, essentially preventing the fruition of universal banking. No longer is this the case with products such as Citibank's 'Citiphone' and Midland Bank's 'Person to Person' providing sophisticated universal account access capability.[19] Personal computers, capable of accessing networks, running software, and even hosting live video teleconferencing that can be utilized for home banking, are also becoming prevalent in today's consumer society, and can now be found in approximately one third of all American households. A significant amount of these households are even beginning to use interactive networks such as Prodigy and America Online at increasing rates to perform duties that traditionally required leaving the home.[20]

Banks such as Citibank—with its 'Direct Access' PC home banking product—are posited to take full advantage of this significant trend in consumer technology awareness and utilization. In other words, the financial services industry is placing full faith in the idea that by the beginning of the third millennium, the majority of consumers will be doing their banking remotely.

All of these developments suggest that the modern North American consumer can no longer ignore, and is actually beginning to embrace, technology as part of its consumer culture. Clearly, this is a trend that is in its infancy with much room to grow in North America, but the transformation is definitely underway. Furthermore, it also suggests that with the decreasing amount of free time (a 40 percent drop in the last 20 years) that most people are now able to enjoy in today's modern lifestyle, banking is one of the areas in which this infusion of technology seems to be welcomed.[21] It is for these reasons that banks must prioritize remaining up to speed with current technology in their field. In short, this cultural change in customer behavior is the key to a financial institution's return on investment in the pursuit of relevant bank technology. Success in North America's very competitive market of the future will be underpinned by a bank's ability to introduce effective user-friendly consumer technology through a small window of opportunity that is rigidly bordered by consumer tastes and technological obsolescence.

Sweetening the pot is the fact that not only does the strategic use of applied technology contribute to a market based approach that seeks to attract customers with the lure of increased convenience and speed, but such an emphasis is also justified from a financial standpoint, with significant cost savings from telephone and ATM transactions versus traditional branch transactions, which are considerably more expensive.[22] In summary, the informed use of applied technology for the delivery of bank services is a clear win-win situation for all involved.

Lending Practices

One of the areas in banking that has been and will continue to be infused heavily with information technology is mortgage lending. Due to the nature of the business as operating on thin margins, management of cost structure amidst a quality customer service environment is particularly important. Toward this end, many lenders have utilized applied technology to their advantage. The premise of this technology is derived from the fact that the mortgage process is somewhat costly due to the manual intervention that is usually required in processing loan applications. Thus, it behooves large lenders to search for a more automated and paperless way in which to conduct the necessities of their business. While this trend has unfortunately led to a shrinking employment base within the industry, due to pressure exerted by the aforementioned slim industry margins, this is not a development that promises to vanish anytime soon. In fact, the opposite can be said with mortgage lenders constantly searching for new technology with which to streamline the loan approval process and keep tight control over vast amounts of information. For the future, the measuring stick of the effective use of information technology in mortgage lending is the same as it is in any other line of business: an organization is not measured by the degree to which it is computerized, but rather on how it uses technology first to improve operational efficiency, satisfy customer needs and corner market share. A case in point is Bankers Trust Company's use of optical imaging to store and immediately access vast amounts of loan closing documentation.[23] This use of applied technology not only lowers overhead costs and solves a large storage dilemma by making optimal use of physical space, but it also provides for improved efficiency and customer service through quicker and easier accessing of documents.

Like in retail banking, mortgage companies systems usually consist of several main components which provide both operational and product support. The first is a large mainframe computer which serves as a kind of central processing unit devoted to transactions and the processing of applications. These transactions are usually limited to basic calculations such as loan amortization schedules that can be repeated ad infinitum for each individual situation. Complementing these applications is a second tier of information technology, usually in the form of proprietary applications—most mortgage companies have thousands—which support a company's various products and services.[24] This wave of technology within the industry has taken such firm hold that even large lenders such as Fannie Mae and Freddie Mac have moved toward routine use of automated appraisal processing and artificial intelligence in loan decision making.[25]

The strategic or competitive significance of this technology is several fold in the North American post-NAFTA market. In addition to the operational efficiency and enhanced ability to serve the customer alluded to earlier, mortgage lending technology also provides access to markets inundated with potential customers through the information superhighway. With respect to Mexico, this has particular relevance because of the technology's ability to link high-tech foreign lenders to a developing nation that will be in constant need of capital. For U.S. and Canadian banks eager to penetrate and test the Mexican market without committing large amounts of initial investment, this technology will provide lower cost access to a market where loans are priced at approximately 30 percent interest on the average. In addition, not only does this technology break down state and national boundaries, but it also dispenses with the traditional requirement of local branch presence to be considered a viable community lender by potential customers. In short, the role of the mortgage banker is evolving to recognize that technology is replacing them as the link between customers (and/or brokers) and lending agencies. Institutions such as GE Capital have taken full advantage of this development and are currently expanding on this concept by actively lending to small and medium sized businesses without having the local branch presence that has been mandatory over the last fifty years.

Pre-Authorized Debits/Credits

Another cutting edge technology in North America which has evolved through increased customer service capability and the emphasis on convenience is pre-authorized debit/credit payment systems. The philosophy on which these services are based is that customer reliance on paper payments and transactions is eliminated. Companies like Checkfree Corporation, based in Columbus, Ohio, are managing electronic bill payment systems that oversee a business within an industry that has grown from between 30 percent and 40 percent during 1994 and 1995. Currently, Checkfree is conducting approximately four million transactions per month. Most of the payment transactions are conducted through home personal computers, but both individuals and businesses are among those that utilize electronic payment services to pay their bills. Checkfree is among a number of companies that are also in the process of developing technology for bill payment through interactive television, but all freely acknowledge that the pace of innovation in this area will surely race ahead of consumer comfort levels with the technology.[26] Nevertheless, such technologies have at their disposal the ability to revolutionize the bill payment and checking process.

Other such developments in this area include direct deposit of salaries, payment of mortgages and loans, as well as point of sale technology that will all aid in dispensing with cash as a cultural icon in North America. The result will be a virtually cashless consumer society much in the mold of what exists in many of the major markets of Europe. An excellent example of this slow transition can be demonstrated through a quick retrospective on the purchasing process at U.S. gasoline stations. What fifteen years ago was a full-service, labor intensive, cash-transacted process, has today become a one-on-one cashless transaction between the customer, a credit or debit card, and a computerized gasoline pump. Simple convenience, customer empowerment, cost reduction, and speedy service have all been achieved effectively through applied technology. It is this same orientation that is the motivation behind what are now called 'electronic purses' or 'smart cards.' These are microchip cards that can be used at ATMs to access accounts and withdraw money, which is then stored on the card to be used instead of cash and coins for future purchases.[27]

Once again, such technologies not only allow for quicker, more convenient, and lower cost transactions, but afford consumers access to what in essence becomes a borderless global marketplace of goods and services. Eventually, a consumer on vacation in Mexico who wants to purchase a product with a smart card from his Florida based bank will be able to do so without hesitation. The technology will make this possible, and one day such processes will be second nature as consumers become more globally conscious and increasingly comfortable with these processes.

Globalization of Equity Markets

This degree of technological advancement also has direct ramifications for the three financial markets of North America in the post-NAFTA world. Within this context, there are two major spheres of influence—information flow and trading operations. In terms of information flow, the effect of applied technology has simply increased the dissemination and accessibility of more and quicker information, which in turn, has led to more informed investment-related decision-making. Many decisions that were previously made on expertise, and what amounted to unsubstantiated hunches, are now made with the aid of easily comprehensible rapid fire quantitative analysis rooted in hard market-based data. The effect has been the both the shrinking of transaction time horizons in trading rooms, and the equalizing of access to information between institutional and individual investors.[28] Both of these trends will surely accelerate in the future.

With respect to trading operations, both scale and scope have been affected by technological applications. Emergent are trends such as the advent of paperless wire trading systems that cut the completion time of a block trade from several hours to two minutes because information can be entered directly to the trading platform; the automation of foreign exchange transactions; and financial services institutions developing a global character by offering access to capital markets on a cross-border basis.[29] Evidence of this globalization can be found in North America through the increase in correlated market activity both during the NAFTA ratification process and after its inception, as well through an increase in American Depository Receipts (ADRs) and the rising number of foreign corporations that are currently listed on the New York Stock Exchange. The eventual result will be the increased integration of the world's markets into one global trading community that can effectively price risk equivalent financial instruments across markets, and which could quite possibly one day operate under the law of one price.

The Redefinition of Competitive Forces

All of these developments in technology are a strong indicator that the factors of competition within the North American financial services sector are amidst a process of great flux. Not only does NAFTA change potential approaches to market strategy, but because applied technology is so strongly and quickly permeating how financial institutions both operate internally and deliver their services, decisions concerning the allocation of resources, cost restructuring, new product development, pricing, distribution channels, and strategic positioning are being revised at almost every level of the industry. It is clear that the aspects of competitive advantage are rapidly evolving to incorporate a dynamic technological component that is sure to mold strategy for many years to come. Consequently, the ability to manage change has become essential. This is because the mere possession of technological capability is not the key to surviving in the North American banking sector moving into the 21st century. It is the proper utilization of applied technology to achieve predetermined, well defined and well communicated strategic objectives for the improvement of business performance. This will be the proper and only context in which technology will develop into a source of competitive advantage.

There are two areas of corporate strategy within the industry that are currently experiencing the greatest degree of dynamic change due to the impact of technology:

- market strategy; and
- profit structure.

Market Strategy

With the opening of the Mexican market as a result of NAFTA, coupled with the overcrowding and fierce competition that already exists in most local banking markets, the revision of market-based strategy is a hot topic in the banking industry. Besides the fact that this is a perpetually ongoing process by its nature in the era of the complex modern consumer, applied technology has complicated the equation all the more. In retail banking, the crux of this new orientation is that adeptness is no longer measured in terms of the efficacy of an organization's penetration and capture of target markets with physical branches, but rather in the ability to reach beyond the traditionally defined 'branch trading area' through technological applications. In other words, the traditional notion of the 'brick and mortar' branch customer service center is outliving its usefulness as the process of linking customers to their banking needs now has a different definition and aspects. All are significantly altering the vital components of competitive advantage and shaking the very foundation of the retail banking structure.

In support of this assertion is extensive market research which essentially reveals that approximately one out of every five bank branches will close by the turn of the millennium, and that more than half of all current bank transactions are conducted outside of traditional bank branches.[30] The material conclusion from such studies is that in all major banking sectors customers are migrating away from the traditional branch to conduct the majority of their transactions.

The result of this industry-wide acknowledgment has been the interim fusion of technological application with the traditional branch concept to produce what has come be known as virtual branches or model branches. Take, for example, Huntington Bancshares' 'Huntington Banks Access' inaugurated in October of 1994. This particular virtual branch is the central component of what has become a more common 'hub and spoke' industry strategy that stresses flexibility and convenience in the banking network's meeting of local needs through technology. Included in the Huntington Bancshares model are three interactive video devices, two advance function ATMs complete with imaging technology, as well as a full wall satellite-fed television screen that shows news, weather, and bank production information. All of these features are housed in a space roughly half the size of a conventional branch (which reduces overhead costs) with a staff size of one employee (which reduces labor costs) who serves in the basic capacity of *concierge*.[31]

Citibank's 'model branch' campaign is another technology-based project whose main focus is to seamlessly integrate and deliver all desired banking elements to any customer, anytime. This objective is accomplished by breaking down the old branch trading area or regionally defined bank branch, and replacing it with a global, technology-based, full-service retail franchise referred to as a model branch. The key to the organization's achievement of this process is the effective application of technology to support more informed and expedient interaction with customers. In other words, within the model branch exists the technology-based distribution strategy that will one day outgrow the brick and mortar walls in which it is housed today.

The strategic significance of such efforts is that the movement of modern day competitive strategy is toward the opportunistic application of technology to enhance and quicken customer service quality, not by the strategic geographic placement of traditional brick and mortar branches in specifically defined target markets. This signifies that the way in which customers are being linked to their banking needs is changing rapidly, thus redefining traditional market segmentation parameters (including breaking down geographic barriers), cost structures, distribution channels, and operational efficiency. Banks that do not embrace these changes and excel in these areas will not be able to compete. They will be forced out not only by their local competition, but by globally-oriented institutions that are able to access virtually any market via the information superhighway. Gone is the day that customers must have a physical presence in a bank to purchase its products. In short, technology is revamping the entire industry to such a degree that the branch concept—in any way, shape, or form—will one day be outdated.

Profit Structure

As a direct result of this evolution of the North American banking industry away from the traditional brick and mortar branch distribution network, the profit structure of the industry is also undergoing a process of change. Today's reality is that banks can no longer afford the large costs associated with extensive branch distribution networks because competitors within the industry are utilizing technology to reduce costs, which thus allows them to engage in more competitive, and often times lower, pricing of similar products. Lower prices translate into reduced spreads—which are one of the main sources of retail bank profits—as banks are forced to alter competitive strategy and generate margins through innovative and differentiated approaches to their various product lines. Consequently, the measure of a bank's profitability has become a dynamic notion of efficiency— efficiency that is a delicate fusion of how well an organization is able to strategically utilize technology in cost reduction, while providing high quality customer service, and accessing information for cross selling and the development of new products.

Carrying the analysis one step further, technology is currently and will continue to impact the four areas that most concretely dictate a bank's degree of profitability.[32]

Cost Control/Reduction

The basis for this conclusion stems from the fact that branch-based servicing is much more costly than automated or technology-driven servicing. This is largely due to the facilities and labor costs associated with servicing, for example, an average household checking account from a local branch. The cost of providing the same service to a household checking account by telephone or other automated service channel is approximately one half of the branch-based cost. Many larger financial institutions and credit card companies such as Citibank are taking this concept one step further by engaging in strategic alliances that are aimed at reducing costly technological support costs for back office operations and transaction processing. These efforts not only cut costs by sharing high-cost technology investments with their partners, but they also allow for the gain of economies of scale.[33] This utilization of technology speaks to the fact that amidst a relatively stagnant industry revenue base, banks will be engaging in any and all activities that assist in the efficient translation of revenue dollars into profit. No doubt that cost-cutting will be a key component in this process.

Pricing

Increased cost savings provide banks with more flexibility in the pricing of their products. This can be a key weapon in attracting new customers or retaining old customers who are thinking of making a change. In addition, because technology carries with it an implied message of value for most customers, banks will not have to decrease product prices at a level that is exactly proportional to the increase in cost savings that they realize due to technology. Thus, this flexibility can directly impact a bank's margin of profitability.

Service Quality

As the cost savings of strategically-placed applied technology are realized, banks can redeploy these savings toward providing their customers with a better and higher quality service experience. This reallocation of cost savings may come in the form of more knowledgeable service representatives or more responsive, more convenient, and faster technology. Consequently, the customer's bank service experience will become more satisfying, thus reducing the need for product price reduction until competitors can match this level of service fulfillment.

Revenue Opportunities

The higher quality service personnel and advanced level of technology resulting from the reallocation of cost savings bring with them the necessary control over information flow to spot opportunities for product cross-selling and new account business development. This, not to mention the additional time that will be available for selling due to the constantly increasing operational efficiency that comes with the ever-evolving technology curve, will greatly improve banks' sales functions.

Consolidation

Accompanying this change in market-based strategy and profit structure is a powerful trend toward consolidation in the North American banking sector. Not only is this trend powerful, but it does not seem to be fleeting in any sense, instead promising to be one of the major forces that shapes the immediate future of the industry. This is the case because of the aforementioned drives toward cost reduction and the resulting change in profit structure due to the infusion of bank technology as the *status quo.* This notwithstanding, the unique aspect of this particular trend is that it is multi-faceted. Not only will consolidation affect the landscape of the industry in the future through merger and acquisition activity, but it will also be a major factor in shaping the regulatory structure according to which banks are mandated to operate.

The Emerging Consolidated Landscape

The emerging competitive landscape in the North American banking sector will be defined by several components. They are the following:

- the increasing presence of global banks in local markets;
- the targeted role of community banks as niche market players; and
- the co-existence of both banks and non-bank financial services providers.

The consolidated nature of this landscape will, first and foremost, reveal that the overall number of banks within the industry will continue to shrink dramatically. These figures have consistently declined since the mid-1980s when there were approximately 14,500 insured banks in the United States—in 1994 there were about 9,900 banks.[34] In order to increase market share and improve profitability and operating efficiency, the wave of merger and acquisition activity that has driven the number of banks downward for almost a decade is likely to continue. The majority of this consolidation activity will take the form of larger banks acquiring well-positioned, medium-sized banks with assets in the $1 billion to $20 billion range. This will be in an effort to build substantial critical mass in targeted geographical markets. The bulk of the rest of the activity should be in the Chemical

Bank-Manufacturers Hanover mold, focusing on the synergy, cost reduction and operational efficiency that large mergers of major institutions in the banking industry provide.

In the same vain, and somewhat more attractive because they do not require as much of a major and permanent allocation of resources as mergers and acquisitions do, will be a continued affinity for strategic alliances, engineered particularly by the larger global banks. The goals here will be technological advancement and operational efficiency as mentioned earlier, but also driving these efforts will be access to local distribution networks. This will be particularly important within the context of accessing the newly-opened Mexican market. The attraction in this scenario is that larger banks get the local market access mentioned earlier without having to build it from the ground up, while the medium-sized banks are the benefactors of cutting edge customer service and delivery technology that is cost prohibitive for them because of their size.

Comprising another facet of the banking landscape in North America will be smaller boutique-type community banks, who will essentially be niche players. These banks will cater to the needs of particular individuals within an extremely well-defined target market. The key to their competitive advantage will be close personal relationships with their clients, as well as an extremely high level of extraordinary and quality-defined customer service.

Adding to the competitive nature of the industry is that many non-bank financial services providers are now expanding their offerings to include several products that were traditionally handled only by commercial banks. It is for this reason that a Towers-Perrin poll of 355 senior bank managers in North America revealed that their greatest concern was competition, particularly from non-bank financial services firms.[35] Not only will banks experience the normal level of competition from known competitors in products such as deposit accounts and commercial loans, but competition from new non-bank entrants such as GE Capital, American Express, and Merill Lynch in those areas, as well as in products such as capital financing instruments, mutual funds, mortgage loans, and credit cards, have already, and will continue to, play a significant role. This fact is evidenced strongly by the decrease in the percentage of intermediary assets held by insured depository banks and thrifts in the United States from a high of 75 percent in 1950 to a current (1994) figure of approximately 25 percent.[36]

The Regulatory Environment

One of the catalysts in the emergence of non-bank institutions into traditional bank territory has been the somewhat less restrictive regulatory framework by which financial services providers are governed. This causal relationship leads directly to the second major way in which consolidation will affect the North American banking sector—namely, in the area of regulation. With the technology-driven emphasis on the distribution and delivery of bank services, the evolution of capital markets, and the widening scope of non-bank offerings, restructuring of both the form and content of the U.S. regulatory environment was virtually imminent. The only question is how far it will go. This area is of particular importance given that banks are among the most regulated entities in the North American market, and as was alluded to earlier, far surpass their non-bank counterparts in the mandated level of regulatory compliance.

In actuality, this process has already begun to take place, having specific ramifications for the entire North American financial services sector. Beginning with the enactment of the Riegle-Neal Interstate Banking and Branching Efficiency Act of 1994, U.S. commercial banks are now able to acquire or merge with banks in most other states. In addition, U.S. banks will be able to freely branch across state lines, while melting existing affiliates under a single national bank charter. This regulatory development is groundshaking within the context of NAFTA's 'national treatment' stipulation, which when combined with this new interstate banking law, effectively completes the formation of a single almost uniform North American banking sector of approximately 370 million consumers.

With regard to the form of the regulatory environment, it is also currently undergoing a process of flux that promises to produce a very different structure in the future. The most prevalent trend that will shape the size and scope of the U.S. banking regulatory framework surrounds addressing the issue of the current structure's institutional orientation, fragmentation, and lack of uniformity. The crux of the problem stems from the fact that each type of U.S. banking institution is regulated by one or more different government agencies: national banks by the Office of the Comptroller of the Currency (OCC); savings and loans and savings banks by the Office of Thrift Supervision (OTS); credit unions by the National Credit Union Administration (NCUA); commercial banks by the Federal Deposit Insurance Corporation (FDIC); and all instructions by the state banking authorities.[37]

The adjustment of the system will consist of the reorientation of the banking regulatory infrastructure toward emphasizing functions, rather than entities. Within this context, all of the jurisdictions and duties of the various bank regulatory agencies mentioned earlier would be folded under the umbrella of responsibilities of one single federal banking commission, organized by functional area. This would leave the FDIC to exclusively administer federal deposit insurance funds and the Federal Reserve free to focus only on the national and international effects of monetary policy.[38] This orientation would eliminate the current overlapping of responsibilities and jurisdictions that is the case under the current structure, in addition to providing for clearer information dissemination and feedback channels. Overall, the end effect is increased efficiency and better management of the bank regulatory process. Moreover, this new framework makes logistical sense with respect to the opening of Mexico and the creation of the North American market because it too will have a functional or transactional—not institutional—orientation as the borders between the three NAFTA nations are meshed together.

Conclusion

By way of conclusion, the main message to be derived from this analysis is that the North American banking and financial services sector is amidst a great period of evolution infused with both internal and external change. Likewise, the competitive landscape of the market is also currently in flux with the keys to sustained future success in this increasingly global environment embedded deeply within this process of evolution. Internally, technology is literally redefining and reconstructing banking as we have known it. Traditional ways of doing business that have been in place for decades are changing in nature and execution. Banking operations, distribution, and profitability are all adopting new components which must be understood quickly and utilized strategically through the effective and flexible management of change as a process. In addition, the focus of the banking sector's efforts—the modern day customer—is much more complex and informed, which makes the corresponding set of requirements in a service industry like banking all the more difficult to satiate.

Externally, the nature and parameters of the North American financial market are also evolving as NAFTA's scope continues to affect the financial markets of the entire continent, and the information highway brings forth a truly universal or global marketplace. NAFTA assumes this particular magnitude of significance because Mexico, a small but very strategically significant Latin American market, could perhaps be the first cog in the machine that will one day integrate the economies of the Western hemisphere. Within this perspective, no bank that strategizes on a global scale can afford to miss an opportunity to get in at the ground level of this process, regardless of the size (or lack thereof) or risks involved in the endeavor. Consequently, NAFTA and Mexico are actually part of a broader competitive framework that stretches far beyond the borders of North America to encompass a much larger technology-driven global framework—an understanding of which is truly essential to being competitive in the marketplace of tomorrow.

Notes

1. Haraf, William S., 'NAFTA Opens Doors to Mexican Markets for U.S. Banks,' Bank Management, January/February 1994, p. 29.
2. Orr, Bill, 'NAFTA—if approved—Would be Good for Banks', *ABA Banking Journal*, November 1993, p. 56.
3. Demographic and economic data taken from the North American section of the World Congress 'Business Intelligence Briefings—1995,' DRI/McGraw-Hill, 1994.
4. Makler, Harry, *Regional Integration and Trends in Financial Services*, Chapter 2 of this book.
5. Makler, Harry, *Regional Integration and Trends in Financial Services*, Chapter 2 of this book.
6. Smith, Geri and Wendy Zellner, 'The Gringo Banks are Drooling,' *Business Week*, September 13, 1993, p.84.
7. Hamid, S. *et al.*, *The Impact of NAFTA on North American Equity Markets*, pp. 167–8.
8. Smith and Zellner, p. 84.
9. Makler, Harry, Chapter 2 of this book.
10. World Congress, 'Business Intelligence Briefings—1995,' p. 61.
11. Smith and Zellner, p. 84.
12. Smith and Zellner, p. 84.
13. Zimmerman, K. A., 'Big Six Accountants Shift Strategy,' *Banker*, February 1991, pp. 13–14.
14. Tracey, B., 'IBM's Unit Mission: Focus on Speeding Technology to Banks,' *American Banker*, May 31, 1994, p. 12.
15. Kutler, J., 'AT&T, IBM, Unisys Join Bank Research Group,' *American Banker*, June 29, 1994, page 14.
16. Ohmae, K. *The Borderless World*, McKinsey & Company, Inc., 1990, p. 114.
17. Gregor, W. and J. M. Sandler, 'Home Banking May Arrive Via Data Superhighway,' *American Banker*, June 20, 1994, p. 18.
18. Corby, C. V., 'Consumer Technology and Its Effect on Banking,' *Bank Marketing*, March 1994, pp. 24–7.
19. Gregor and Sandler, p. 19.
20. Corby, p. 25.
21. Gregor and Sandler, p. 18.
22. Gregor and Sandler, p. 18.
23. Cisney, K. M., 'The Marriage of Mortgage Lending and Technology,' *Mortgage Banking*, April 1993, p. 66.
24. Cisney, p. 66.
25. Prakash, S., 'Big Lenders Fear They'll Be Cut Out As Fannie, Freddie Build Technology,' *American Banker*, February 14, 1994, p. 10.
26. Mastrull, D., 'Banks are Banking on Technology,' *Philadelphia Business Journal*, May 13–19, 1994, p. 29.
27. Mastrull, p. 29.
28. 'Financial Information: Moving Markets,' *Fortune Magazine-Information Technology Special Report: Special Advertising Supplement*, Autumn 1993, p. 88.

29. Strachman, D., 'Bankers Trust Installs Wire Trading Systems,' *American Banker*, August 16, 1994, p. 13.
30. Study based on 1993 analysis of transactions made from more than 3500 accounts at 10 U.S. banks including Banc One Corp. and Huntington Bancshares, Inc.—Cited in *Business First* newspaper's article 'Bank Technology Makes Branches Less Popular' November 29, 1993.
31. Marjanovic, S., 'Huntington Bancshares Inaugurates Its First Full Service "Virtual Branch",' *American Banker*, October 17, 1994, p. 26.
32. Bowen W. J., 'The Direct Route to Improved Retail Profitability,' *The Bankers Magazine*, July/August 1994, pp. 49–50.
33. Zack, J., 'More Big Banks Team Up for Processing,' *American Banker*, September 28, 1994, pp. 1–15.
34. Barnett, R. E., 'Government—The Third Party in Consolidation Discussions,' *The Banker's Magazine*, July/August 1994, p. 7.
35. Zuckerman, S. 'What Worries Bankers Now? Mostly, It's the Competition,' *American Banker*, October 7, 1994, pp. 1–2.
36. Crone, R., 'Technology Is Bringing Banking Without Banks,' *American Banker*, September 8, 1994, page 16.
37. Barth, J. *et al.*, Chapter 4 of this book.
38. Barth, J. *et al.*, Chapter 4 of this book.

8

Beyond NAFTA: Banking Trends in Latin America

EMMANUEL N. ROUSSAKIS

Introduction

The early 1990s mark the beginning of a period of dramatic changes for the commercial banking industry in Latin America. Economic reforms launched by the governments of Latin America to restructure their economies are breaking down the traditional and legal barriers that have long separated financial institutions and are thrusting banks as the catalysts for the consolidation of the financial sector. More important, as individual economies are becoming increasingly interlinked, market forces are fostering the emergence of regional players in the market for financial and banking services.

This study discusses the development of commercial banking in Latin America. It reviews the forces responsible for the transformation of the banking industry and addresses the current trends. Although the pace of change currently affecting the banking industry in Latin America varies somewhat from one country to another, its direction is consistent with trends in other parts of the world.[1] Consolidation of commercial banks has been the key characteristic of the banking industry in Latin America. The move toward regional integration in the framework of the Southern Cone Common Market (Mercosur) and the prospect of the Free Trade Area of the Americas (FTAA) by year 2005 provide impetus for the emergence of regional financial conglomerates that will compete aggressively in hemispheric markets.

Development of Commercial Banking

Although individual banks appeared earlier, the development of the financial services industry in Latin America dates from the 1920s and 1930s, when central banks were established to exercise monetary policy and regulate banking systems. These systems were composed of a mixture of private and public financial entities. By 1960, there were 22 monetary authorities in Latin America that supervised and regulated 465 commercial banks and 15 official development banks. Among the commercial banks, 118 were official and mixed banks, 286 were private national banks and 61 were foreign banks.[2]

From a functional perspective, the financial system was divided into a number of discrete components that did not compete directly with each other. Each type of financial institution attracted certain kind of funds and offered rather specialized types of services. This compartmentalization was especially true with credit institutions. Commercial banks, for example, relied on sight deposits from individuals and corporations to extend loans to businesses; mortgage banks and savings and loan associations received savings deposits and offered mortgage loans; and credit unions (cooperatives) pooled member savings to make installment loans to their members. Businesses accounted for a sizable part of the local credit demand, although there was heavy competition from governments for a limited amount of local currency financing. Commercial bank loans to businesses were generally of short-term maturity and were extended for financing trade or carrying working capital. Medium- and long-term financing was generally limited. The main source of longer-term credits, to the extent available, was from state-owned development banks for priority projects. In certain countries, some medium- and long-term credits were also available through investment banks, private development banks, finance companies (*financieras*) and similar institutions. Long term security and equity markets were generally thin, and little local capital was available from these sources.

For other financial intermediaries, the situation was no different. Laws and regulations ensured that the functional division was fairly clear and that each type of institution operated as a separate line of commerce. That segmentation contributed to very specialized financial systems with minimal competition throughout.

The growth of group banking in the United States and the consequent enactment of legislative reforms had a profound effect on the manner in which financial services were delivered in Latin America. One type of group banking is the multi-bank holding company—a corporate entity that controls two or more banks. U.S. banks made increasing use of this vehicle in the early 1950s as a substitute for branching in states that limited or prohibited branch banking. The U.S. Bank Holding Company Act of 1956 subjected the formation, expansion and merger of multibank holding companies to regulatory control. As this law did not address corporations that held a single bank, the ensuing years witnessed a spectacular increase in the number of one-bank holding companies. The latter type of group banking evolved in response to the competitive environment in which U.S. banks operated and to the increased public demand for the delivery of varied banking and financial services. One-bank holding companies enabled banks in the United States to establish affiliated institutions (that is bank holding company subsidiaries) engaged in traditionally nonbanking business. This development prompted legislative reforms in 1970 that amended the 1956 law in a manner that erased, for all practical purposes, the regulatory distinction between multi-bank and one-bank holding companies. Moreover, the 1970 reforms provided regulators with a framework for determining the permissible activities in which bank holding companies could engage. The list of permissible activities has grown considerably over the years to include a wide range of financial services, such as leasing, credit cards, factoring, data processing, and financial advisory services.

The U.S. approach in the delivery of financial services has been referred to as 'supermarket banking,' 'supermarket of financial services,' and 'financial supermarket.' These terms have been used loosely to describe one-stop shopping for financial services, similar to supermarket retailing of food and other products. The U.S. concept of a financial supermarket is no different from the European approach to banking—the German concept of 'universal banking.' Reputedly coined by Deutsche Bank, universal banking refers to the extension of a full range of banking and financial services by one legal entity.

That system in the delivery of financial services was also introduced in Latin America. In some countries banking laws were amended to allow for the formation of financial groups through holding companies. In Mexico, for example, legislative reforms enabled institutions that were associated or were part of the same consortium to be brought together to provide a broad range of financial services. In other countries there were no effective regulatory barriers to such groups; as a result, their formation came much earlier. In Brazil, for example, the financial group Bradesco was established in 1943 by 39 companies and covered a wide spectrum of financial services, ranging from loans to agriculture, commerce and tourism, to leasing, insurance, and data processing. Bradesco and other similar groups were created to perform a basic function: the mobilization of financial resources. The nascent state of domestic capital markets prompted many innovative businessmen to establish such groups to secure the self-financing of their undertakings. In many countries, textile, food, beverage and other industries became the springboard for the establishment of financial institutions (e.g., banks, investment companies, and insurance companies) as well as financial groups offering a wide array of services. Whatever the circumstances that prompted their creation, financial groups played an important role in the mobilization and allocation of financial resources in each country.

By the mid-1970s there was a considerable increase in the number and variety of financial institutions operating in Latin America. That increase manifested in all the sectors and fields of banking—central banks, commercial banks and other financial institutions. Specifically, by 1975, there were 24 monetary authorities in Latin America presiding over systems composed of 720 commercial banks and 547 other institutions. The commercial banking systems included 168 official and mixed banks, 406 private national banks, and 146 foreign banks.[3] Although institutional development was characteristic in all cases, in relative terms, two categories stood out between 1960 and 1975: foreign banks and other financial institutions. The participation of foreign banks in the commercial banking systems of Latin America rose from 61 (13.1 percent of the total) in 1960 to 146 (20.3 percent) in 1975. This rise was primarily due to the increased presence of foreign banks in Panama and its emergence as an international banking center. Institutional development was even more rapid in the case of other financial institutions which comprised such entities as public development banks, specialized banks, mortgage banks, and savings banks. The relative participation of these institutions in the financial systems of Latin America increased from 15 (3 percent of the total) in 1960 to 547 (42.4 percent) in 1975. Leading in the development of these institutions were Brazil (151), Mexico (100), Argentina (85) and Venezuela (39). Some of these institutions were established by the government while others were a product of private initiative.

The increase in the number of commercial banks and other financial institutions during this period reflected the pace of economic and social development in the region. As a result of this momentum, not only the number and variety of financial institutions increased, but also the volume and growth rate in the financial assets held. Between 1960 and 1975, the financial assets of the commercial banking system alone increased from $18.7 billion to $65.2 billion (constant 1973 dollars). This increase represented an average annual real rate of growth of 9.3 percent—a rate that implies a sustained and rapid expansion for the period under consideration. Most of the growth occurred from 1964 on. Specifically, between 1964 and 1967, real growth averaged 9.1 percent per annum, compared to 4.3 percent for the years 1960–63. Growth continued unabated for the remainder of the period attaining a record average real rate of about 12 percent per year during 1968–75.[4]

Evidence suggests that, at least through the 1970s, the Latin American financial system functioned well in meeting the developmental challenges of the region. The economic momentum of the 1960s and 1970s played an important role in developing manufacturing and industry and transforming the region's economies. This momentum attracted foreign capital, which continued to flow into Latin America even after the onset of the energy crisis. Indeed, the drastic increase in oil prices in 1973–74 had a profound effect on the economic growth of industrial countries and the European Community, in particular, a favored destination of U.S. investment funds in the postwar decades. As the oil-dependent economies of Europe began to slow down, the flow of U.S. foreign direct investment was funneled elsewhere, with part of it directed toward developing countries. Latin America received a large share of these funds, because of its growth momentum relative to that of the industrialized countries. The region's rapid economic growth in the 1960s and early 1970s increased income levels and expanded national markets, creating significant investment opportunities to foreign capital, which government policy generally favored over imports. The Latin American governments of the 1970s, although bureaucratic and authoritarian, welcomed foreign investment and appeared to guarantee political stability. By the end of the 1970s, that combination of economic and political factors had caused Latin America to account for about half of the total stock of foreign direct investment located in the developing world.[5] Within Latin America, foreign direct investment was concentrated in the relatively more industrialized economies with large domestic markets—countries like Argentina, Brazil, Chile and Mexico.

Consolidation of the Banking Industry

Although the flow of foreign capital to Latin America grew significantly during the 1970s, its composition underwent radical changes during that decade and through the early 1980s. Foreign direct investment, traditionally the major source of foreign capital for developing countries, accounted for a declining share of the total capital flows to the region during that period. Debt capital from commercial lenders replaced equity as the major component of capital inflows. The increased supply of petrodollars from the Organization of Petroleum Exporting Countries (OPEC) countries prompted U.S. banks active in international lending to engage in a large scale secondary recycling.

OPEC funds thus found their way to oil-dependent developing countries which had incurred record balance of payment deficits that had to be financed.

Commercial bank lending to Latin America grew rapidly until the early 1980s. Pursuit of a tight monetary policy in the United States to curb inflationary pressures led the country into a deep recession, which reduced the demand for imports and adversely affected world commodity prices. Similar conditions in other industrialized countries accentuated those trends and contributed to the collapse of the export markets of debtor nations, with drastic consequences on their ability to service their debt to major banks around the world. When, in August 1982, Mexico announced to the world its inability to meet scheduled external debt payments, it set off an international debt crisis. That announcement produced a chain reaction and within a year, 30 other debtor countries—including the major countries in Latin America—followed suit. With the onset of a debt crisis, new lending to the region dried up and many U.S. banks took large losses.

The recession of the industrialized countries and the debt crisis ushered a period of contraction for the economies of Latin America. High real interest rates and increased indebtedness precipitated the failure of many private firms, leading to serious liquidity and solvency problems for many banks and other financial intermediaries. As the crisis deepened it triggered a wave of failures among banks and other financial institutions, resulting in significant consolidation of the industry. In Argentina, for example, more than 30 banks and 500 other financial institutions ceased operation between 1977 and 1987, while 93 institutions were intervened by the central bank. In Chile, more than 50 conglomerates and their associated banks came under direct governmental control, and 15 banks and other financial institutions closed. In Mexico, the financial crisis precipitated the nationalization of the country's major banks. The end result of those developments was a general decline in the number of financial institutions operating in Latin America and an increase in the role and importance of official banks. Banking systems were *de facto* nationalized and economic policy moved back toward controls.

Austerity programs introduced by several Latin American governments depressed domestic demand and slowed growth to a trickle. As local conditions became distinctly unattractive to foreign investment and the economies deteriorated further, a number of major countries began a transition to democratic regimes. The new regimes were pressured by the U.S. government and the international lending organizations (the World Bank and the International Monetary Fund) to adopt the appropriate micro- and macroeconomic measures necessary for successful economic reforms and debt resolution. These pressures yielded drastic changes in the domestic policies of debtor nations. Latin American governments committed to restructure their economies in order to restrict government influence on price setting, to foster greater reliance on market forces, and to promote private ownership across the economy. Typical of the new policies adopted were major market-opening measures that, in combination with broad fiscal reforms, bolstered the return of flight capital and spurred foreign investments. Those measures encouraged the foreign acquisition of domestic firms and the participation of foreign capital in sectors that were once reserved exclusively to domestic private or public ownership. The governments of Latin America sought to benefit from the contribution of foreign direct investment to specific development priorities.

Consistent with their new policies, many governments announced ambitious plans to privatize government-owned banks and other firms. Privatization was viewed as the vehicle to eliminate the large number of state enterprises, yield billions of dollars in cash revenues and contribute to debt reduction by requiring buyers to effect partial payment in foreign debt paper traded in the secondary market. Privatization was also expected to reduce government subsidies and budgetary deficits, while strengthening the institutional structure of the region's financial markets and encouraging the creation of more competitive industries. Although the timing of that reform process has varied from country to country, its effects have been felt by most of the countries within the region. The earliest privatization efforts are associated with Chile, Argentina and Mexico. These embody the challenges inherent within the process.

Chile

Privatization in Chile occurred during two phases. The first took place between 1974 and 1978, and came after General Pinochet's military coup removed the socialist regime of Salvador Allende that had nationalized many banks and other corporations in the early 1970s. During its 'reprivatization,' the Pinochet regime returned some of the companies and banks to their original owners, especially those corporate groups and individuals who were among the domestic business elite. In many instances, the government received no reimbursement. In other instances, companies and a large number of banks were sold to private investors. Most of these sales were conducted by auction, but some assets were awarded by direct, noncompetitive sales, and most purchases were made by a relatively small number of domestic conglomerates known as *grupos*. The total sales netted some $543 million, and are estimated to have provided a 30 percent subsidy to the buyers, almost all of whom were Chilean.[6]

Because the government imposed no limits on the amount of equity these groups could acquire, and because it agreed to accept payment in installments, it assumed a major portion of the risk. Many of the *grupos* highly leveraged their acquisitions and further borrowed heavily to modernize them. Thus, when recession struck in the early 1980s, a large number of firms and financial institutions failed, and the Pinochet regime was compelled to renationalize them.

The second round of Chilean privatization took place in the mid-1980s. Having learned from its earlier experiences, the Pinochet regime made sure that the privatization process was better regulated and resulted in a wider distribution of ownership that included nearly all sectors of the economy. Reprivatization was accomplished by the sale of small packages of stocks to numerous investors; sale of large stock packages to a smaller number of certifiably solvent domestic and foreign investors; and a mixture of both approaches. Many corporations were sold on Chile's stock exchange, and opportunities to purchase stock were offered to employees and workers. Whereas domestic *grupos* had acquired most of the banks and companies during the first round of privatization in the 1970s, foreign investors played a major role in the 1980s, obtaining up to 10 percent of the equity of corporations offered on the stock exchange. Their participation was facilitated by their access to Chile's debt/equity swap program which allowed the exchange of foreign debt for equity in domestic firms. Chileans were excluded from this program.

By 1990, more than 500 state-owned corporations and banks were privatized, placing some 75 percent of the GNP in private hands. Among the most prominent banks to be privatized were Banco de Chile and Banco de Santiago, shares of which were sold to the public at large. Other major banks like Banco Concepcion and Banco Internacional were sold directly to domestic investors. The banks completed their recapitalization by 1987, by which time Banco de Chile had some 39,000 shareholders, and Banco de Santiago had 16,000. Generous credit facilities to small investors had encouraged their participation, and limits on stock sales ensured diverse ownership (popular capitalism), avoiding the concentration of divested assets experienced in the 1970s. As a result, by the end of the decade, private banks dominated a banking system that was closely regulated by the Central Bank and the Superintendent of Banking.

A robust local economy, banking reforms and the most stringent regulatory oversight in the region enabled the Chilean banking system to become the strongest in the area. By providing for repatriation requirements and other capital controls, Chile discouraged foreign short-term capital flows. Consequently, unlike other countries in Latin America—and for that matter other emerging economies in Asia and

Central Europe—Chilean financial markets did not suffer from the effects of the Mexican peso devaluation and faltering investor confidence in the first months of 1995. Uninterrupted growth of the economy, at an average annual rate of 7 percent in real terms from the mid 1980s forward, fostered the continued growth of the banking sector. This growth, combined with the strong credit culture of Chilean banks, resulted in high asset quality and, consequently, low provisioning pressures. This, in turn, contributed to the increased profitability of the banking sector, the highest in the region. In 1996, the Chilean banking system reported a 16.7 percent return on equity, with a 1 percent ratio for past due loans to total loans.

The strong performance of the banking system attracted foreign banks and intensified competition, which has in turn increased pressure on profit margins. To enhance their competitive position, some large banks sought to merge. For example, Banco Santander Chile—a subsidiary of Banco Santander of Spain—absorbed Banco Osorno in 1996, to form Banco Santander Chile. The same year, Banco O'Higgins and Banco de Santiago merged to establish Banco Santiago. The latter merger created the largest commercial bank in Chile, with a market share of 17.6 percent of the total loans in the system, compared to Santander's 13 percent. The merger will enable institutions to take advantage of improved efficiency and economies of scale, while offsetting continued pressure on profit margins from competition.

Consolidation is expected to continue, especially among the smaller institutions, as foreign banks or larger domestic banks try to build their market share. Consolidation will bring about further concentration in a system where the top seven banks account for 69 percent of the market. A recent banking law (General Banking Law, 1997) enables Chilean banks to move toward a universal banking model by allowing them to engage in activities including leasing, factoring and insurance. As holding company structures already permit banks to have affiliated institutions engaged in these related areas, the advantages of this law lie in cost benefits and improved efficiency. This legislation also permits bank expansion abroad through such vehicles as branches and subsidiaries. Chilean banks would have a comparative advantage over their neighbors as their banking system is more established, and has a track record of stability and a sophisticated regulatory system in place.

Argentina

Like Chile, Argentina experienced two waves of bank privatization, a less successful one in the 1970s and a more successful one in the 1980s.

The first phase began in 1977, when, for ideological reasons, the military initiated a program of financial liberalization. A new policy of 'decentralization of deposits' reduced reserve requirements, expanded the range of financial activities, offered deposit insurance, and opened markets to nonbank financial institutions. This policy rapidly increased the number of financial institutions operating in Argentina, as banks and other institutions increased profits by securing international financing at interest rates below domestic rates. Continued reliance on foreign financing increased the vulnerability of those institutions, and ultimately produced adverse consequences for the economy in the wake of the debt crisis. High domestic interest rates and high levels of debt undermined many private companies, and their inability to meet their payments ultimately led to numerous bank failures.

In 1987, the Alfonsin administration inaugurated a second phase of privatization by authorizing the Central Bank to auction 147 branches that had belonged to banks taken over by the state in the 1970s and early 1980s. Only nationally-owned, private banks were allowed to participate in the auctions, which occurred between December 1987 and March 1988. These resulted in the sale of 119 banks for $19.5 million.[7]

In addition, from as early as 1985, the Central Bank began selling off an assortment of assets it had acquired from liquidated financial entities, including real estate, vehicles, and fixed assets. It also supported the sale or merger of banks initiated by the parties themselves, while in other cases the Central Bank put out for bid banks it had acquired and restructured encouraging their merger with the buyer. Through this second process, foreign banks were able to acquire Argentinean institutions (e.g., Bank of America absorbed Banco Internacional). The terms of the two kinds of mergers and acquisitions differed significantly in price, forms of payment, financing, and facilities provided by the Central Bank to the purchaser. Altogether, the cost to the Central Bank of this restructuring has been estimated at $15.8 billion.[8]

Carlos Saúl Menem was elected president in 1988, and in 1990, his administration introduced its own economic program by relaxing legal restrictions to make the privatization process more flexible. Through the mid-1990s, Menem's program focused primarily on selling public utilities and services and did not greatly affect the banking sector. By accepting foreign debt at face value when that debt was presented as payment for state assets, the administration was able to keep the nominal sale price of the firms high, while significantly reducing the amount actually paid by the buyer. This practice encouraged foreign participation and the infusion of flight capital.

At the same time, it significantly reduced Argentina's outstanding foreign debt.

In addition to foreign investors, well-established domestic business groups were initially able to accrue a concentration of market power by forming conglomerates. However, later use of the stock exchange as a vehicle for achieving privatization provided greater diversity of ownership, while simultaneously increasing the market's depth and level of activity.

In 1994, the effects of Mexico's devaluation ('tequila effect') reverberated across Latin America, roiling financial markets and raising concerns about the stability of currencies throughout the region. Argentina, which like Mexico, depended on foreign short-term capital to finance its current-account deficit, was especially affected. As confidence in the country's financial system diminished, depositors—initially foreign and subsequently domestic—withdrew their savings and sparked a wave of bank runs. Ultimately, they withdrew some $8 billion from local banks, about 18 percent of deposits, and threatened to precipitate the collapse of the entire banking system.

To rectify the situation, the government implemented emergency financing measures that included tightening reserve requirements and forming a multibillion dollar fund to ensure liquidity. These measures were later replaced with a deposit insurance system and a $6 billion credit facility from international banks to be used for emergencies. In addition, the Central Bank introduced a new approach to bank oversight, in which the private and public sectors shared the burden of auditing the banks. Banks were required to be regularly rated by private credit-rating agencies, and to issue bonds worth at least 2 percent of their deposits each year. The price of the bonds thereby established an indicator of the market's perception of each bank's fiscal health.

Bank consolidation was another step taken to improve the health of the banking system. Some banks were forced to close while others were encouraged to merge. Banks owned by the provincial governments were restructured and privatized (with financial assistance from international development organizations), or are in the process of being sold off. Since 1995, the number of banks operating in Argentina fell from 200 to under 150. Experts anticipate an additional drop in the number of banks by 50 or so in the next few years. Moreover, foreign banks were allowed to acquire local banks and thereby infuse foreign capital into the system. As a result of these developments, the banking system is now more sound than in the past. The top 10 banks, benefiting from a flight to quality, now account for 75 percent of deposits, compared to about 60 percent when the Mexican crisis hit. Estimates indicate that Argentineans still hold some $50 billion in banks outside the country, as many citizens retain greater faith in foreign financial institutions than in Argentina's. Luring back these funds to domestic banks is not an easy task. Yet the greater presence of highly respected foreign institutions in Argentina will have a positive effect in this regard. Moreover, the presence of foreign banks will intensify the trend toward consolidation and competition for customers.

Mexico

Though in early 1983 the Mexican government began to close small, unprofitable public sector companies, significant divestiture did not start until the mid-to-late 1980s. Between 1989 and 1992, some of the most prominent state-owned enterprises were sold, including the telephone company, the largest steel producing company, and 12 of the country's 18 nationalized banks. Banks sold at auction commanded higher prices than initially anticipated, reflecting the market's confidence in Mexico's program, and the privatization process succeeded in facilitating Mexico's reentry into international financial markets. Foreign ownership in Mexican banks was tightly restricted. As in the initial privatizations in Chile and Argentina, a small number of wealthy, Mexican investors and domestic conglomerates gained control of most of the banking assets.

To protect investors from undetected bad loans in the banks' portfolio at the time of sale, the government provided rebate provisions. This practice had been followed in European privatization, since government accountants were not always as stringent as those working for private companies, and problem loans sometimes went undetected while the banks were under government ownership.

Many of the bidders sought to take advantage of Mexico's movement toward universal banking, in order to establish full service financial institutions. So fierce was the bidding for Mexican banks that buyers paid steep prices. The sale of 12 banks, for example, generated about $10 billion of proceeds for the government. This represented a price to earnings ratio of about 20, which far exceeded international averages for banks.[9] Payment of excessive prices placed banks under pressure to generate higher returns, which in turn encouraged aggressive lending and investing practices.

The extent of banks' exposure to risk became apparent in late 1994, as political uncertainty arising from the assassinations of three prominent leaders and serious economic woes undermined the faith in the economy. To restore investor confidence in the market, the government freed the peso from the narrow band within which it had previously traded. By March 1995, it had lost more than 50 percent of its value. This devaluation provoked a massive exodus of foreign short-term capital, even after the United States and international organizations injected $52 billion in loans and loan guarantees. Mexico's faltering peso quickly shook investor confidence in other Latin American nations, as investors perceived these countries to be vulnerable to similar economic conditions as those that spawned the Mexican crisis. In response, both domestic and foreign investors removed their capital from the region's financial markets and institutions.

Subsequently, Mexico took a number of steps to restore confidence in its economy and make it competitive once again. The government tightened its fiscal and monetary policies with steep budget cuts and a reduction in the monetary base. Moreover, a package of reforms gave private investors access to a new range of infrastructure sectors that had previously been solely in the government's domain. As a result, the economy bounced back in 1996, with a growth rate of 5.1 percent, employment levels increased, and credit demand was expected to rise again.

The crisis exacerbated problems already facing the banking sector. In spite of privatization, Mexico's banking industry was suffering from weak regulation, poor credit-risk analysis, indiscriminate lending, and inexperienced management, all of which had resulted in the growth of credit and a consequent escalation of non-performing loans. The crisis and the soaring interest rates that followed worsened the condition of Mexican banks by making it difficult for them to fund existing portfolios, or for borrowers to make loan payments. In 1995 and 1996, the government launched a series of comprehensive programs to support debtors and help out troubled banks. Although these measures provided significant relief, banks' financial condition remained weak. Moreover, new accounting requirements similar to the U.S. generally accepted accounting principles (GAAP) are expected to delay the banks' recovery further, even as these procedures bring Mexico into greater conformity with international banking standards. The requirements, which took effect on January 1, 1997, are expected to diminish the banks' asset quality ratios, as they require banks to place entire loans on nonperforming status once they are 90 days past due, or, in the case of mortgages, 180 days past due. Previously only overdue payments were placed on nonperforming status. As a result of the new standards, banks' total past due loans are expected to double, according to some analysts, mainly because of the impact of mortgage loans. Moreover, as interests may not be accrued once a loan becomes past due, banks' net interest margins are expected to suffer accordingly. In an environment of low credit demand, loan loss provisioning and declining net interest margins will place additional strains on profitability.

Pressure to raise more capital, especially among smaller and regional banks, is contributing to the consolidation of the banking sector and the increased participation of foreign shareholders. Repeated capitalizations have diluted the traditional family networks of bank owners to the point where a growing number of foreign investors have equity stakes in local banks. From just one non-Mexican bank (Citibank) at the start of the decade, foreign institutions now control 10 percent of the banking system. This figure, according to local bankers, might easily rise to half the total by year 2000. While providing necessary capital infusions, foreign shareholders are transferring technology, thus helping in the development of systems and operating procedures.

The Move Toward Regional Banking

The economy of Latin America in the late 1990s promises to be vibrant, and this expectation bodes well for the region's banking sector. In particular, Argentina, Brazil, and Mexico, which collectively account for 79 percent of Latin America's GDP, are rebounding from their financial crises of the mid-1990s, as increased foreign and domestic investment reinvigorates their economies. The region's GDP is expected to grow by 4.2 percent in 1997, up from 3.1 percent in 1996, and 1.2 percent in 1995. The increased growth rate will make Latin America one of the fastest growing regions in the world. At the same time, tight fiscal and monetary policies are expected to reduce the rate of regional inflation to about 12.8 percent, down from 16.4 percent in 1996.[10]

The strong growth rate is anticipated to produce greater regional integration, which in turn will generate new business opportunities throughout Latin America. The Southern Cone Common Market (Mercosur), the dominant economic bloc in the region, has a GDP of over $1 trillion, and accounts for almost 70 percent of the Latin American market. In addition to its original member nations—Brazil, Argentina, Uruguay, and Paraguay—Mercosur now includes Chile and Bolivia. Venezuela and Peru may join later. The expanded membership, along with greater trade among the original members, should increase Mercosur's intraregional trade to over $45 billion in 1997, up from $28.5 billion in 1995.[11] Moreover the recent addition of Chile to the Latin American common market allows the member nations to take advantage of Chile's fast track trade entry into the North American Free Trade Agreement (NAFTA).

Attracted by the new opportunities to do business in the region, multinational corporations are becoming major players within Latin American markets. The reduction in trade barriers, privatization of state-owned companies, local corporate restructuring, and the emergence of expanded markets created by Mercosur have contributed to the multinationals' entry into the region. For instance, with the expansion of such new regional industries as automobile, energy, consumer goods, and banking, multinationals are increasingly viewing Mercosur nations as bases for exporting their products throughout all of Latin America.

Pushed by the new competition from the outside, and without the trade barriers and protected markets, they had enjoyed for decades, local companies will have to focus on core businesses and divest non-strategic subsidiaries. Local family-owned conglomerates will be compelled to consolidate and restructure while expanding their core products and markets throughout the region. An increasing number of Brazilian and Argentine firms are affiliating to serve the Mercosur market, while others are forming joint ventures or business alliances with foreign corporations. As a result, mergers and acquisitions are expected to increase significantly. This trend is already evident, as merger and acquisition activity at the beginning of 1996 was 50 percent greater than during the same four-month period in 1995, and much of that growth resulted from foreign investment. For example, foreign investment in Brazil accounted for half of the corporate acquisitions in 1996, compared to less than 35 percent in 1995.[12]

Regional integration in the framework of Mercosur is initiating liberalization of financial markets. The complexity of the regulatory frameworks of member countries and the restructuring taking place within their domestic banking markets are likely to slow the pace of integration of financial markets. Nevertheless, the groundwork has been laid with the adoption by the Mercosur members of the uniform capital adequacy requirements for banks, agreed upon by the major industrialized countries in Basle, Switzerland. Moreover, central banks of member countries have agreed to broad policy goals for the year 2000 that entail the liberalization of financial transactions and the free flow of capital within Mercosur.

Banking Strategies

Individual banks have already taken the lead in the process for regional expansion. Some banks have made outright acquisitions, while others have been opening branches, or are forming strategic alliances. For example, Chile's Banco Santiago has invested in Argentine and Peruvian banks; the Brazilian Banco Itau, a technologically-advanced and one of the best managed institutions within the region, is creating a large branch network in Argentina where it plans to invest over $70 million and open a new branch every month; and Infisa, a Chilean financial group that owns Banco Concepcion in Chile and Banco

Consolidado in Venezuela, has announced an agreement with an investor group to purchase banks in other countries and launch Latin America's first regional retail banking network.

Outside investors still promise to make the greatest impact within the region. Canada's Bank of Nova Scotia and Bank of Montreal have made significant investments in Latin American banks. However, Spain's Banco Santander, Banco Bilbao Vizcaya, and Banco Central Hispanoamericano have made the largest investments. The Canadian interest in Latin American banks has stemmed in part from the 1993 North American Free Trade Agreement (NAFTA), which has stimulated trade between Canada and Mexico. The Spanish, on the other hand, are taking advantage of the linguistic and cultural similarities they share with Latin Americans, and seek to garner profit margins that are considerably greater than in their home market. Moreover, the recent crises have offered them opportunities for acquiring Latin American banks at bargain prices. Banco Santander, which eventually plans to invest about a quarter of its capital in Latin America, has taken the strongest position in the market. It has already acquired banks in Chile, Mexico, and Venezuela, and, unlike its rival Spanish banks that rely on joint ventures, loose alliances, and minority ownership, Santander has purchased full control of its acquisitions and plans to integrate them into a regional network under its own name that will operate out of Chile. Table 8.1 identifies recent major purchases by the Spanish banks in Latin America.

Foreign banks are targeting medium-sized businesses and a huge, untapped consumer market. The retail-banking business may prove to be among the most lucrative for foreign banks, as a growing middle class emerges within the region. Low inflation and a projection of continued economic growth have created an attractive environment for retail banking to serve this new class of consumers. The huge potential of this market may be evident in the ratio of total bank loans to gross domestic product, which is presented as Table 8.2, for selected Latin American countries. As seen in this table, except for Chile, at 52 percent, the ratio for all other countries was very low. In the case of Venezuela, the ratio did not even exceed the 10 percent mark. By contrast, in the United States, the ratio was about 80 percent. This situation has contributed to interest rate margins that are two or three times the size of those earned in industrialized nations.

Citicorp, the most important U.S. bank to respond to this potential, has already announced plans to purchase retail banks to strengthen its existing network within Latin America. It will compete not only with local banks, but also with emerging regional banks such as Infisa. London-based Hong Kong and Shanghai Banking Corporation (HSBC) Holdings plc is also entering new retail-banking markets by

TABLE 8.1 *Major Acquisitions by Spanish Banks in Latin America, 1995–97*

Institution	Country	Percentage Ownership	Price ($ millions)
Banco Bilbao Vizcaya SA			
Grupo Financiero Probursa (1995)	Mexico	90%[1]	$495
Banco Continental (1995)	Peru	35	130
Banco Ganadero (1996)	Colombia	40	328
Banco Provincial (1996)	Venezuela	40[2]	n.a.
Banco Frances (1996)[3]	Argentina	30	350
Banco Santander SA			
Banco Mercantil and Banco Interandino (1995)	Peru	100	90
Banco Osorno (1996)	Chile	Merger	483
Banco Mexicano (1996)	Mexico	75	425
Banco de Venezuela (1996)	Venezuela	90	338
Banco Rio de la Plata (1997)	Argentina	35[4]	594
Banco Comercial Antioqueno (1997)	Colombia	55	144
Banco Geral do Comercio (1997)[5]	Brazil	51	220
Banco Central Hispanoamericano			
Banco de Colombia	Chile	75[1]	250
O'Higgins Central Hispano[6]	Chile	50	n.a.

[1] Purchase of shares began in 1991.

[2] May rise to 57 percent as a result of an agreement with Credit Lyonnais of France for an additional 17 percent stake valued at $300 million.

[3] In August 1997, Banco Frances del Rio de la Plata acquired 72 percent of Banco de Credito Argentino. BBV's intent was to merge both institutions into a single entity.

[4] May rise to 50 percent, as a result of an option to acquire an additional stake.

[5] In August 1997, Banco Geral paid about $500 million for a slightly higher than 50 percent stake in Banco Noroeste, thereby providing Santander with a presence in southern Brazil.

[6] Holding company for Banco Santiago and Banco O'Higgins.

Source: J. Friedland and C. Vitzthum, 'Spanish Banks Push into Latin America,' *Wall Street Journal,* October 25, 1996, p. A11; T. Vogel and C. Vitzthum, 'Venezuela Banks Snag Foreign Investors,' *Wall Street Journal,* December 20, 1996, p. A12; *Wall Street Journal,* May 8, 1997, p. A18; J. Friedland, 'Foreign Acquirers Bolster Argentina's Banking System,' *Wall Street Journal,* May 28, 1997, p. A15.

expanding its investment beyond Chile. In addition to a stake in Mexico's Grupo Financiero Serfin SA and an equity position in Peru's Banco del Sur, HSBC has acquired Banco Bamerindus of Brazil and Roberts SA de Inversiones of Argentina, a diversified financial group. The combined assets of these banks amount to $49 billion.

Regulatory Trends

For these and other foreign banks, the region presents a very different opportunity than it did 20 years ago. Chastened by their earlier experiences, some Latin American governments are implementing regulations to avoid bank failures similar to the 1970s, 1980s, and mid-1990s.

TABLE 8.2 *Ratio of Total Bank Loans to Gross Domestic Product for Selected Latin American Countries in 1996*

Country	Percentage
Chile	52
Colombia	35
Brazil	30
Mexico	30
Argentina	23
Peru	17
Venezuela	9

Source: Thomas T. Vogel, Jr., 'Foreign Banks Target the Little Guy in Latin America', *Wall Street Journal*, October 9, 1997, p.A15.

They have increased capitalization requirements to ensure that banks are able to sustain losses during economic slumps and to encourage investors to monitor banks more closely. Argentina and Colombia, for example, have raised their capital requirements to 11.5 percent and 9 percent, respectively, well above the 8 percent international minimum standard set by the Basle Accord, and even above the standards in most industrial countries. Other Latin American countries employ the same capital levels as in the United States and Europe, despite the riskier environment. Many Latin American nations have also adopted more stringent accounting standards modeled after those used in the United States, although Brazil and Venezuela's procedures are more porous and leave greater room for bad loans to go undetected. Peru, on the other hand, has the most rigorous accounting system in the region. In several countries, banks are required to be regularly rated by private credit-rating agencies, and this likewise increases pressure for them to conform to responsible procedures. Table 8.3 identifies current regulatory trends in Latin America which are contributing to the creation of sounder banking systems.

Although the current trends have created a conservative regulatory regime they have not resulted in overregulation. In fact, as Table 8.4 shows, banks in the countries with the most conservative regulatory environment have earned the highest profits.

As seen above, Argentina, Peru, Colombia and Chile have imposed the most conservative banking regulations and their banks have been the most profitable. Forecasts for the next several years indicate sustainable profitability for the banks in these countries.

TABLE 8.3 *Current Trends in Regulation*

Trend	Relevant countries
Consolidated supervision of all entities owned by a bank or controlled by common shareholders	Chile, Peru
Increased sharing of credit information	Argentina, Peru
General provisions to reflect inherent loan risk	Peru
Mechanical rules for judging nonaccrual status of loans	Mexico
Stricter capital adequacy guidelines	Chile
Maintenance of high reserve (liquidity) requirements	Argentina, Brazil

Source: Brian R. Pearl, 'Latin American Banks,' *Industry Analysis,* J.P. Morgan Securities Inc., January 22, 1997, p. 6.

TABLE 8.4 *Regulatory Ranking and Real Return on Equity*

Country	Regulatory ranking	Real return on equity (%)	
		4Q/93–3Q/96	Next 5 years
Argentina	1	14.0	20.0
Brazil	5	13.3	18.0
Chile	4	16.9	18.0
Colombia	3	20.8	20.0
Mexico	6	–13.9	15.0
Peru	2	23.3	22.0

Note: Countries are ranked from 1 to 6, with 1 reflecting the most conservative, and hence least risky, environment.
Source: Brian R. Pearl, 'Latin American Banks,' *Industry Analysis,* J.P Morgan Securities Inc., January 22, 1997, p.1.

Conclusion

Economic reforms and regional trade agreements have encouraged the flow of foreign investments and have created a momentum for economic stability and deregulation. Open markets have increased the size and scope of banking services thrusting banks as the catalysts in the consolidation of the financial system. Latin American countries are witnessing the slow emergence of regional banking structures offering a complete range of financial services, modeled after the universal banking system of Europe, or the financial supermarket approach in the United States. This trend is expected to gain momentum in the years ahead, as the Free Trade Area of the Americas agreement is implemented. This trend will contribute further to the internationalization of the industry and the development of a hemispheric market which aspires to become the most important trade bloc of the next century.

This prospect for the future is the result of many years of privatization, stricter regulation and tighter accounting procedures, consolidation, greater diversification of ownership, greater foreign investment, and a move toward regionalism. As the economies within Latin America strengthen, inflation subsides, and Mercosur grows, the emergence of an expanding credit-hungry middle class is expected to increase the demand for a range of banking services and the number of domestic-based regional institutions. One result will be the dominance of the universal banking, or the financial supermarket, model. At the same time, the greater role of foreign banks will provide much needed infusions of capital and introduce new technologies and higher standards for assessing and granting loans. In turn, these new technologies and higher banking standards should push domestic banks, now operating in comparatively open markets, to higher levels of performance.

Increased competition is also expected to advance the current trend toward consolidation, as weaker banks become absorbed by their more successful and more efficient rivals. In particular, as multinationals and other large banks continue to upgrade their technology, many small and medium-sized local banks will not be able to compete. Many of those banks are acting forcefully to address these challenges, expanding their range of activities through mergers and acquisitions. Their capacity to successfully manage expansion will be continually tested, however, by increasing pressure from their larger and better-established competitors. These larger banks will continue to diversify their activities by building a growing portfolio of financial services that should allow them to protect and expand their market shares.

Squeezed between the larger and smaller banks, mid-level institutions will survive as niche players, concentrating on specific segments of the market, such as the needs of the middle-class or high-income customers.

Finally, as the earlier runaway inflation falls further under control, banks that once made easy profits, regardless of the soundness of their loans, now must master the arts of credit assessment and efficiency. Furthermore, bank supervision and regulation has now become more prudent and better enforced. At the same time the stronger presence of foreign banks and their ensuing competition with local banks will create an efficient banking environment. The ultimate beneficiaries will be Latin American corporations, small businesses and consumers.

Notes

1. E. N. Roussakis, 'The Banking Consolidation Trend in the United States, Europe and Japan,' *Academia*, No. 18, 1996, pp. 39–54.
2. Mario Rietti, *Money and Banking in Latin America* (New York: Praeger Publishers, 1979), pp. 76–77.
3. Rietti, pp. 76–77.
4. Rietti, pp. 40–41.
5. Bank for International Settlements, *Annual Report*, 1992, p. 93.
6. Melissa H. Birch, 'Foreign Direct Investment in Latin America during the 1990s,' in *Privatization in Latin America*, ed. Werner Baer and Melissa H. Birch (Westport, Conn.: Praeger, l994), p. 106.
7. Javier Gonzalez Fraga, 'Argentine Privatization in Retrospect,' in *Privatization of Public Enterprises in Latin America*, ed. William Glade (San Francisco: ICS Press, 1991). p. 86.
8. Kenneth P. Jameson, 'The Financial Sector in Latin American Restructuring,' in *Privatization of Public Enterprises in Latin America*, ed. William Glade (San Francisco: ICS Press, 1991), p. 124.
9. Birch, p. 107.
10. James Livingstone and Ellena Ochoa, 'A Brighter Future: Economic and Trade Outlook for Latin America,' *Latin America Trade Finance—A Latin Finance Supplement*, September 1996, p. 12.
11. Livingstone and Ochoa, p. 14.
12. Livingstone and Ochoa, p. 16.

9

Mexico and the IMF: Regional Banking Crisis—Global Consequences

JOHN A. ADAMS, JR

The function of the International Monetary Fund in the years since World War II has gone through a number of subtle evolutionary areas of emphasis, but none so pronounced as its role since the late 1994 devaluation of the Mexican peso. Global financial markets and national economies—both emerging and industrialized—were briefly but dramatically impacted by the seemingly sudden ramifications and aftermath of the economic turmoil brought on by the 'tequila effect.' A closer look at the role and reaction of the IMF in the wake of the Mexican crises is paramount for an understanding and the resolution of future debt crises and economic disturbances that can have disruptive consequences on banking in North America and beyond.

In the fall of 1994 it appeared that there was little that could derail the spectacular recovery and growth of the Mexican economy. All of Latin America, as well as emerging economies worldwide, looked to Mexico as a shining example of how to begin the transition from Third World status to emerging as a more internationalized economy. Two-way commerce with its trading partners (especially the United States) had risen significantly for five consecutive years, direct investment into infrastructure and industrial projects had exceeded the most optimistic projections, and portfolio investment in the newly rejuvenated Mexican stock market made the country the area of choice for investors worldwide. The ratification of the North American Free Trade Agreement (NAFTA) was to seal Mexico's emergence among the leading nations worldwide. The Mexican banking sector, on questionable footing until the reprivatization in the early 1990s, sensed a reprieve from the debt-devaluation cycles of the 1970s and 1980s.

Political upheaval during the year preceding the 1994 presidential election had caused concern among North American bankers and investors, but no apparent alarm. The Salinas technocrats and central bank gauged the hyper-levels of foreign investment activity in Mexico as the by-product of their successful economic recovery after years of stagnation and low growth. Yet, behind the scenes concern was raised that the peso was both over-valued and artificially pegged at a rate that did not reflect the true course of the Mexican economy, or the reality that the current account balance required the constant daily attention during 1994 by the Banco de Mexico to stabilize the value of the peso. The primary concern of the Salinas administration was to control the 1994 presidential transition. The failure to adhere to timely reporting on the true nature and condition of the Mexican economy raised investor expectations to a level such that the resulting crash in late December 1994 was that much more devastating. To this end, a post-devaluation assessment by the Mexican central bank lay blame for the crisis on the 'political difficulties' of 1994, and not on foreign exchange, a weak banking sector, or monetary policy.[1]

While volumes will be written to chronicle the events of 1994 and 1995 and the resulting reaction to the repercussions of the Mexican peso crisis, one element that has resurfaced as a pivotal component is the role of the International Monetary Fund (IMF) during and after the Mexican banking and currency crisis. The resulting assessment will strongly impact the role of the IMF during all future currency crises. While these post-devaluation events to recovery involved the intervention of the U.S. Treasury, the World Bank, the Bank of International Settlements, as well as a host of other financial intermediaries, the focus of this pre-sentation will be on the role of the IMF. The IMF is at the forefront of country specific economic performance, as well as the orderly review of economic policy and planning for over 120 developing countries. As the monitor of currency/economic stability, the IMF has emerged as the provider of lender-of-last-resort accom-modations for banks and 'explicit and implicit' government guarantees of bank liabilities. The scope of the 1994–95 currency crisis was beyond the ability of any bank, or group of banks, in North America to buttress the deterioration of the Mexican financial sector and currency. Furthermore, the final NAFTA agreement did not include either solutions or guidelines in the event of a currency or banking crisis like that which unfolded in 1995. NAFTA, however did provide a more open cross-border financial services environ-ment.[2]

Background

The Mexican role and association with the IMF has unwittingly made Mexico the center of, and an example of, debt crisis management and recovery over the past three decades. The oil-price shocks and devaluations of the 1970s, followed by the debt crisis of the mid-1980s, focused on the sensitive and fragile nature of balancing growth and development with the pressures of the global market place. In the wake of this series of crises, lending by multinational banks nearly halted as payment reorganization plans called for debt service schedules that demanded a range of solutions spanning debt forgiveness to long term repayment that over time diminished the future value and recovery of the investor. For their part, foreign commercial banks, prior to 1987, had violated a cardinal rule of prudent banking to reduce risk by avoiding the concentration of loans to a small number of similar customers. Awash with petro-dollars deposits from the boom days of the Organization of Petroleum Exporting Countries (OPEC), many North American banks allowed themselves to accept a great deal of foreign loan exposure. To return investor confidence, the IMF (with aid primarily from the U.S. Treasury via the Brady Bond debt restructuring agreements) endeavored to right the Mexican economy by lowering risk and devising measures to combat the harmful effects generated by factors outside of the control of the Mexican economy—such as rising interest rates sensitivity, irregular trade flows (or trade imbalances), and the management of investment flows (portfolio as well as direct foreign investment) that could possibly disrupt the fragile growing economy.[3]

Increasingly through the late 1980s, the IMF had worked with Mexico and a host of emerging nations to encourage stable economic conditions. The lessons of the 1980s stressed the fact that the return of foreign commercial banks and foreign investors (both corporate and individuals) hedged on country stability, largely in the form of open access to international credit facilities. The disruption of ready channels of capital in times of currency instability, inflation spurts, or political intrigue was paramount. In this regard the IMF and the World Bank both worked to reduce 'country risk' by encouraging and in some cases requiring the need for the continuous flow of timely economic and monetary data. These efforts to collect and require economic information, in the case of Mexico were prudent in concept yet short of timely reporting of key data. The lack of economic data transparency proved pivotal to a precise assessment and forecast of the true nature of the currency situation in Mexico during the early 1990s. By 1994, the void of timely reporting from Mexico proved critical.[4]

The last 'consultation' by the IMF in Mexico prior to the December

1994 devaluation took place in February 1994. Following this visit 'a lot happened' according to the IMF. A key indicator noted after the Mexican devaluation is that many IMF members do not fulfill the data reporting obligations 'particularly when they are in trouble.' IMF Executive Director Karin Lissakers noted that, 'the surveillance function [by the IMF] did not work as it should have in the Mexican crisis.'[5] The IMF had been viewed by investors and central bankers as an agency that would help gauge economic transitions within its member countries, as well as issue warning signals in advance of a potential crisis. The 1994–95 crisis pointed to the importance of such early warning for the resolving of future crises. While international capital markets and currency valuations will fluctuate and at best be imperfect, the added dimension of investor rationale or lack thereof, such as the Mexico-type currency crisis, will challenge each country to report the best available data on capital flows, portfolio investment, and government debt.[6]

IMF Response to the 1994–95 Crisis

It became apparent that the currency crisis and exodus of foreign investment from Mexico in early 1995 could have an extensive impact on not just Mexico and Latin America but markets worldwide. The magnitude of investment from the U.S. and other money centers in Europe and Asia was tremendous. North American investors, attracted by the high return on investments in tesobonos and cetes, had millions of dollars of pension funds tied to the Mexican stock market. While most foreign banks were not as exposed as they had been in the 1970s and 1980s, there were nonetheless significant loans in not only Mexico but throughout Latin America, that could be placed in jeopardy if Mexico could not restructure its loans and/or defaulted on debt obligations. Private, almost secret, consultations between officials at the IMF and the U.S. Treasury had begun in late 1994 to review a possible course of action in the event of a crisis. The conclusion of both agencies by late November and early December 1994 was that Mexico could not continue the flawed currency policy that artificially supported the overvalued peso.[7]

Initial efforts by the Clinton administration in January 1995 to develop a rescue plan (the old plan) fell short of fruition due to a reluctant U.S. Congress dominated by a Republican majority. By February, the situation in Mexico was critical. It became apparent that, first, action was needed to prevent a wholesale default, and second, no one agency was able to provide the financial resources needed to shore up the crisis. In late February, with Mexico on the verge of default, a joint plan (the new plan) by the U.S. Treasury and the IMF made available over $50 billion in currency swaps, loans, and guarantees to the Mexican government. The IMF, in the biggest loan ever granted to a nation, established a $17.8 billion facility in conjunction with $20 billion from the U.S. Treasury. Additional funds were provided in time to address the short and medium-term needs of Mexico[8] (see Table 9.1).

With a total financial disaster avoided, Mexico was placed under strict economic reporting and loan payment provisions. Even with the bailout package in place, financial markets in other emerging countries reeled from the so-called 'tequila effect', created by the shock of capital flight and investor disintermediation of funds from any market that was felt to mirror the Mexican situation. For example, all of Latin American, Thailand, Malaysia, the Philippines, South Korea, and most of the Eastern European countries were at once suspect. The recovery of the Mexican economy during all of 1995 and most of 1996 was painful. Furthermore, calls were made for the IMF to go beyond its obsession with price stability in debt countries. Shortly after the implementation of measures to correct the Mexican crisis

Table 9.1 *The Old and the New: A Comparison of the Mexico Plans.*

Funding Source	Old Plan	New Plan
U.S. Treasury	Guarantees of up to $40 billion of long-term Mexican bonds. Commitment of $9 billion from Exchange Stabilization Fund for short-term swaps of dollars for pesos.	Commitment of $20 billion from Exchange Stabilization Fund for: • Short-term swaps • Mid-term swaps • Guarantees of long-term Mexican bonds.
International Monetary Fund	$7.8 billion in direct loans.	$17.8 billion in direct loans.
Bank of International Settlements	$5 billion in direct loans.	$10 billion in direct loans.
Latin American Countries	None.	$1 billion in short-term swaps.
Canada	None.	$1 billion in short-term swaps.
Commercial Banks	$3 billion in new loans.	$3 billion in new loans.
Total	$64.8 billion.	$52.8 billion.

Source: Washington Post

the central bank noted the following impact on the budget balances and scarce credit:

> A surplus or at least a balanced budget was absolutely necessary to prevent the federal government from increasing its share of the scare financing available, thus avoiding both additional pressure to the already high interest rates and the crowding out of a credit hungry private sector. Also it was prudent to accumulate resources that could be necessary to support essential activities whose existence could be jeopardized by the crisis as was the case of the financial system.[9]

In the case of Mexico, inflation soared, construction and investment came nearly to a halt, unemployment rose to the highest levels in decades, and non-performing loans skyrocketed at all Mexican banks. The middle class was squeezed, average real wages plunged by more than 20 percent, over one million mortgage loans were in peril of default, and infrastructure development projects that had hallmarked the growth of Mexico during the early 1990s came to a standstill. The Mexican miracle touted by both economists and investors worldwide was, for the near term, over.[10]

Global Watchdog

The first substantive evaluation of the impact of the Mexican crisis and the future role of the IMF began in the spring of 1996. The role of the IMF was to fill a void. North American banks in 1994 and 1995, unlike in previous devaluations and currency crises, remained guarded in their estimation of the situation. A post-crisis assessment of the reaction of North American banks and the IMF involvement with Mexico resulted in an internal review of the means and measurements to better identify and manage future crises. Even more so after the Mexico crisis, the IMF was called on to be the 'global watchdog' of economic performance—ready to sound the alarm in the event of crisis. The primary weak points of the Mexican economy are: (1) lack of an institutional standard to attract investor confidence, (2) high inflation, (3) pressured public finances, and (4) complications and delays with the privatization process. These are issues other emerging nations face. As the primary holder of Mexican debt, the IMF had a vested interest. Total external Mexican debt was estimated to be $165 billion. Thus, the debt, along with the contraction of the Mexican economy by 6.9 percent in 1995, was reason for concern.

To address Mexican-style crisis prevention and detection, the IMF began to gauge all its programs, planning, and crisis response to a broader perspective on how to detect and mitigate future calamities. Country risk assessment and timely economic and financial information were paramount. In the weeks prior to the October 1996 annual meeting of the IMF (held jointly with representatives from the World

Bank) broad debate began on the means to address pre-crisis situations. The discourse was accented by the fact that the agency's financial liquidity was shrinking due to a record level of commitments of $26 billion (primarily to Mexico and the old Soviet bloc states) during the fiscal year ended April 30, 1996. Improvements included a wide range of initiatives:

- allowing more access to country specific economic data to investors, private industry, and government agencies via an electronic bulletin board;
- more frequent on-site country IMF inspections;
- more frequent IMF executive board meetings;
- selling up to 5 million ounces of the IMF's gold reserves (about 5 percent) to assist with the financing of long-term, below-market-rate loans;
- consideration for ways to issue outright financial grants;
- a move to double the General Agreements to Borrow facility from $25 to $50 billion;
- consideration to move toward a new issue of special drawing rights to shore up international accounts.[11]

These plans, while generally accepted, received mixed reviews from those nations that invest more heavily in the over $200 billion IMF revolving fund. Major decisions are driven primarily by the foreign ministers from the Group of Seven (G-7) industrialized nations composed of the United States, Japan, France, Italy, Germany, Great Britain, and Canada. While all were in agreement that adequate resources were needed by developing nations in light of the dynamic global course of trade and financial service, Germany and Italy opposed the sale of gold to create more ready funds and loans for multilateral debt-relief initiatives. The concern of these two nations hinges on the 1996–97 economic conditions in each country, that now boast raising expenses for social services and double digit unemployment. Notwithstanding, in late 1996 thirteen nations (Australia, Austria, Belgium, Denmark, Finland, Hong Kong, South Korea, Luxembourg, Malaysia, Norway, Singapore, Spain, and Thailand) agreed to contribute a combined total of $25 billion to a new IMF emergency credit line facility to be called the New Arrangements to Borrow. This action was intended to enhance the existing program known as the General Arrangements to Borrow financed by the G-7 and Saudi Arabia.[12]

However, the key issue that gained a significant amount of treatment was the need for transparent economic data and timely reporting on the part of all member nations. In the future, to be eligible for debt relief via bridge loans and grants, each country would have a stronger requirement to report economic trends. Furthermore, debtor nations will be required to maintain strict programs of market reforms. Debt relief for the world's heavily indebted poor countries (HIPCs) will cost in excess of $8 billion annually by the turn of the end of 1999. HIPCs have a debt-to-export ratio of over 500 percent—more than three times as high as the average for all developing countries. Objections to such seemingly harsh measures have been voiced by some to remove the fate of such emerging and reforming economies like those of eastern Europe and Russia 'out of the hands of inept and incapable economists at the IMF and devise a serious, direct program of Western aid and trade to the emerging democracies.'[13] Contrary to this view, many assume that the IMF is the post World War II vehicle to coordinate Western aid and financial assistance to emerging countries in time of crisis.[14]

With the introduction of an on-line bulletin board (on which each member country is 'required' to post valid, honest, up-to-date economic data), IMF members agreed to shift the burden of risk management increasingly to private sector investors and monitoring agencies. This move was directly related to the Mexican currency crisis, which opponents to the February 1995 U.S.-IMF package viewed as a bailout of private sector investors who need to assess their own risk and take their own losses. The financial markets of Wall Street, in a not-so-convincing argument, felt that they were 'caught by surprise' in December 1994 by the Mexican government's announcement to widen the band (i.e. devalue) in which the peso was traded. Experienced North American banks, fresh from the debt restructuring and Brady Bond era of the 1980s, knew differently. Regional and multinational banks had, during the early 1990s, begun to enhance their credit criterion, thus reducing loan exposure in Mexico. The most salient consequence of these new measures on the private sector is that the IMF in its assessment has put investors on notice—*caveat emptor.*[15]

Banking: Bedrock of Stability or Source of Crisis

The 1994–95 peso crisis had broad implications for not only Mexican banks, but also North American financial institutions with exposure in all parts of the globe. One sector that was impacted and continues to be under scrutiny is the banking sector in all developing countries. One in five banks in developing nations during 1995–97 faced a banking crisis. None can be more acute than the Mexican-style banking crisis that the IMF hopes to avoid in the future. The range of solutions to the core currency concerns in each emerging country have received a broad menu of measures to ensure stability. In most cases, the central bank (government-controlled) of these nations is linked directly to the currency control, reserve requirements, and exchange polices dictated to the member private banks.[16] In times of currency imbalances such as strained trade flows, increased foreign direct and portfolio investment, or capital flight, it is the IMF who has been the lender-of-last-resort. Such imbalances often compound to create secondary problems such as the rise of bad loans, unemployment, and crime.[17]

The resolution to localized banking problems in small economies is not as simple as one solution fits all. As was seen in Mexico, increased foreign investment did not bring about, nor insure, stability. Furthermore, the micro-management by the Mexican government and central bank to artificially prop up the peso did not insure currency equilibrium. 'Hot money' in the Mexican stock market—attracted there by the prospects of high return on investment and always prone to a rapid exit in cases of economic downturn—boosted investor interest in the country, but did not guarantee stability. One popular argument lively debated during 1994–96 was to install a currency board scheme that would peg the currency to a 'hard' currency such as the dollar. Often cited is the case of Argentina, where a currency board pegged to the U.S. dollar dropped inflation from over 2,000 percent to near zero. The currency board concept became a much debated critical element as a possible measure to stabilize the banking sector in Thailand during the 1997–98 Asian economic crisis. However, while Argentina felt the impact of the 1994–95 Mexico tequila effect, the currency board and financial planning of Menen-Cavallo team weathered the crisis. In the case of Thailand, a currency board was viewed as a quick fix. However, there were inadequate assets to allow a credible peg of the currency, thus the idea was turned down by the IMF (as well as by the U.S. Treasury officials who were closely monitoring the crisis).[18]

While Mexico has declined to establish such a currency board, it did set a new trend in further opening the domestic market to attract direct foreign investment, especially in the banking sector. Direct investment in the financial services sector was first expanded by the New Investment Law of December 1993, and further enhanced by market opening policies in early 1995. The net result has been a gradual, yet substantial, investment by foreign banks in partnership with existing institutions. In early 1997, the Mexican banking system began a modified use of generally accepted accounting principles (GAAP) standards that introduced consistency in reporting on balance sheets, asset valuation, mark-to-market pricing of security portfolios, and a stricter approach to charging off non-performing loans. By 1998, a weak banking sector, due primarily to a large unresolved portfolio of non-performing loans, further delayed the full implementation of GAAP. Notwithstanding, the primary source of this new foreign investment in Mexican banking continued to flow in from the United States, Canada, Spain, Japan, and Italy.[19]

Seven Factors: Measures of Potential Financial Crisis

It is imperative that North American banking institutions, both localized and multinational, clearly appreciate the factors that have, and that will, create exposure and country risk. The Mexican crisis of 1994–95 reinforced the need to evaluate fundamental factors to determine currency and economic stability.[20] By early 1998, the financial conditions of South Korea, Thailand, the Philippines, Poland, Indonesia, and Malaysia were routinely compared to the Mexican economy before and after the crash. The lessons learned by the IMF in Mexico in 1995 proved instructive during the Asian crisis of 1998. An understanding of these dynamics helped reduce or limit North American banking exposure. Thus, it has been the intent of experts and planners at the IMF to be more vigilant. In this regard, seven key factors will be stressed in the evaluation of financial turmoil and are important means to measure the course and stability of a nation's economy:

- *Current account deficit*—A large current account deficit (CAD), such as the one in Italy, is potentially the dilemma; however, a large deficit coupled with a high level of foreign debt and a sluggish economy can be problematic. As with the imbalance in Mexico in 1994, the current account deficit becomes a problem when it grows to a level greater than 5 percent of GDP. Thus, the CAD in Thailand at 7.7 percent, and in Malaysia at 9.7 percent, during 1996 was cause for concern.[21]
- *Mismatched short-term debt vs. foreign reserves*—In 1994 Mexico found itself in the predicament that daily investors became reluctant to rollover maturing debt if there becomes a possibility that the obligation could not be meet. In addition to hyper-investment and high rates of return, Mexico was faced with a daily vigil of selling more debt instruments to meet shorter and shorter maturing issues. In an effort to maintain confidence, measures were established to allow dollar-denominated payments; even this mechanism lost favor as the political intrigue and assassinations during the presidential campaign raised investors' fears. Furthermore, Mexican foreign exchange reserves covered less than 20 percent of their short term obligations. In contrast, countries on the watch list, such as South Korea, Indonesia, Thailand, the Philippines and Malaysia, have maintained varying

amounts of reserves to cover debts.[22] Much like Mexico, the IMF has required radical reforms of the tight relationship between the government and business conglomerates. At issue are a number of factors to include: first, the interest rate structure and controls, second, the role and power of an independent monetary authority; and third, a clearer method to distinguish between government 'planning' of national economic activities versus 'projections' of performance of the economy as a whole.[23]

- *Consumption vs. investment*—High levels of unchecked consumer spending and low, or no, savings can spell disaster for any country. In the five years prior to the December 1994 crisis in Mexico, spending and the extension of credit (most notable in the form of credit cards) outpaced savings and payments by consumers. While inflows of capital investments was significant, it did not match the country's ability to individually, or collectively, repay timely debt requirements. Another area that suffered was the new and growing middle class mortgage market that became over-extended as early as mid-1994. It should be noted that the level of unchecked spending and poor credit quality was much more of a factor than the level of consumer savings. In fact, Mexico has had a higher level of savings than the United States (see Table 9.2).

- *Budget deficit*—A current account deficit is cause to worry only if it reflects a budget deficit as opposed to private sector decisions about savings and investment. In 1994, Mexico's budget deficit to GDP ratio was 0.7 percent; in 1996, Indonesia's budget deficit forecast was 2.4 percent.[24] Banking problems and budget concerns continued into 1996–97. Progressively the problem escalated, even though in Thailand, for example, the central bank fended off attacks on the baht by spending in excess of $40 billion in foreign reserves by early 1997. Indonesia, the recipient of a $43 billion

Table 9.2 *International Average Savings Rates (Percent of GDP)*.

	1988-84	1988-91	1991-94
Japan	33.88	33.43	33.51
Developing Countries	25.10	25.55	25.47
Industrial Countries	21.00	19.73	20.36
European Union	21.12	19.30	20.26
Mexico	18.25	15.35	16.69
United States	15.90	14.93	15.41

Source: Baring Securities

bailout program from the IMF, hoped to cap its budget deficit at 3.2 per cent of GDP by early 1998.[25] Similar problems began to surface all over the Asian region. U.S., Mexican, and Canadian banks could ill afford to increase exposure outside obligations in North America.

- *Overvalued exchange rate*—The Mexican peso was overvalued even until late 1993. Investment flows and the Banco de Mexico's ability to manage the value of the peso within a narrow trading band were not apparent to the investing public until mid-1994. By July 1994, a number of private economists and governmental agencies by July 1994 pointed to a peso overvaluation of 17–21 percent. It was determined by the Salinas administration that a readjustment in the peso, or devaluation during 1994, would impact the electoral process. In terms of the dollar, currencies in the Philippines and Thailand were undervalued during 1996. Generally, undervalued currency runs a small chance of becoming a target of speculation. In contrast, South Korean currency by 1997 was overvalued in the 15–19 percent range. Mexican economist Roberto Salinas-Leon stresses the magnitude of the importance of a nation's currency valuation, noting that, 'In the final analysis, credibility is the key to maintaining the public's confidence in the future value of money.'[26] It should be noted that one significant result, seldom mentioned, of the post-Mexican crisis was the further dollarization of foreign currencies worldwide. Additionally, by early 1998, Asian currency uncertainties caused Mexican banks to place pressure on the central bank to consider a more expansionary fiscal policy. There was a major concern that liquidity in international financial markets was hampering the Mexican recovery—in spite of the poor bank loan portfolios.
- *Capital inflow composition*—The composition of foreign investment is paramount in a growing, emerging nation. It is preferable to have the largest percent of investment in foreign direct investment (FDI) that enhances the manufacturing, distribution, and infrastructure base of the country. In the case of Mexico and other attractive markets, investments tended to be short term portfolio capital in liquid investments—movable at a moment's notice in times of crisis. During 1993–94 Mexico averaged in excess of $7 billion per year in foreign investment inflows, mostly in the short term portfolio category. As reserves were depleted, there was more likelihood of a devaluation and capital flight. Direct industrial investment in South Korea, Malaysia, and the Philippines has trended toward long term industrial and infrastructure inflows. In contrast, the current account deficit of Thailand is composed almost exclusively of short-term capital.[27]

- *Rapid monetary growth*—During 1994, Mexico allowed its money supply to increase by 23 percent from the prior year. Large money supplies, as witnessed in Asia in 1997–98, are hazardous. The imbalance can bring on inflation, cheapen the value of exports, and disrupt a banking system that holds a high level of bad loans. The percentage of excess cash in the economies of the Philippines, Indonesia, and Thailand during 1996 averaged 21 percent. By late 1997, problem loans, currency weakness, and a failure to monitor current account balances resulted in instability. The Asian 'approach' of not clearly understanding (nor accepting) the dynamics of economic changes due to cultural considerations *can* and *will* have a tremendous impact on North American banking if there is a wholesale failure of a large number of Asian banks.[28] North American banking, in the NAFTA environment, will be presented with a broad array of tough decisions and competition for a stabilizing investment flows. In like fashion, the Latin American banking sector, that has always had tremendous reverberations on the overall exposure of North American banking, is 'squarely on a collision course with the world's other emerging markets for a limited supply of cash.'[29]

Conclusion

In the wake of the 1994–95 Mexican crisis, the IMF has once again reassessed the means to detect and manage future currency predicaments. While the diagnosis is at times difficult, the IMF and World Bank have entered a new era where it is paramount to have the transparency of economic data and financial/trade flows to help head off crisis situations. Policies and procedures, established in 1995–96 after the Mexican crisis, proved vital in addressing the Asian crisis of 1997–98. Such procedures were crucial in preventing banking and financial services operations in North America from being overly impacted. Like Mexico, the central banks and economic planners will become more accountable for fiscal policy. Mexico, in the aftermath of its crisis, now reports over 100 sets of statistical, money supply, and financial indicators weekly. Thus, such indicators as the current account deficits in emerging countries will no longer be viewed as benign.[30]

The impact of a regional economic crisis on North American banking has long involved an understanding of the secondary repercussions gestated from such events as the Asian crisis; most elements of which banks in the NAFTA region can not control.[31] The globalization of banking and financial services has, to some degree, spread the exposure, while at the same time casting concern on portfolio management and credit policies. As the IMF again learned, the Asian crisis of 1997–98 is but a prime example of how regional off-shore economic events can have broad global consequences. One important result is that North American banking was better prepared, both operationally and psychologically, to enhance regional banking, in spite of the spill-over effect from Asia.[32] A wave of merger and consolidation in North American banking (as well as new foreign direct investment[33]) and related financial services was very dramatic in the 1996–98 time frame. The result has been a series of changes in Canada, Mexico, and the United States. Direct foreign investment and merger mania, along with a more transparent national treatment approach to banking services, has prevailed[34] (see Table 9.3).

Finally, the aftermath of the radical currency devaluation and banking crisis in Mexico is that the post-crisis period to recover from a trauma can take years, even decades. While the IMF has been bullish in its efforts to encourage economic stability, it is clear that each such currency crisis will have lasting scares. Mexico was not the first, and will not be the last, to experience such upheaval. As other regions and economies adjust, so too does Mexico. In addition to yearly increasing the allowable percentage of foreign investment in the banking sector, Mexico will, for example, sell over $2 billion in problem assets during 1998, a process that will be closely watched by the IMF, as well as banks throughout the region. These activities will once again provide an advanced real-time market-tested means to attempt to improve the banking industry in Mexico. Such liquidation of bank

Table 9.3 *Foreign Capital Participation in Mexican Commercial Banks.*

Bank	Foreign Bank	% Equity Position
Citibank	Citibank, N.A.	100
Banco Alianza	GE Capital	100
Banco Santander Mexicano	Banco Santander	80
BBV Probursa	Banco de Bilbao y Vizcaya	65
Bancrecer	Allianz Bank Group	60
Inverlat	Bank of Nova Scotia	51
Banca Confia	Citibank, N.A.	50
Banca Serfin	Hong Kong Shanghai Bank & J.P. Morgan & Co.	28.5
Bital/Banco del Atlantico	Banco Central Hispanoamericano & Banco Central Portugues	28
Bancomer	Bank of Montreal	16

Source: National Banking and Securities Commission

assets will be yet another milestone in an ongoing series of significant actions directed at the bank restructuring activity since the reprivatization activities of the early 1990s.[35]

Notes

1. Robert S. Gay, 'Too Much Pessimism on Mexico?' *Perspectives on the Americas*, Bankers Trust Research, July 21, 1994, pp. 16–17; David Malpass, '20 Reasons Mexico Won't Devalue,' *Latin America Watch*, April 21, 1994, pp. 7–8; Debbie Galant, 'Why Wall Street Missed Mexico,' *Institutional Investor*, May 1995, pp. 73–6. See also John A. Adams, Jr. *Mexican Banking and Investment in Transition* (Westport: 1997).

2. *North American Free Trade Agreement Between the Government of the United States of America, the Government of Canada and the Government of the United Mexican States*, 1993, Chapters 11, 12, 14; 'Highlighting the Link Between Bank Soundness and Macroeconomic Policy,' *IMF Survey*, May 20, 1996, pp. 165–177. Note: More than two thirds of IMF member countries have experienced significant banking sector problems.

3. Luis Rubio, 'Stability and Stabilization in Mexico: A Historical Perspectives' as seen in James A. Dorn and Roberto Salinas-Leon *Money and Markets in the Americas: New Challenges for Hemispheric Integration* (Vancouver: 1996), pp. 79–99. See also Peter Korner, Germ Maass, Thomas Siebold and Rainer Tetzlaff *The IMF and the Debt Crisis: A Guide to the Third World's Dilemmas* (London: 1986) and Richard E. Feinberg and Valeriana Kallab, eds. *Uncertain Future: Commercial Banks and the Third World* (New Brunswick: 1984).

4. Steve Hanke and Kurt Schuler, 'Monetary Systems and Inflation in Developing Countries,' as seen in Dorn and Salinas-Leon *Money and Markets in the Americas*, pp. 235–58.

5. Sara Kane, 'Living with the Reality of Integrated Global Capital Markets,' *IMF Survey*, April 3, 1995, pp. 105–6.

6. Graham Bird, 'The International Monetary Fund and developing countries: a review of the evidence and policy options,' *International Organization*, Summer 1996, pp. 477–511.

7. Adams, *Mexican Banking and Investment in Transition*, pp. 87–106.

8. Press release: 'Camdessus Welcomes Advance Repayment of Loans by Mexico, Positive Developments in Mexican Economy,' International Monetary Fund, Washington, D.C.: January 15, 1997.

9. Guillermo Guemez, 'Comments to the Border Trade Alliance on the Strategy and the Evolution of the Economic Adjustment in Mexico,' Banco de Mexico, Mexico City, April 1996.

10. 'New Financial Order,' *The Journal of Commerce*, September 27, 1996, p. 8A.

11. Richard Lawrence, 'IMF acts on several fronts to shore up financial system,' *Journal of Commerce*, September 13, 1996, p. 2A; Lawrence, 'IMF: World financial system stronger; emerging-market nations still lagging,' *Journal of Commerce*, September, 19, 1996, p. 2A; Blair Pethel, 'Deferring Debt Relief,' *Journal of Commerce*, September 26, 1996, p. 11A.

12. Wire reports: Blair Pethel, ' G-7 "committed" to financing IMF debt relief plan,'

Knight-Ridder Bridge News (hereafter *KRBN*), September 30, 1996; Pethel, 'IMF Focus: Ensuring funds, spurring growth on agenda,' *KRBN*, September 30, 1996; Ned Stafford, '13 Nations set as contributors to new IMF $25 bln credit line,' *KRBN*, September 30, 1996.

13. Catherine Qwin and John Howell, 'The heavy burden of external debt,' *Journal of Commerce*, September 30, 1996, p. 5A; Jack Kemp [Republican vice presidential candidate in 1996] 'IMF's "velvet tyranny",' *Journal of Commerce*, December 16, 1996, p. 6A. See also Richard Lawrence, 'Discord at IMF, World Bank,' *Journal of Commerce*, October 10, 1996, p. 8A.

14. Michael R. Pakko, 'Debt Relief,' *International Economic Trends*, Federal Reserve Bank of St. Louis, November 1996, p. 1. Note: The World Development Report of 1996 has identified the following HIPCs: Bolivia, Ethiopia, Mali, Mozambique, Nicaragua, Tanzania, Uganda, and Zambia. See also Communique: Inter-governmental Group of Twenty-Four on International Monetary Affairs, IMF, Washington, D.C.: April 27, 1997.

15. Wire report: Pethel, 'IMF Focus,' September 30, 1996; Richard Lawrence, 'IMF-World Bank talks mostly upbeat but some thorny questions remain,' *Journal of Commerce*, October 1, 1996, p. 2A; Robert Collier, 'Bullish Investors Pouring Billions Back Into Mexico,' *San Francisco Chronicle*, July 5, 1996.

16. George W. Grayson, 'Mexican central bank challenge,' *Journal of Commerce*, December 23, 1997, p. 7A.

17. Stephen Fidler, 'Concern over credit health of Mexican banks,' *Financial Times* (London), August 2, 1996; Alicia Salgado, 'Demand for Banking Services Drops 47 percent,' *El Financiero Weekly International*, August 4, 1996; Richard Lawrence, 'World Bank and IMF targeting corruption, weak banking systems,' *Journal of Commerce*, October 2, 1996. Note: Non-performing loans in the Mexican banking sector jumped from 13.8 percent in July 1996 to over 25 percent in January 1997.

18. Wire report: John Lipold, 'Mexico Bank System Remains Strained, U.S. Treasury Says,' *KRBN*, October 1, 1996; John A. Adams, Jr., 'Impact of the Mexican Peso Crisis On Argentina,' as seen in Farok, J. Contractor, ed. *Economic Transformation In Emerging Countries: The Role of Investment, Trade, and Finance* (Elsevier: 1998).

19. 'Mexico's Banks Seek Foreign Partners,' *Financial Times* (London), August 8, 1996.

20. Alan Greenspan, Statement before the Subcommittee on Capital markets, Securities and Government-Sponsored Enterprises of the Committee on banking and Financial Services, U.S. house of representatives, March 19. 1997 as seen in *Federal Reserve Bulletin*, May 1997, pp. 373–8.

21. 'Thai Stability: Policy Credibility is Paramount,' *Asia Window*, Bankers Trust Research, New York: April 1997, pp. 44–50.

22. 'Third World Debt,' *The Washington Post*, editorial, September 28, 1996, p. A16; Pakko, 'Debt Relief,' *International Economic Trends*, November 1996, p. 1.

23. Cletus C. Coughlin, 'Homer Jones' Views on South Korean Crisis,' *Monetary Trends*, Federal Reserve Bank of St. Louis, March 1998, p. 1.

24. 'The Other Asias: How they Stack Up Financially,' *Global Risk Monthly Review*, Minneapolis: October 1996, p. 2.

25. Paul Handley, 'Is the Bank of Thailand Part of the Problem?' *Institutional Investor*, December 1996, pp. 163–4; William H. Overholt, 'Is the Asian Crisis Over?' *Bankers Trust Research*, December 1997, pp. 10–14; Jay Solomon and I. Made Sentana,

'Indonesia, IMF Tentatively Loosen Targets,' *The Wall Street Journal*, April 2, 1998, p. A14.

26. Roberto Salinas-Leon, 'The Importance of Money,' *Journal of Commerce*, October 16, 1996, p. 6A.

27. Communique: Intergovernmental Group of Twenty-Four on International Monetary Affairs, IMF, Washington, D.C.: April 27, 1997.

28. Francis Fukuyama, 'Asian Values and the Asian Crisis,' *Commentary*, February 1998, pp. 23–27.

29. Leon Lazaroff, The Debt Roulette,' *LatinFinance*, March 1998, pp. 23–28.

30. U.S. Treasury, *Semi-Annul Report to Congress by the Secretary of the Treasury on behalf of the President: Pursuant to the Mexican Debt Disclosure Act* (Washington, D.C.: December 1995), pp. 1–21; Press release: 'Camdessus Welcomes Advance Repayment of Loans by Mexico,' IMF, Washington, D.C.: January 15, 1997.

31. John V. Duca, David M. Gould and Lori L. Taylor, 'What Does the Asian Crisis Mean for the U.S. Economy?' *Southwest Economy*, Federal Reserve Bank of Dallas, March–April 1998, pp. 1–6.

32. Ron Corben, 'Stronger Thai Currency Points to a Recovery,' *Journal of Commerce*, March 25, 1998, p. 2A; Gene Marlowe, 'A bitter pill for Japanese banks,' *Journal of Commerce*, p. 6A.

33. Jaideep Anand and Bruce Kogut, 'Technological Capabilities of Countries, Firm Rivalry and Foreign Direct Investment,' *Journal of International Business Studies*, 1997, Vol. 28, No 3, pp. 445–465.

34. NAFTA, Chapters 11 and 14; G. Flores, 'Megarrescate bancario en manos del Congreso,' *El Financiero*, April 1, 1998, p. 1.

35. Craig Torres, 'For Sale in Mexico: $2 billion in Bank Assets,' *The Wall Street Journal*, March 6, 1998, A. A11; Scott E. Pardee, 'Bet on Mexico in 1998, ' *Journal of Commerce*, December 31, 1997, p. 4A; Rick Wills, 'Giant Bank Bailout Is Proposed,' *El Financiero*, April 6, 1998, p. 1.

10

The Effect of NAFTA on the Entry of Foreign Banks in Mexico and in the United States

SATURNINO E. LUCIO, II

I. Introduction

Among its many other goals, the North American Free Trade Agreement (NAFTA) between the United States, Canada and Mexico was designed to eventually create a 'borderless' regional financial market in which the banks and other financial institutions of one country would be able to quickly and easily establish operations in the other member countries. This, however, has not happened for a number of important reasons which are detailed in this chapter, which focuses solely on the experience of two of the NAFTA member countries, namely, the United States and Mexico.

In order to determine its impact upon the legislative and regulatory framework which existed in both of these two countries prior to NAFTA, a historical explanation is necessary.

II. Mexico

1982 coincided with the first substantial economic decline in Mexico in over fifty years. It was apparent to many observers that Mexico was experiencing widespread capital flight (most of it apparently coming to the United States) and dropping oil prices (Mexico's largest source of export revenues), and these factors led to a substantial devaluation of the Mexican peso. Rightly or wrongly, much of the blame for the economic crisis in Mexico was laid at the doorstep of the private commercial banks operating in Mexico at that time.

A. Nationalization of Mexican Banks

These economic pressures (or perhaps as a way of deflecting criticism of his administration) caused Mexican President José López-Portillo, on September 1, 1982, to decree the nationalization of all of the Mexican commercial banks. The one exception granted was for Citibank, a U.S. bank which had operated in Mexico since 1929, and which was considered 'grandfathered' under Mexican law. Otherwise, banking was declared an activity reserved for the Mexican state and foreign banks were excluded from establishing operations in Mexico.

For a variety of reasons, Mexico's economy and banking system improved between 1982 and 1989. During this time, Mexico also engaged in a concerted effort to reform its banking system and to consolidate the number of Mexican banks. From a high of over 150 commercial banks operating in Mexico prior to 1982, the total number of Mexican banks dropped to below 20 institutions by 1990.

B. Privatization of Mexican Commercial Banks[1]

By 1990, the political climate had also changed in Mexico, and there developed pressure to privatize the Mexican banks by returning them to private ownership. Between 1989 and 1992, the Mexican Government adopted various constitutional and other legal reforms which:

1. excluded commercial banking from the list of activities reserved for the Mexican state;
2. established a bidding procedure for the eventual privatization of the Mexican commercial banks; and
3. permitted foreign investors to acquire limited rights in the equity of the Mexican banks.

The privatization of the Mexican banks occurred between 1990 and 1992. The successful bidders were very important Mexican private economic groups and individuals, who reportedly paid the Mexican Government substantial monies to acquire the Mexican banks. All in all, 18 Mexican banks, with an aggregate of nearly $130 billion dollars in assets, were sold by the Mexican Government through an auction process in exchange for approximately $12.4 billion dollars.

C. Foreign Investment in Mexican Banks[2]

Immediately prior to 1992, with the exception of Citibank, no foreign banks were allowed to establish permanent operations in Mexico and no foreign persons were allowed to invest in existing Mexican banks. Commencing that year, however, foreign investors were allowed to acquire certain kinds of specially-designated shares of Mexican banks (e.g., 'L' shares), with limited voting rights and other restrictions. But no matter the particular share designation, no foreign investor could acquire more than 30 percent of the voting and nonvoting capital of a Mexican bank. Foreign banks were also not allowed to establish their own banking institutions in Mexico, or to acquire control of any Mexican bank.

This was the situation in Mexico when NAFTA was ratified and entered into effect in 1994.

III. United States

A. International Banking Act of 1978[3]

A year before the federal International Banking Act of 1978 (IBA 1978) was adopted, several states, including Florida, enacted legislation permitting foreign banks to establish international banking branches, agencies and representative offices in those states. The adoption of IBA 1978, among other things, created a dual chartering option for foreign banks. Such banks could apply for a license to establish a federal international banking agency, or could opt for a state licensed agency. Since there were some differences between the federal and the state legislation, there were various factors that could lead a foreign bank to select one type of agency over another, but such a discussion is beyond the scope of this chapter.

Pursuant to IBA 1978 and the various state laws, numerous foreign banks were allowed entry into the United States. Less than four years later, over 300 different foreign banks had established a U.S. presence, consisting of 602 branch and agency offices, 90 domestic bank subsidiaries, 20 other banking affiliates and 243 representative offices. A good summary of the various economic benefits to the United States resulting from the entry of the foreign banks can be found in the Internet web page of the U.S. Institute of International Bankers, which can be accessed at: *http://www.iib.org/summ93.htm.* The New York State Banking Department, which has authorized the largest number of foreign banks to establish a presence in that state, also has a report entitled 'Foreign Banks in New York' which is also available for downloading from the Department's web page at: *http://www.banking.state.ny.us/booklet.htm.*

Prior to December 1991, a number of Mexican banks had also opted to enter the United States banking market, and had established direct banking operations as well as acquired subsidiary banks, in states such as California, New York and Texas. At the time of this writing (in 1997), for instance, Banco Nacional de Mexico (Banamex) maintains a subsidiary bank in Los Angeles (California Commerce Bank) and banking agencies in Houston, Los Angeles and New York City. Banca Serfin and Bancomer maintain banking agencies in Los Angeles, and Bancomer, Banco Internacional (Bital) and Banca Serfin, among others, also maintain bank agencies in New York City.

B. Foreign Bank Supervision Enhancement Act [4]

On December 1991, the U.S. Congress adopted the Foreign Bank Supervision Enhancement Act (FBSEA). FBSEA was prompted in part by fears that foreigners were poised to take over a substantial portion of the U.S. banking system. In addition, the global bank scandals associated with the collapse of Bank of Credit and Commerce International (BCCI), and the improper loans made by Banca Nazionale del Lavoro (BNL) convinced the U.S. Congress that many international banks were under no centralized regulation and could be operating in defiance of international banking norms. The sense of crisis that these developments provoked was a key factor in the U.S. Congress picking up an old Federal Reserve proposal to strengthen U.S. banking supervision of foreign bank activities and to limit the entry of foreign banks in the U.S.

FBSEA is generally concerned with worldwide banking organizational structures which are not accountable to a single banking regulator. Prior to FBSEA, it was feared that no one single banking regulator could see an entire banking organization at once and determine if the organization was headed for problems.

Building on the structure of the Basle Concordat, the Federal Reserve and the U.S. Congress therefore determined that the best way to tackle this problem was to require that foreign banking organizations prove that they were subject, in their home country, to 'comprehensive supervision on a consolidated basis' (the CCS standard). Since the U.S. Congress could not require foreign countries to adopt laws or reform existing banking laws to provide for such a regulatory system, it opted to permit entry into the U.S. banking market only to banks from countries where such supervision was in effect.

Consequently, FBSEA provided that any foreign bank applicant which desired to establish a United States office had to present an application for approval not only to the primary licensing authority, but also to the Federal Reserve Board. Under FBSEA, the Federal Reserve has to consider a variety of factors in deciding whether or not to approve a particular application. Some of these factors are mandatory on the Federal Reserve; i.e., if the applicant could not establish that it met a particular test, the Federal Reserve was required by the U.S. Congress to disapprove a foreign bank's application (even if the application could be or was granted by the primary state or federal licensing authority pursuant to its regulatory conditions).

Among the mandatory factors *requiring rejection* by the Federal Reserve of an application by a foreign bank to establish a new office in the United States (even if said bank already maintained other U.S. offices) were that the foreign bank:

1. was not engaged directly in the business of banking outside the United States;
2. was not subject to the CCS standard by the home country banking regulator; and/or
3. refused or failed to provide 'adequate assurances' to the Federal Reserve Board that it would provide information upon request.

Several other 'optional factors' were left to the discretion of the Federal Reserve, such as whether the foreign bank had the requisite amount of capital, profitability, level of indebtedness, future prospects and general financial condition to be able to operate successfully an office in the United States.

C. Comprehensive Consolidated Supervision

As noted above, one of the most important factors to be considered by the Federal Reserve in reviewing a foreign bank application, is that which effectively requires the Federal Reserve to assess the home country bank regulatory system by determining whether such system adequately complies with the CCS standard. There is no definition of the CCS standard in FBSEA, nor is any clarification of its meaning found in the short legislative history. The final regulations, promulgated by the Federal Reserve Board in January 1993, attempted to shed some light on what was meant by that phrase, but rather than establishing any parameters or elements that would guide a foreign bank applicant, the Federal Reserve instead opted for a case-by-case determination, given the particular situation of a foreign bank and the regulatory context within which it operates.

Based on the few approvals which have been granted since the adoption of FBSEA, the Federal Reserve appears to have been satisfied in the case of Spain, Switzerland, England and Taiwan, among others. But between 1992 and 1997, few Latin American banks which had applied for permission to establish a U.S. office after FBSEA became applicable, other than Banco de Chile (international banking agency) and Banco Bandeirantes of Brazil (representative office), had received favorable approvals from the Federal Reserve. That dynamic should be contrasted with the typical four to six foreign bank applications which had been granted by the State of Florida alone from 1977 to 1990 (many of them from Latin American banks).

Based on the Federal Reserve regulations, the CCS standard requires a showing that the home country banking regulator has a monitoring and supervisory system in place for assessing the global risk exposure and capital of its banking organizations, including their non-bank affiliates. At the very least, the home country regulator must require regular information on the condition of a particular bank, and its affiliates inside the country and outside the country as well. At the most, the home country supervisor was required to have actively monitored and controlled the operations of one of its banks (in and out of the country) and conducted examinations of such domestic and overseas operations. Although the U.S. Congress could not very well order foreign banking regulators to alter their laws and methods of doing business, unless they were engaged in a substantial effort to do so, their local banks would be denied the ability to establish a United States office.

According to the Federal Reserve regulations, there are several '*indicia*' relevant (but not determinative or all-inclusive) to determining whether a particular foreign bank is considered to be subject to the CCS standard:

a. Whether the foreign banking authority requires that the foreign bank has adequate procedures for monitoring and controlling its worldwide operations;
b. Whether the foreign authority regularly receives information on the condition of the foreign bank and its affiliates;
c. Whether the foreign authority obtains information on all dealings between a foreign bank and its domestic and overseas affiliates;
d. Whether the foreign authority obtains financial reports which are consolidated for the banking organization on a worldwide basis;
e. Whether the foreign authority evaluates prudential standards such as capital adequacy and risk asset exposure on a worldwide basis.

Theoretically, the same standards apply to the formation of a new United States office by a foreign bank as to the possible closing of the U.S. operations of said bank which are currently in existence, if the home country banking regulator does not meet the CCS standard of bank regulation. It is noteworthy, however, that since FBSEA was adopted, not a single U.S. office of any foreign bank has been required by the Federal Reserve to be closed for failing to meet the CCS test—even though at the same time new applications of foreign banks to establish an office in the United States have been held up for a long period of time without being approved. So these termination provisions remain as a form of 'big gun,' which the Federal Reserve can use with respect to any problematic bank, even though it appears the Federal Reserve has been very reluctant to invoke the power to close an existing foreign bank office.

Consequently, there has developed the anomaly that new applications by foreign banks from a particular foreign country have gone unapproved for a long period of time (and in some cases the applications have been 'voluntarily' withdrawn after years of fruitless waiting), while other banks from the same country—and even the same bank which had submitted the pending application—maintained existing bank offices operating in the United States. For example, when Banamex applied for a Miami international banking agency, its application was processed for over four years, until it was withdrawn by said bank (perhaps because it could not prove that Mexico applied the CCS standard and therefore Banamex was not likely to receive eventual Federal Reserve approval). At the same time, Banamex currently maintains several banking offices in the United States and even owns a subsidiary bank in California. It is open to question whether any U.S. bank regulatory purpose is served by not allowing Banamex the opportunity to establish an additional banking office in Miami, however.

Thus, this was the regulatory context in Mexico and in the United States governing foreign bank entry at the time of the adoption of NAFTA by the countries of Canada, Mexico and the United States (each a 'Party').

IV. North American Free Trade Agreement ('NAFTA')

To be sure, NAFTA is a comprehensive trade agreement which governs a lot of different commercial operations, such as the duty-free entry of goods, the offering of transportation services and many other areas. With respect to financial services, Chapter XIV of NAFTA was intended to eventually create a single transparent financial market in the region, in which financial institutions (including commercial banks, insurance companies and securities firms) from one NAFTA country would be granted equality of treatment when entering into the financial markets of the other NAFTA countries and conducting a financial service business in those countries. NAFTA was supposed to eliminate the existing barriers to entry of foreign banks in all three member countries over a six-year transitional period concluding on January 1, 2004.

A. 'National Treatment'

Chapter XIV of NAFTA concerns 'Financial Services' and applies to measures adopted, or maintained by a Party, relating to financial institutions (e.g., banks, insurance companies, and securities providers) of another Party or investors of another Party in financial institutions in the Party's territory (Article 1401).

The 'national treatment' standard of NAFTA is set forth in Article 1407(1):

> Each Party shall accord to investors of another Party and financial service providers of another Party national treatment with respect to the establishment, acquisition, expansion, management, conduct, operation and sale or other disposition of investments in financial institutions in that territory.

Although the term 'financial institution' was intended to cover a broad range of institutions offering financial services, the focus on this article will be on the establishment of crossborder commercial banking operations. Similar but somewhat different rules govern insurance companies and securities firms.

The term 'national treatment,' which has a long history in international law, is defined in Article 1407(4) and (5) as follows:

> 'National treatment' means treatment no less favorable than that accorded by a Party to its own investors, financial service providers and financial institutions in like circumstances.
>
> A measure of a Party, whether it accords to financial institutions of another Party different or identical treatment compared to that it accords to its own providers or institutions in like circumstances, shall be deemed to be consistent with [national treatment] . . . if it accords equal competitive opportunities.

Thus, according to this determination, a United States financial institution could one day, theoretically, be able to establish operations in Mexico, and engage in financial operations in that country, similar and to the same extent that would be the case for a Mexican financial institution. And consequently the U.S. bank would not be limited to a maximum of 30 percent of the capital of the Mexican bank.

B. Limitations on Establishment of Crossborder Operations

NAFTA did not expressly grant financial institutions of one country the *carte blanche* right to enter the financial markets of other parties to NAFTA. First, NAFTA allowed particular countries to make reservations, such as creating transitional periods, regarding allowing foreign financial institutions access to its financial markets. Since the United States (and Canada) already provided national treatment for the entry of foreign banks into its country, the United States did not seek to reserve its rights in this regard. Neither did Canada.

Mexico, however, provided that access to its financial markets by foreign financial institutions occur over a ten-year transitional period, as follows:[5]

1. Any foreign bank could, immediately upon obtaining permission, establish a 100 percent wholly-owned subsidiary in Mexico, but could not own less than 100 percent of that new institution. If a foreign investor or foreign bank was going to invest in an existing Mexican bank, then it would be limited to a 30 percent equity interest.
2. At the commencement of the 'transitional period' ending on January 1, 2004, the maximum capital of Mexican banks owned by a foreign investor (including a foreign bank), measured as a percentage of the aggregate capital of all Mexican banks, could not exceed 1.5 percent.
3. At the end of the transitional period, the maximum capital of Mexican banks owned by foreign investors (including foreign banks), measured as a percentage of the aggregate capital of all Mexican banks, could not exceed 4 percent.
4. At the commencement of the transitional period, the aggregate maximum capital of Mexican banks owned by foreign investors, including foreign banks, measured as a percentage of the aggregate capital of all Mexican banks, could not exceed 8 percent.
5. At the end of the transitional period in 2004, the aggregate maximum capital of Mexican banks owned by foreign investors, including foreign banks, measured as a percentage of the aggregate capital of all Mexican banks, could not exceed 15 percent.
6. After the end of the transitional period, Mexico reserved the further right, once during the four years following the end of the transitional period (but for no longer than for three years thereafter) to freeze the aggregate capital percentage held by all foreign banks in Mexico to a maximum of 25 percent.

The second general limitation under NAFTA regarding financial services was that each country was free to adopt or maintain reasonable regulatory measures for prudential reasons (Article 1403), such as for:

(a) the protection of investors, depositors, financial market participants, policy-holders, policy-claimants or persons to whom a fiduciary duty is owed by a financial service provider or financial institution;
(b) the maintenance of the safety, soundness, integrity or financial responsibility of financial service providers or financial institutions; and
(c) ensuring the integrity and stability of a Party's financial system.

A final limitation was that each NAFTA Party was free to impose other terms, conditions, and procedures on the establishment of a financial institution's presence within a country (such as requiring the use of a locally-incorporated subsidiary) provided that such limitations were consistent with 'national treatment' as defined under Article 1407—see Article 1404(3)(a) and (b).

V. Post-NAFTA

A. Mexico

The above constituted the conditions and limitations on entry to the Mexican banking market available to foreign investors by the end of 1994. As everyone knows, Mexico suffered a truly severe economic crisis commencing in December 1994, which resulted in a substantial devaluation of the Mexican peso by February 1995 (the peso lost approximately 40 percent of its value between December 1994 and February 1995).[6] Much has been written about this period in Mexican history, but for present purposes it is sufficient to note that the viability of the entire Mexican financial system came into question. In order to shore up the Mexican financial system with foreign investment, Mexico significantly amended its banking regulations in 1995 in order to permit greater foreign investment in the Mexican financial system.[7]

Under the NAFTA rules, foreign banks could really only acquire the two smallest Mexican banks. Even at the end of the NAFTA transitional period, when the individual market limit would be raised to 4 percent of the Mexican banking market controlled by banks from the NAFTA countries, the top six Mexican banks would still be unable to be acquired by foreign bankers. These top six banks currently control over 70 percent of all of the Mexican banking assets.

These limitations were substantially relaxed by the Mexican Government on February 6, 1995, when it provided that:

1. NAFTA member banks could, in any one case, acquire control over one or more Mexican banks, provided that the foreign bank did not exercise control over more than 6 percent of the capital of all Mexican banks.
2. NAFTA member banks could, in the aggregate (counting all foreign bank participations in Mexican banks), acquire control of Mexican banks having up to 25 percent of the capital of all Mexican banks.
3. NAFTA member banks could enter into joint ventures with Mexican banks whereby the foreign bank could maintain control over 51 percent or more of the equity of the Mexican bank (rather than limiting investments to 100 percent subsidiaries).
4. NAFTA member investors and banks could acquire up to 49 percent of the capital of any Mexican bank, including the largest Mexican banks.

These changes resulted in a widening of the pool of available investors; only the three largest Mexican banks continued to be off-limits to foreign investors and foreign banks seeking to obtain control of such institutions, but even then the foreign investors or foreign banks could make noncontrolling investments in such banks.

Ever since the adoption of NAFTA, there has been generated a great deal of enthusiasm for foreign bank entry into Mexico.[8] By the end of 1994, for instance, over 50 applications by foreign financial institutions (19 of them banks) to establish bank subsidiaries in Mexico and/or to invest in Mexican banks had been approved by the Mexican Finance Ministry. All in all, over 100 applications were filed by foreign financial institutions. No applications were rejected by the Mexican Finance Ministry, although some were returned to the applicants with requests for additional information. The peso crisis in Mexico, however, dampened many of those expectations, particularly because it had a major negative effect upon the Mexican banks.[9] Less than one year after the application had been approved by the Mexican Government, however, few U.S. banks (or other foreign banks) had formally launched banking operations in Mexico. In recent years, however, the situation has changed, and Citibank has acquired a substantial Mexican bank.

The widespread economic problems affecting the Mexican banking industry also prompted a number of governmental programs in Mexico to attempt to rescue such industry.[10] These measures have begun to have a positive effect on the Mexican banks, although it is estimated that the total amount of Mexican government support may eventually reach $80 billion. This gain in confidence has resulted in greater foreign investment in the Mexican banking system—although to date most of it has come from European banking groups rather than from NAFTA member banks. Currently, the Mexican Banking Commission estimates that over 15 percent of the Mexican banking system was in foreign hands by the end of 1997.

So what effect did NAFTA have on the opening of the Mexican banking market to U.S. banks? To be sure, NAFTA provided a delicate compromise, at the time, whereby the Mexican banking market opened itself in a significant fashion to foreign investment. Remember that even as late as the first quarter of 1990, banking was still regarded as an official state activity of the Mexican Government, and not a private function in which both Mexicans and foreigners could engage. But the peso devaluation in Mexico, commencing in late 1994, probably did more to change the perceptions of Mexican lawmakers and produce greater interest in the acquisition of depressed and/or undervalued Mexican banking assets and stocks. The opening of the Mexican banking sector which has followed has, therefore, rendered NAFTA largely unnecessary—and its somewhat restrictive limitations have already been superseded by subsequent developments in Mexico.

B. United States

Since the United States permitted 'national treatment' to Mexican banks even before NAFTA, the enactment of NAFTA did not change the conditions whereby Mexican banks could establish a presence in this country. Whether due to FBSEA or perhaps other factors, however, no Mexican bank has received the requisite approvals to establish any new office in the United States since 1991.

As for the United States, NAFTA has really not assisted the Mexican banks in entering into this country. First, such entry was possible prior to FBSEA, and a number of Mexican banks took advantage of such opportunity in establishing banking operations in California, New York and Texas. Second, FBSEA created a high hurdle for the Mexican banks which, thus far, they have been unable to meet to the satisfaction of the Federal Reserve. Third, the 1994–95 peso devaluation certainly made matters more difficult for the Mexican banks (and their regulators), who worried more about survival in their domestic market than expansion into the more competitive U.S. banking market. So NAFTA really has not done much to ease Mexican bank entry into the United States.

IV. Concluding Remarks

NAFTA has had a major role, however, in how the citizens of each nation view the others' participation in their domestic market. This perception may be negative or positive, depending upon one's perspective, but it has nonetheless drawn the two countries closer together, as other chapters in this book can attest. The effect of such greater involvement may not be measured in terms of how many financial institutions of one country have to date successfully entered the other's banking market; but, by bringing the economies more closely together, NAFTA has led to a functional amalgam of U.S., Mexican and other foreign banks, which participate in a broader range of cross-border activities and transactions than before NAFTA was adopted. This dynamic may, in time, truly lead to the borderless regional financial market envisioned by the NAFTA drafters, but not immediately, and not directly.

Notes

1. For a discussion of the Mexican bank privatization process, see, H. Unal and M. Navarro 'The Technical Process of Bank Privatization in Mexico', Wharton Financial Institutions Center paper 97–42. This study is available for downloading from: *http://wrdsenet.wharton.upenn.edu/fic/wfic/papers/97/p97242.html*.
2. For a discussion of the differing treatment of foreign banks in Mexico over time, see D. R. Fraser, 'Whither the Mexican Banking System?', Center for the Study of Western Hemispheric Trade Insight Paper, p.1. This paper is available for downloading from *http://www.lanic.utexas.edu/cswht/TIP6b.html*.

3. The International Banking Act of 1978 was enacted by Public Law No. 95–369, 92 Stat. 607 (codified in scattered sections of Title 12 of the U.S. Code). For a discussion of the International Banking Act and the general experience of foreign banks in the United States, see, Note, The International Banking Act of 1978: Federal Regulation of Foreign Banks in the United States, 8 GA. J. INT'L & COMP. L. 145 (1978); Recent Developments: Banking—The International Bank Act of 1978, 19 HARV. INT'L L.J. 1011 (1978). IBA 1978 also permitted foreign banks to form Edges, either individually or in consortium with other banks.

4. FBSEA was adopted by the 102nd U.S. Congress on December 19, 1991. S.1019, 102nd Congress, 1st Sess. (1991).

5. For a complete recitation of the various reservations made by Mexico, see Schedule of Mexico to NAFTA, Annex VII, Part A (Sector: Financial Services) and Part B (Transitional Exceptions), especially Part B, paragraphs 2, 5, 9, 13.

6. For a discussion of the 1994 Mexican peso devaluation and its effects on Mexican banks, see P. Rose, 'The Impact of the Peso's Devaluation on Bankers' Access to Mexico Under NAFTA', Center for the Study of Western Hemispheric Trade Paper (hereinafter '*Impact*'), available for downloading from: *http://www.lanic.utexas.edu/cswht/TIP4b.html*. *See also*, Dr. S. Weintraub, 'The Peso Devaluation: What Happens Next?', Speech before the LBJ School of Public Affairs of the University of Texas on March 10, 1995, which is available for downloading at: *http://www.utexas.edu/lbj/usmex/pesostyle.html*. *See also*, J. E. Hazleton, 'The Peso Devaluation in Retrospect', Center for the Study of Western Hemispheric Trade Paper, available for downloading at: *http://www.lanic.utexas.edu/cswht/TIP2b.html*.

7. For a discussion of the post-NAFTA Mexican legislative and regulatory changes permitting foreign banks to acquire a greater participation in the Mexican banking market, see the summary prepared by the Federal Reserve Bank of Dallas Financial Industry Issues First Quarter 1995 Report entitled 'Mexican Banks Open to Foreign Investors', which can be downloaded from: *http://www.dallasfed.org/publications/fi/txt/fi_95_1q.html*.

8. For one U.S. bank's view of the effects of NAFTA on foreign bank entry in Mexico, see 'NAFTA and its Effects on Banking in Mexico', which can be downloaded from Bank of America's web page at: *http://www.bankamerica.com/corporate/cash_management/nafta.html*.

9. For a discussion of the 1994 Mexican peso devaluation and its effects on the entry of foreign banks in Mexico, *see* M. Peck, 'Where are the Foreign Banks?', article available for download at: *http://daisy.uwaterloo.ca/~alopez-o/politics/banksys.html*. See also P. Rose, *Impact*, p. 6 (as cited in Note 6).

10. For a discussion of the steps taken by the Mexican Government to assist its troubled financial industry as a result of the peso devaluation, see A. De Palma, 'Mexico Tries to Rescue Sick Banks,' *New York Times* article reprinted at: *http://www.latino.com/mexban.html*. *See also* J. Hamburg, 'Bancomer, Banamex to Receive Government Bailout', p. 3, which is available for download at: *http://www.latinolink.com/biz/biz97/0124bmeb.htm*. These efforts have caused an improvement in Mexican banks, and made them more attractive to foreign acquisition. See G. Smith, 'Mexican Banks Pull Out of a Dive', 44 *BUSINESS WEEK* September 2, 1996, available for download at: *http://www.fgvsp.br/cursos/CMAPG/ingles2.htm*; 'Mexican Banks on the Mend?', 2 *LATIN AMERICAN BANKING REPORT* 1, pp. 2–3, which is available for download at: http://www.riskconcepts.com/latinam2.html.

11

Conclusion

JERRY HAAR AND KRISHNAN DANDAPANI

Banking in North America continues to be driven by four sets of dynamics:

1. the globalization of financial services;
2. the regional integration of finance and banking;
3. change and reform within individual country markets; and
4. the development and expansion of new products, technologies and services.

Within this mix, the pattern, speed and intensity of change vary widely by country, region and sector (e.g. trade finance); additionally, non-bank entities such as securities, investment banking, real estate, insurance, leasing and factoring firms further invigorate the competitive environment of domestic and international banking.

At the national and cross-national level, as well, the cause and effect relationships between banking and macroeconomic and regulatory policies are more closely linked than ever before; this is especially true in North America where the political economies of Canada, the United States and Mexico have experienced dramatic shifts during the last decade.

In the United States, the most important change to occur in recent years is the option for states to opt out of the McFadden Act, which prohibits interstate banking; and while repeal of the Glass-Steagal Act at one time looked imminent, at best only minor modifications by Congress are envisioned. The same may be said for the Foreign Bank Supervision and Enforcement Act (FBSEA), passed in the wake of the Bank of Credit and Commerce International (BCCI) scandal; in this case, rather than congressional changes, a more flexible interpretation and enforcement of the Act by federal regulators is more likely.

Far more important to the evolution and competitiveness of U.S. banking in North America are the accelerating strategic, operational, and product and service delivery trends. Large mergers and acquisitions, the proliferation of non-bank services offered by commercial banking institutions, the quest for additional fee income (e.g. foreign exchange transactions, and derivatives) and the application of technology, such as the ATM machine and banking at home by computer, are permanently altering the landscape of U.S. banking. Mirroring the sweeping changes in the manufacturing, telecommunications, health services, and entertainment industries, the largest banks are becoming even larger, medium-sized institutions prey to acquisitions and takeovers, resulting in the new mega-banks offering a wide-range of products and services to both retail and commercial customers. Small banks with strong balance sheets are surviving—many are doing quite well—due to a particular geographic advantage, a niche position or specialty in a specific banking service, and excellent customer relations. Recognizably, also, many profitable small banks, even in growing markets, are less desirable merger or acquisition candidates for larger banks than other financial institutions whose size and product complementarity (as well as customer base and composition of loan portfolio) offer a greater degree of attractiveness. Inadequately capitalized banks and those whose clientele and loan portfolios are predominantly agricultural and/or natural resource-based (such as soybeans, wheat, or oil) carry a significantly higher degree of risk and are far more likely to experience collapse and liquidation (rather than acquisition), as vividly illustrated by the savings and loan crisis of the late 1970s (due to inadequate capital) and the oil-based Texas and Oklahoma bank failures in the early 1980s (due to the drop in world petroleum prices).

Unquestionably, one of the most dramatic developments in American banking during the last two years has been the scale of consolidation, which has leapt to a new level. Superregional and money center banks both have been on a merger binge. In April of 1998, BankAmerica/ NationsBank ($570 billion in assets), BancOne/First Chicago ($240 billion), Citicorp/Travelers Group ($698 billion) all chose to merge. When combined with mergers within the last two years of Chase Manhattan/Chemical ($366 billion) and First Union/Corestates ($206 billion), these banks along with J.P. Morgan ($262 billion) comprise the 'megabanks' of the American banking establishment.

The Canadian banking system is also experiencing changes which will affect its future performance both within its domestic as well as wider North American markets. Unhampered by either McFadden or Glass-Steagall-type restrictions, Canadian banks were allowed into the securities business in 1987; three years later, they were permitted to sell private banking and asset management services along with limited powers to sell insurance. They have long been able to open branches wherever they please.

Nevertheless, Canadian banks will not be permitted to sell insurance directly through their 6,000 plus branches until at least 2002; banking margins have traditionally been thin, and continue to be so; and foreign competition within the Canadian market is expected to increase.

Canadian banks, however, are bracing for change—some positive and some negative. A government white paper on financial institutions has recommended a variety of amendments to the Bank Act. Among the most important are those pertaining to foreign banks, electronic banking and automobile leasing. In the first instance, the government proposes putting the 46 foreign banks in Canada on the same footing as Canadian banks, permitting them to open branches across the country. Currently, offshore banks are required to establish subsidiaries in Canada that are totally independent from the parent firm, with their own directors and accounting firms. Restrictive regulations can be attributed to the departure from the market in 1996 of such banks as Standard Chartered Bank and Lloyds Bank (both British institutions) and Banca Nazionale del Lavoro (an Italian bank). Deregulation would provide the Canadian people with a much wider array of banking services and, quite possibly, lower fees. Electronic banking would also be deregulated, opening the market to retailers, brokerages and other interests. Presently, a quasi-monopoly exists whereby the Canadian Payment Association, consisting of banks and other deposit-taking institutions, controls the country's check-clearing system; and, through Interac, the six major banks also dominate automated teller machines and other electronic transactions. The proposed deregulation of the C$9 billion automobile leasing market is a change which Canadian banks have sought for some time. From 1989 to 1994 the number of leases jumped from 44,000 to 245,000; one in three new cars in Canada is leased rather than purchased. Canadian banks are allowed to finance leases only on vehicles weighing more than 21 tons. The leasing market is dominated by two U.S. subsidiaries: General Electric Capital Leasing and General Motors Acceptance Corporation.

Unquestionably, 1998–99 will go down as a landmark period in Canadian banking. In January of 1998, Royal Bank of Canada and Bank of Montreal announced plans to merge. Three months later, Canada's second largest bank, Canadian Imperial Bank of Commerce (CIBC) and its fifth-largest bank, Toronto Dominion, announced plans to merge. The two mergers would create banks that would have 62 percent of the assets in the banking sector. By June of 1999, the government will implement legislation to allow foreign banks to establish branches in Canada. As Canadian banks can offer trust, brokerage, and insurance services, and a 10 percent limit exists on single ownership, the increased concentration through mergers *within* the Canadian banking sector raises the specter of oligopolistic practices, which will impact pensioners and individual investors.

Nevertheless, most Canadian banking executives believe that concentration is not the answer, favoring instead a more open banking market (allowing for cross-border mergers and international expansion), which will more than compensate for tougher competition at home and stagnant asset growth.

Although Canadian banks have traditionally focused on the domestic market, they have long been active in international banking, as well, concentrating on niche markets. The Royal Bank of Canada, in addition to private banking, is a force in foreign exchange; Canadian Imperial Bank of Commerce is emerging as a major player in derivatives; and the Bank of Nova Scotia, with an extensive branch banking network throughout the Eastern Caribbean, has been prominent in leading international lending syndicates and in trade finance. The Bank of Montreal purchased a 16 percent stake in Mexico's Grupo Financiero Bancomer, that nation's second largest bank, and could well be increasing its international business activity in selected markets.

In Mexico, the banking crisis which erupted following the drastic devaluation of the peso, announced by President Zedillo on December 20, 1994, has whipsawed an already depressed economy. Nearly every one of Mexico's 18 largest banks has been hurt; losses exceed 12 percent of the country's 1995 output. Worse still, there is potential damage to free-market reform efforts; for the total cost of the bailout of Mexican banks could well exceed the $12 billion realized by the government from its bank sales when the system was privatized in the early 1990s. Thirteen of eighteen banks have gone bust since the peso devaluation of 1994.

No doubt the bank privatization process itself has exacerbated the banking crisis. To begin with, the government allowed buyers to pay inflated prices, instead of ensuring adequate capitalization on the part of the new financial groups, as well as the knowledge and experience of the groups' banking executives to manage a bank. The average sale price of a privatized bank was 3.1 times its book value and 15 times its earnings. In an attempt to achieve a quick payback on their investments, many bank executives pursued overly liberal and expansive lending policies; and even as loan portfolios deteriorated, they sought to placate shareholders with dividend payments instead of boosting bank capital.

There was fraud, as well, the most glaring example being Banco

Union-Cremi, SA, then the fourth-largest banking group. In all, seven banks had been seized or supported by early 1996, at a cost in excess of $5 billion. In June of 1996, the National Banking and Securities Commission, CNBV, seized Grupo Financiero Sureste SA and Grupo Financiero Capital SA after the institutions failed to meet capital and reserve requirements.

Even relatively healthy banks, such as Grupo Financiero Banamex-Accival SA, are plagued by large past-due loan portfolios. In the case of Banamex, past due loans are 13 percent of total loans (as of 1998). (A U.S. bank, by comparison, is considered unhealthy if the past-due loan rate exceeds 3 percent.) The Mexican government has strengthened Banamex by purchasing $2 billion worth of low-quality loans; in response, Banamex has pledged to increase capital by $1.1 billion. Several other banks, including Mexico's third-largest bank, Grupo Financiero Serfin SA, have also taken advantage of the government's loan-for-capital program. In fact, government incentives helped banks attract $4.8 billion in new private capital in 1995, an 88 percent increase over 1994. Reserves against past-due loans increase from 48 percent, to 63 percent, and overall capitalization rose to 12 percent. Other government efforts, exceeding a cost of $24 billion, have assisted mortgage-holders, industries, and local governments to extend their payments and control interest increases.

The Mexican government has also instituted two long overdue measures, which should improve the present and future situation. First, it has created a new agency, similar to the Resolution Trust Corporation in the United States, to create a secondary debt market and dispose of the bank assets in its control. Second, the banking commission is requiring higher reserve levels and adoption of U.S. generally accepted accounting principles, which provide a more accurate picture of the health of a bank's loan portfolio. By Mexican accounting standards, only the total amount of interest owed is considered past-due; in the U.S., the entire amount of the loan is considered non-performing, when a borrower misses a payment and it is outstanding for more than ninety days.

Nevertheless, it will be some time before the ailing Mexican banking system recovers. Banks are making very few new loans; and business executives claim they cannot self-finance indefinitely—without fresh credit they cannot break out of their cut-back mode and begin to grow to where they were prior to the peso devaluation. Consumers, as well as businesses, are outraged over loan costs; this has even led to a middle-class resistance movement of bank debtors who pledge to make principal payments on their loans but not interest. Known as 'El Barzon' (a yoke for oxen), the group has captured widespread attention, and has mobilized political support.

To date, despite a government bailout and cash infusions from investors such as the Bank of Montreal and Banco Santander, the banking system remains poorly capitalized and plagued with overdue loans. Plans are in the works to bolster the national banking commission, strengthen the autonomy of the central bank, establish a comprehensive deposit insurance plan and remove restrictions on foreign ownership. However, there is strong opposition to the provision which would transform outstanding liabilities of the Banking Fund for the Protection of Savings (Fobaproa) into public domestic debt. Mexican deposit insurance and bankruptcy laws protect depositors and borrowers from practically all risk. Not surprisingly, moral hazard is rampant.

Also troublesome has been the 1998 U.S. money-laundering indictment against three Mexican banks (Banca Serfin, Grupo Financiero Bancomer, Banca Confia) and dozens of bankers; this is unlikely to help Mexico improve the quality and supervision of its banking system.

Recognizably, an unfinished agenda of reform remains in North America. Of the 50 largest countries economically, only Canada and Mexico do not allow branch banking. Foreign banks must have separately capitalized units, effectively limiting the size of the loan they can make. This remains a significant impediment to an open and competitive banking system, and results in disadvantages to both commercial and retail customers. The U.S. is not exempt from the need to institute reforms with respect to the Glass-Steagall, the FBSEA, and money-laundering and other illegal activities.

NAFTA and European Banking

An important question is the implication for competition between the NAFTA regions and the new European Monetary Union. While NAFTA has been restricted to three countries, its impact and implementation have clear implications for European banking. The competition between the institutions in the two trade regions should clearly await the consolidation of operations of the financial institutions. But the beneficial lessons and solutions for cooperation and collaboration are already emerging. For example, from a regulatory perspective, the four major lessons of NAFTA that are pertinent to the European Monetary Union are the following. The first lesson is the revised definition and measurement of structure and risk. In place of the traditional measure of interest rate risk, the underlying asset and liability risk measure becomes more relevant and important for valuation. Second, the evaluation of risk should be based on the overall portfolio approach, and not on exclusive opportunities. Third, the expansion into newer markets and investment options necessitate the re-examination and relevance of interest rate contracts and foreign exchange derivative securities for risk management. Finally, the effective use and regulation of such derivatives underscore the need for the development and implementation of a reward structure based on risk-adjusted exposure.

Author Index

Subject Index